WRITING SKILLS SUCCESS
IN 20 MINUTES A DAY

6th Edition

LEARNING EXPRESS®

NEW YORK

Cataloging-in-Publication Data is on file with the Library of Congress.

ISBN 978-1-61103-065-5

Printed in the United States of America

9 8 7 6 5 4 3 2 1

Sixth Edition

For information on LearningExpress, other LearningExpress products, or bulk sales, please write to us at:
  LearningExpress
  224 W. 29th Street
  3rd Floor
  New York, NY 10001

Contents ▶

CONTENTS

Introduction ▶

Since you bought this book, you probably want or need to learn more about the process of writing and how to become a better writer. This book will help you acquire the coveted power of the pen in 20 easy steps. It covers the basics of writing: punctuation, usage, diction, and organization. You'll find no fluff in this book; it's for busy people who want to learn as much as they can as efficiently as possible. Each lesson contains enough illustrations for you to get the idea, opportunities to practice the skills, and suggestions for using them in your daily life.

Many people fear a blank sheet of paper or an empty computer screen. "I just don't know what to write. Even when I know what I want to say, I'm afraid it will come out looking wrong or sounding stupid."

But that's one of the things to love about writing. Writing is a process. The first time you write a draft, it doesn't matter if your writing comes out wrong or sounds stupid to you because you can change it as often as you want. You can go over it until you're completely satisfied or until you need to shift gears. You can show your draft to your friends or family and get a response before you ever make it public.

Don't put pressure on yourself by thinking you're going to write a perfect first draft. No one can sit down and write polished memos, reports, or letters without changing (or revising) them at least slightly. Even professionals have to revise their work. For instance, writer Ernest Hemingway had to revise the last page of his famous novel *A Farewell to Arms* 39 times before he was satisfied. You probably won't want to revise anything that many times before the final copy, but even if you write two or three drafts, you certainly aren't alone in your need for revision.

Writing has three distinct advantages over speaking:

1. In writing, you can take it back. The spoken word, however, cannot be revised. Once you make a statement verbally, it affects your listeners in a particular way, and you can't rephrase it to the point that the first statement is forgotten. However, if you write a statement, look at it, and realize that it sounds offensive or incorrect, you can revise it before giving it to the intended audience. Writing is a careful, thoughtful way of communicating.

2. Writing forces you to clarify your thoughts. If you're having trouble writing, it's often because you're not yet finished with the thinking part. Sometimes, just sitting down and writing whatever is on your mind helps you discover and organize what you think.

3. Writing has permanence. Ideas presented in writing carry far more weight than do spoken ideas. Additionally, they can be reviewed and referred to in their exact, original form. Spoken ideas rely upon the sometimes inaccurate memories of other people.

Writing is nothing more than thought on paper—considered, organized thought. Many people are protective of their thoughts and, therefore, prefer to keep them hidden inside their heads. Many great ideas and observations are never born because their creators won't express them. This book can help you express your ideas in clear, grammatically correct ways. After you learn how to insert commas and semicolons correctly, use verbs to create strong images in your writing, and the other basic skills taught in this book, you'll gain confidence in your writing ability. In fact, you'll be able to move forward and master more complex writing concerns after you get the basics down. More and more jobs these days require at least some writing, so the skills you learn in this book will be put to good use.

The lessons in this book are designed to be completed in about 20 minutes each. If you do a lesson every weekday, you can finish the whole course in about a month. However, you may find another approach that works better for you. You'll find you make more progress, though, if you complete at least two lessons a week. If you leave too much time between lessons, you'll forget what you've learned. You may want to start with the pretest that begins on page 1. It will show you what you already know and what you need to learn about grammar, mechanics, and punctuation. Then, when you've finished the book, you can take a posttest to see how much you've improved.

If you practice what you've learned in this book, it won't take long for other people to notice the new and improved you. So dive into the first lesson and get ready to improve your writing skills. Good luck!

Pretest ▶

Before you start your study of grammar and writing skills, you may want to get an idea of how much you already know and how much you need to learn. If that's the case, take the pretest that follows. The pretest consists of 50 multiple-choice questions covering all the lessons in this book. Naturally, 50 questions can't cover every single concept or rule you will learn by working through these pages. So even if you answer all of the questions on the pretest correctly, it's almost guaranteed that you will find a few ideas or rules in this book that you didn't already know. On the other hand, if you get a lot of the answers wrong on this pretest, don't despair. This book will show you how to improve your grammar and writing, step by step.

So use this pretest for a general idea of how much of what's in this book you already know. If you get a high score, you may be able to spend less time with this book than you originally planned. If you get a low score, you may find that you will need more than 20 minutes a day to get through each chapter and learn all the grammar and mechanics concepts you need.

There's an answer sheet you can use for filling in the correct answers on page 3. Or, if you prefer, simply circle the answer numbers in this book. If the book doesn't belong to you, write the numbers 1–50 on a piece of paper, and record your answers there. Take as much time as you need to complete this short test. When you finish, check your answers against the answer key that follows. Each answer tells you which lesson of this book teaches you about the grammatical rule in that question.

1.	ⓐ	ⓑ	ⓒ	ⓓ
2.	ⓐ	ⓑ	ⓒ	ⓓ
3.	ⓐ	ⓑ	ⓒ	ⓓ
4.	ⓐ	ⓑ	ⓒ	ⓓ
5.	ⓐ	ⓑ	ⓒ	ⓓ
6.	ⓐ	ⓑ	ⓒ	ⓓ
7.	ⓐ	ⓑ	ⓒ	ⓓ
8.	ⓐ	ⓑ	ⓒ	ⓓ
9.	ⓐ	ⓑ	ⓒ	ⓓ
10.	ⓐ	ⓑ	ⓒ	ⓓ
11.	ⓐ	ⓑ	ⓒ	ⓓ
12.	ⓐ	ⓑ	ⓒ	ⓓ
13.	ⓐ	ⓑ	ⓒ	ⓓ
14.	ⓐ	ⓑ	ⓒ	ⓓ
15.	ⓐ	ⓑ	ⓒ	ⓓ
16.	ⓐ	ⓑ	ⓒ	ⓓ
17.	ⓐ	ⓑ	ⓒ	ⓓ

18.	ⓐ	ⓑ	ⓒ	ⓓ
19.	ⓐ	ⓑ	ⓒ	ⓓ
20.	ⓐ	ⓑ	ⓒ	ⓓ
21.	ⓐ	ⓑ	ⓒ	ⓓ
22.	ⓐ	ⓑ	ⓒ	ⓓ
23.	ⓐ	ⓑ	ⓒ	ⓓ
24.	ⓐ	ⓑ	ⓒ	ⓓ
25.	ⓐ	ⓑ	ⓒ	ⓓ
26.	ⓐ	ⓑ	ⓒ	ⓓ
27.	ⓐ	ⓑ	ⓒ	ⓓ
28.	ⓐ	ⓑ	ⓒ	ⓓ
29.	ⓐ	ⓑ	ⓒ	ⓓ
30.	ⓐ	ⓑ	ⓒ	ⓓ
31.	ⓐ	ⓑ	ⓒ	ⓓ
32.	ⓐ	ⓑ	ⓒ	ⓓ
33.	ⓐ	ⓑ	ⓒ	ⓓ
34.	ⓐ	ⓑ	ⓒ	ⓓ

35.	ⓐ	ⓑ	ⓒ	ⓓ
36.	ⓐ	ⓑ	ⓒ	ⓓ
37.	ⓐ	ⓑ	ⓒ	ⓓ
38.	ⓐ	ⓑ	ⓒ	ⓓ
39.	ⓐ	ⓑ	ⓒ	ⓓ
40.	ⓐ	ⓑ	ⓒ	ⓓ
41.	ⓐ	ⓑ	ⓒ	ⓓ
42.	ⓐ	ⓑ	ⓒ	ⓓ
43.	ⓐ	ⓑ	ⓒ	ⓓ
44.	ⓐ	ⓑ	ⓒ	ⓓ
45.	ⓐ	ⓑ	ⓒ	ⓓ
46.	ⓐ	ⓑ	ⓒ	ⓓ
47.	ⓐ	ⓑ	ⓒ	ⓓ
48.	ⓐ	ⓑ	ⓒ	ⓓ
49.	ⓐ	ⓑ	ⓒ	ⓓ
50.	ⓐ	ⓑ	ⓒ	ⓓ

Pretest

1. Which version of the sentence is correctly capitalized?

   a. Since you're here, you and Denise should plan to pay a quick visit to aunt Janice, uncle Don, and your Cousin Ray.

   b. Since you're here, you and Denise should plan to pay a quick visit to Aunt Janice, Uncle Don, and your cousin Ray.

   c. Since you're here, you and Denise should plan to pay a quick visit to Aunt Janice, uncle Don, and your Cousin Ray.

   d. Since you're here, you and Denise should plan to pay a quick visit to Aunt Janice, Uncle Don, and your Cousin Ray.

2. Which of the underlined words in the following sentence should be capitalized?

   The <u>governor</u> gave a speech at the <u>fourth</u> of July picnic, which was held at my <u>cousin's</u> farm five miles <u>east</u> of town.

   a. governor
   b. fourth
   c. cousin's
   d. east

3. Which of the underlined words in the following sentence should be capitalized?

   "Last <u>semester</u>, I wrote my <u>history</u> report on the Korean <u>war</u>," my <u>sister</u> told me.

   a. semester
   b. history
   c. war
   d. sister

4. Which version uses periods correctly?

   a. Dr Harrison will speak at a hotel in Chicago, IL, on Thurs at 3:00 P.M.

   b. Dr. Harrison will speak at a hotel in Chicago, IL., on Thurs at 3:00 PM.

   c. Dr Harrison will speak at a hotel in Chicago, IL., on Thurs. at 3:00 P.M.

   d. Dr. Harrison will speak at a hotel in Chicago, IL, on Thurs. at 3:00 P.M.

5. Which version uses punctuation correctly?

   a. Wow, that was a terrific novel? What other books has this author written!

   b. Wow! That was a terrific novel. What other books has this author written?

   c. Wow? That was a terrific novel! What other books has this author written?

   d. Wow. That was a terrific novel? What other books has this author written?

6. Which of the following is a sentence fragment, or NOT a complete sentence?

   a. Hearing the thunder, the lifeguard ordered us out of the water.

   b. Turn off the lights.

   c. Sunday afternoon spent reading and playing computer games.

   d. I was surprised to see that my neighbor had written a letter to the editor.

7. Three of the following sentences are either run-ons or comma splices. Which one is NOT a faulty sentence?

   a. The newspapers are supposed to be delivered by 7:00, but I am usually finished before 6:45.

   b. I called the delivery service this morning, they told me the shipment would arrive on time.

   c. Look in the closet you should find it there.

   d. I was the first to sign the petition Harry was second.

8. Which version is punctuated correctly?
   a. Charlotte, who ran in the Boston Marathon last year will compete in this year's New York Marathon.
   b. Charlotte who ran in the Boston Marathon, last year, will compete in this year's New York Marathon.
   c. Charlotte who ran in the Boston Marathon last year, will compete in this year's New York Marathon.
   d. Charlotte, who ran in the Boston Marathon last year, will compete in this year's New York Marathon.

9. Which version is punctuated correctly?
   a. The park service will not allow anyone, who does not have a camping permit, to use this campground.
   b. The park service will not allow anyone who does not have a camping permit to use this campground.
   c. The park service will not allow anyone, who does not have a camping permit to use this campground.
   d. The park service will not allow anyone who does not have a camping permit, to use this campground.

10. Which version is punctuated correctly?
   a. As soon as she finished her dinner, Lisa, who is a volunteer at the hospital, reported for her shift.
   b. As soon as she finished her dinner Lisa, who is a volunteer at the hospital reported for her shift.
   c. As soon as she finished, her dinner, Lisa who is a volunteer at the hospital, reported for her shift.
   d. As soon as she finished her dinner, Lisa who is a volunteer at the hospital reported for her shift.

11. Which of the underlined portions of the following sentence is punctuated incorrectly?

My mother was born on (**a**) <u>December 15, 1944,</u> in Kingwood, West (**b**) <u>Virginia, when</u> she was (**c**) <u>five, her</u> family moved to (**d**) <u>347 Benton Street, Zanesville, OH</u>.

   a. December 15, 1944,
   b. Virginia, when
   c. five, her
   d. 347 Benton Street, Zanesville, OH

12. Which version is punctuated correctly?
   a. Yes I would like to receive the credit card application and please send it as soon as you can to my home address.
   b. Yes, I would like to receive the credit card application and please send it, as soon as you can to my home address.
   c. Yes, I would like to receive the credit card application and, please send it as soon as you can to my home address.
   d. Yes, I would like to receive the credit card application, and please send it as soon as you can to my home address.

13. Which version is punctuated correctly?
   a. It seems, Brian, you have not been completely honest about the amount of time you've been spending on your studies. That is disappointing.
   b. It seems Brian you have not been completely honest about the amount of time you've been spending on your studies that is disappointing.
   c. It seems, Brian, you have not been completely honest about the amount of time you've been spending on your studies, that is disappointing.
   d. It seems Brian you have not been completely honest about the amount of time you've been spending on your studies. That is disappointing.

14. Which is the correct punctuation for the under-lined portion?

The weather forecasters are predicting 10 inches of snow <u>tonight therefore</u> the annual chili sup-per will be rescheduled for next week.

a. tonight, therefore
b. tonight, therefore,
c. tonight; therefore,
d. tonight, therefore;

15. Which is the correct punctuation for the under-lined portion?

You may choose to read any two of the follow-ing <u>novels The</u> Great Gatsby, Song of Solomon, Sophie's Choice, The Color Purple, The Bell Jar, and The Invisible Man.

a. novels, *The*
b. novels: *The*
c. novels; *the*
d. novels. *The*

16. Which version is punctuated correctly?
a. One of my complaints—if you really want to know is that the recycling bins are not clearly labeled.
b. One of my complaints—if you really want to know—is that the recycling bins are not clearly labeled.
c. One of my complaints, if you really want to know—is that the recycling bins are not clearly labeled.
d. One of my complaints if you really want to know is that the recycling bins are not clearly labeled.

17. Which version is punctuated correctly?
a. The childrens' books are located on the first floor.
b. The children's books are located on the first floor.
c. The childrens books are located on the first floor.
d. The childrens's books are located on the first floor.

18. Which version is punctuated correctly?
a. Whose coat is this? Is it yours or Eric's?
b. Whose coat is this? Is it your's or Eric's?
c. Who's coat is this? Is it your's or Eric's?
d. Who's coat is this? Is it yours or Eric's?

19. Which version is punctuated correctly?
a. "May I ride with you?" asked Del. "I can't get my car started."
b. May I ride with you? asked Del. "I can't get my car started."
c. "May I ride with you? asked Del. I can't get my car started."
d. "May I ride with you"? asked Del, "I can't get my car started."

20. Which of the following items should be placed in quotations marks and should NOT be italicized or underlined?
a. the title of a book
b. the title of a story
c. the title of a movie
d. the title of a newspaper

21. Which version uses hyphens correctly?
- **a.** The well-known singer-songwriter gave a three hour concert.
- **b.** The well known singer songwriter gave a three-hour concert.
- **c.** The well-known singer-songwriter gave a three-hour concert.
- **d.** The well known singer-songwriter gave a three hour concert.

22. Which of the following should NOT be hyphenated?
- **a.** forty-five dollars
- **b.** one-hundredth of an inch
- **c.** a ten-minute break
- **d.** five-pieces of gum

23. Which version uses parentheses correctly?
- **a.** I plan to do my geography report on the Central American country of Belize (formerly known as British Honduras).
- **b.** I plan to do my geography report on the (Central American country of) Belize, formerly known as British Honduras.
- **c.** I plan to do my (geography) report on the Central American country of Belize, formerly known as British Honduras.
- **d.** I plan to do my geography report on the Central American country (of Belize) formerly known as British Honduras.

For questions 24 and 25, choose the correct verb form.

24. Last night, Rita _____ a standing ovation for her performance.
- **a.** has gotten
- **b.** gotten
- **c.** will get
- **d.** got

25. Brandon _____ his camera so he could photograph the basketball game.
- **a.** brang
- **b.** brought
- **c.** bring
- **d.** had brung

26. Which of the following underlined verbs is NOT written in the correct tense?

Last year, I (**a**) <u>vacationed</u> in Jamaica. I (**b**) <u>sunbathe</u> on the beach every morning. In the afternoons, I (**c**) <u>explored</u> the island, and when evening came, I (**d**) <u>couldn't wait</u> to change my clothes and try another local restaurant.

- **a.** vacationed
- **b.** sunbathe
- **c.** explored
- **d.** couldn't wait

27. Choose the version that correctly rewrites the following sentence in the active voice.

I was taken to the public library by my sister before I was able to read.

- **a.** Before I was able to read, I was taken to the public library by my sister.
- **b.** Before learning to read, my sister took me to the public library.
- **c.** Before I was able to read, my sister took me to the public library.
- **d.** I was taken to the public library before I knew how to read, by my sister.

28. Which of the following sentences is in the passive voice?

    a. Maya hoped that her party would not be ruined by the impending thunderstorm.

    b. Maya was hoping that her party would not be ruined by the impending thunderstorm.

    c. Maya is hoping that her party won't be ruined by the impending thunderstorm.

    d. Maya has hoped that her party won't be ruined by the impending thunderstorm.

For questions 29 and 30, choose the verb that agrees with the subject of the sentence.

29. Neither of the boys _____ to basketball camp.

    a. have been

    b. were

    c. is been

    d. has been

30. Christian and Jennifer _____ to go canoeing next Saturday.

    a. are trying

    b. is trying

    c. tried

    d. have tried

31. Choose the subject that agrees with the verb in the following sentence.

    _____ of the customers have complained about poor service.

    a. One

    b. Neither

    c. Each

    d. Some

32. In which of the following sentences is the underlined verb NOT in agreement with the subject of the sentence?

    a. Where <u>are</u> the forms you want me to fill out?

    b. Which <u>is</u> the correct form?

    c. Here <u>is</u> the forms you need to complete.

    d. There <u>are</u> two people who still need to complete the form.

33. In which of the following sentences is the underlined pronoun incorrect?

    a. Alicia and <u>me</u> want to spend Saturday at Six Flags Amusement Park.

    b. Either Sam or William will bring <u>his</u> CD player to the party.

    c. She and <u>I</u> will work together on the project.

    d. Why won't you let <u>her</u> come with us?

34. In which of the following sentences are the underlined pronouns correct?

    a. Would <u>he</u> or <u>me</u> be a better bowling partner?

    b. Would <u>he</u> or <u>I</u> be a better bowling partner?

    c. Would <u>him</u> or <u>me</u> be a better bowling partner?

    d. Would <u>him</u> or <u>I</u> be a better bowling partner?

For questions 35–38, choose the option that correctly completes the sentence.

35. Four band members and _____ were chosen to attend the state competition. One of _____ will do the driving.

    a. me, we

    b. me, us

    c. I, we

    d. I, us

36. Marcus _____ the bags of groceries on the kitchen table 15 minutes ago.

    a. had sat

    b. set

    c. sit

    d. sat

37. About five minutes after the sun _____,
my alarm goes off, and _____ time to
get up.
  a. raises, it's
  b. raises, its
  c. rises, it's
  d. rises, its

38. Julian ran _____ in the race today, but Kyle
wound up with a _____ score.
  a. good, better
  b. good, best
  c. well, better
  d. well, best

39. Which of the sentences is clearly and correctly
written?
  a. Driving along the country road, a deer ran in
  front of us.
  b. A deer ran in front of us while driving along
  the country road.
  c. As we were driving along the country road, a
  deer ran in front of us.
  d. Running in front of us, we saw the deer, driving along the country road.

For questions 40–46, choose the option that correctly
completes the sentence.

40. If we divide this pizza _____ the five
people here, there won't be _____ pieces
left over.
  a. among, any
  b. among, no
  c. between, any
  d. between, no

41. Yesterday, I _____ the campers to the
_____ we had chosen near the river.
  a. lead, cite
  b. lead, site
  c. led, cite
  d. led, site

42. As we have done in the _____, we will
_____ at the coffeehouse at 10:00 A.M.
  a. past, meet
  b. past, meat
  c. passed, meet
  d. passed, meat

43. As you can _____ see, there has been a
_____ in the water pipe.
  a. planely, brake
  b. planely, break
  c. plainly, brake
  d. plainly, break

44. Do you know _____ Teresa will
_____ to join our organization?
  a. weather, choose
  b. weather, chose
  c. whether, choose
  d. whether, chose

45. Did you _____ the team jacket you were
supposed to _____ to the meet this afternoon?
  a. loose, wear
  b. lose, where
  c. loss, wear
  d. lose, wear

46. Do you _____ if Serena Williams
_____ the tournament?
  a. know, one
  b. know, won
  c. no, one
  d. no, won

47. Which of the following phrases contains a redundancy? (It expresses the same idea twice, with different words.)

   a. I did not go to the shopping mall.

   b. She always does very well in school.

   c. The judges have temporarily delayed the competition until later.

   d. Liz and Lauren have both contributed greatly to the fundraising campaign.

48. Which of the following sentences contains a cliché?

   a. Why not start now? There's no time like the present.

   b. Just keep trying. You'll catch on.

   c. Whew! I'm tired.

   d. I'm as shocked at the news as you are.

49. Which version has a consistent point of view?

   a. The history of English is divided into three periods. You could mark the earliest one at about the fifth century A.D.

   b. You can say that the history of English could be divided into three periods, and I know the earliest one begins about the fifth century A.D.

   c. The history of English is divided into three periods. The earliest one begins at about the fifth century A.D.

   d. I learned that the history of English is divided into three periods and that you begin the earliest one at about the fifth century A.D.

50. Which version has a parallel structure?

   a. We write for a variety of purposes: in expressing our feelings, to convey information, to persuade, or to give pleasure.

   b. We write for a variety of purposes: to express our feelings, convey information, persuasion, or giving pleasure.

   c. We write for a variety of purposes: an expression of our feelings, conveying information, persuade, or to give pleasure.

   d. We write for a variety of purposes: to express our feelings, to convey information, to persuade, or to give pleasure.

Answers

If you missed any of the answers, you can find help for that kind of question in the lesson shown to the right of the answer.

1. b. Lesson 1	**26. b.** Lesson 10
2. b. Lesson 1	**27. c.** Lesson 11
3. c. Lesson 1	**28. b.** Lesson 11
4. d. Lesson 2	**29. d.** Lesson 12
5. b. Lesson 2	**30. a.** Lesson 12
6. c. Lesson 3	**31. d.** Lesson 12
7. a. Lesson 3	**32. c.** Lesson 12
8. d. Lesson 4	**33. a.** Lesson 13
9. b. Lesson 4	**34. b.** Lesson 13
10. a. Lesson 4	**35. d.** Lesson 13
11. b. Lessons 5, 6	**36. b.** Lesson 14
12. d. Lesson 5	**37. c.** Lesson 14
13. a. Lesson 5	**38. c.** Lesson 14
14. c. Lesson 6	**39. c.** Lesson 15
15. b. Lesson 6	**40. a.** Lesson 15
16. b. Lesson 7	**41. d.** Lesson 16
17. b. Lesson 7	**42. a.** Lesson 16
18. a. Lesson 7	**43. d.** Lesson 16
19. a. Lesson 8	**44. c.** Lesson 17
20. b. Lesson 8	**45. d.** Lesson 17
21. c. Lesson 9	**46. b.** Lesson 17
22. d. Lesson 9	**47. c.** Lesson 18
23. a. Lesson 9	**48. a.** Lesson 18
24. d. Lesson 10	**49. c.** Lesson 19
25. b. Lesson 10	**50. d.** Lesson 19

Answer Explanations

1. Choice **B** is correct. *Aunt* and *Uncle* are being used as names, whereas *your cousin* is describing Ray; it's not part of his name.

   Choice **A** is incorrect. *Aunt* and *Uncle* should be capitalized because they are used as names here; *cousin* should not be capitalized because it is being used as an adjective describing your relationship to Ray.

   Choice **C** is incorrect. *Uncle* should be capitalized because it is being used as a name; *cousin* should not be capitalized because it is being used as an adjective describing your relationship to Ray.

   Choice **D** is incorrect. *Cousin* should not be capitalized because it is being used as an adjective describing your relationship to Ray.

2. Choice **B** is correct. The Fourth of July is a holiday, which makes the entire phrase a proper noun that should be capitalized.

   Choice **A** is incorrect. Because *governor* is preceded by the article *the*, it is not a proper noun. Therefore, it should stay lowercase.

   Choice **C** is incorrect. *Cousin* is not a proper noun unless it's a direct part of a name or title. It should not be capitalized here.

   Choice **D** is incorrect. *East* is given as a direction here, not a specific geographical region, so it should not be capitalized in this sentence.

3. Choice **C** is correct. The war in question is a specific one: the Korean War. This should be capitalized as a proper noun.

   Choice **A** is incorrect. *Semester* is not a proper noun and should not be capitalized.

   Choice **B** is incorrect. Your sister is not referring to a particular history class, but rather a general history report; therefore, the word should not be capitalized.

   Choice **D** is incorrect. Your sister is not named here, so *sister* should not be considered a proper noun in this case.

4. Choice **D** is correct. All abbreviations in this sentence except *IL* should be punctuated with a period.

   Choice **A** is incorrect. The abbreviations *Dr.* (doctor), *Thurs.* (Thursday), and *P.M.* (*post meridiem*) should always be followed by a period.

   Choice **B** is incorrect. State abbreviations like *IL* should not be followed by a period, but abbreviations for days of the week like *Thurs.* should be followed by a period.

   Choice **C** is incorrect. State abbreviations like *IL* should not be followed by a period, but the abbreviation *Dr.* (doctor) should always be followed by a period.

5. Choice **B** is correct. *Wow* is an exclamation and is punctuated correctly with an exclamation point. *That was a terrific novel* is a statement, so the period is correct. And *What other books has this author written* is a question, so the question mark is correct.

   Choice **A** is incorrect. The first sentence, *Wow, that was a terrific novel*, is a statement, not a question, and should not end with a question mark. The second sentence is a question, not an exclamatory statement, and should end with a question mark instead of an exclamation point.

   Choice **C** is incorrect. *Wow* is an exclamation, not a question, so it should end with an exclamation point.

   Choice **D** is incorrect. *Wow* is an exclamation, not a statement, so it should end with an exclamation point. Also, *That was a terrific novel* is a statement, not a question, and should end with a period instead of a question mark.

6. Choice **C** is correct. *Saturday afternoon spent reading and playing computer games* is not a complete sentence. It is missing a verb and does not express a complete thought: *Who spent Saturday afternoon reading and playing video games? Saturday afternoon spent reading and playing computer games is what?* The information is incomplete, and so this is a sentence fragment.

Choice **A** is incorrect. *Hearing the thunder* is a fragment, but it is followed by a complete sentence (*the lifeguard ordered us out of the water*). Therefore, it is an independent clause and not a fragment.

Choice **B** is incorrect. *Turn off the lights* is an order directed at the listener (an implied *you*), so it is considered a complete sentence.

Choice **D** is incorrect. This choice contains all the necessary elements of a sentence: subjects (*I* and *my neighbor*), verbs (*was* and *had written*), and a complete thought.

7. Choice **A** is correct. This choice contains two complete thoughts, joined by the conjunction *but*. Therefore, it is a compound sentence, not a faulty one.

Choice **B** is incorrect. *I called the delivery service this morning* is a complete sentence, as is *they told me the shipment would arrive on time*. However, there is no coordinating conjunction to connect the two thoughts, so this choice is a comma splice.

Choice **C** is incorrect. There is no punctuation to tell you where one statement ends and the other begins, which makes this a run-on sentence.

Choice **D** is incorrect. *I was the first to sign the petition* is a complete thought, and *Harry was second* is another. However, because there is no

separation between the two thoughts, this is a run-on sentence.

8. Choice **D** is correct. The subordinate clause is correctly set off by commas, and *year's* has the correct apostrophe.

Choice **A** is incorrect. There should be a comma after *year* to set off the subordinate clause *who ran in the Boston Marathon last year*. Additionally, there should be an apostrophe in *year's* because it is possessive.

Choice **B** is incorrect. There should be a comma after *Charlotte* to set off the subordinate clause *who ran in the Boston Marathon last year*. Also, the comma after *Boston Marathon* which should not be there.

Choice **C** is incorrect. There should be a comma after *Charlotte* to set off the subordinate clause *who ran in the Boston Marathon last year*.

9. Choice **B** is correct. *Who does not have a camping permit* is a restrictive clause (meaning it offers essential information), so it should not be set off with commas. The sentence is punctuated correctly.

Choice **A** is incorrect. *Who does not have a camping permit* is a restrictive clause (meaning it offers essential information), so it should not be set off with commas.

Choice **C** is incorrect. The comma after the word *anyone* is incorrect and confusing—it doesn't set off a subordinate clause, and it separates the information into two disjointed parts.

Choice **D** is incorrect. The comma after *permit* incorrectly separates the sentence into two parts without indicating a clause or forming any particular order.

10. Choice **A** is correct. The commas in this sentence group the clauses correctly: *As soon as she finished her dinner* is the introductory clause, *who is a volunteer at the hospital* is a nonrestrictive clause, and *Lisa . . . reported for her shift* is the independent clause that holds the sentence together.

Choice **B** is incorrect. Because *who is a volunteer at the hospital* is a nonrestrictive clause (it offers extra information about Lisa that is not essential to the sentence), a comma is needed after *hospital* to set it off.

Choice **C** is incorrect. *Her dinner* is not a clause on its own and should not be set off by commas.

Choice **D** is incorrect. Because *who is a volunteer at the hospital* is a nonrestrictive clause (it offers extra information about Lisa that is not essential to the sentence), commas are needed after *Lisa* and after *hospital* to set it off.

11. Choice **D** is correct. When punctuating a street address you should always use a comma after the street address and after the town name.

Choice **A** is incorrect. Although a date should always have a comma after the day (*December 15,*) it is not essential to have a comma after the year unless the date is part of a subordinate clause.

Choice **B** is incorrect. Using a comma instead of a semicolon or a period here creates a run-on sentence.

Choice **C** is incorrect. *When she was five* is a restrictive, or essential, clause that tells you when the speaker's mother moved, relative to her birth date. Therefore, it shouldn't be set off with a comma.

12. Choice **D** is correct. *Yes* is an introductory clause and should be followed by a comma. This is a compound sentence: *I would like to receive the credit card* is the first independent clause, and *Please send it as soon as you can* is the second independent clause. The comma should come before the coordinating conjunction (*and*) that connects the sentence's two independent clauses.

Choice **A** is incorrect. With no punctuation at all, this is a run-on sentence.

Choice **B** is incorrect. *And* is used as a coordinating conjunction connecting the sentence's two independent clauses. The comma should come before the coordinating conjunction, not after *it*.

Choice **C** is incorrect. *And* is used as a coordinating conjunction connecting the sentence's two independent clauses. The comma should come before the coordinating conjunction.

13. Choice **A** is correct. The independent clause (*It seems . . . you have not been completely honest about the amount of time you've been spending on your studies*) surrounds an appositive (*Brian*). This appositive is set off by commas because it is restating the name of *you*, the person to whom the speaker is addressing. *That is disappointing* is correctly separated as its own sentence.

Choice **B** is incorrect. Without commas, semicolons, periods, or anything else separating the parts of the sentence, the meaning is incredibly difficult to figure out. This is a run-on sentence.

Choice **C** is incorrect. While *Brian* is correctly set off with commas, the comma after *studies* incorrectly turns the sentence into a comma splice (two independent clauses joined by a comma).

Choice **D** is incorrect. The sentences are correctly split into two, but the appositive *Brian* should be set off by commas because it is restating the name of *you*, the person to whom the speaker is addressing.

14. Choice **C** is correct. The semicolon divides the independent clauses into separate (but related) thoughts without needing a conjunction. Because *therefore* becomes an introductory word after the semicolon, it is correctly punctuated with a comma.

Choice **A** is incorrect. A comma between *tonight* and *therefore* (without a coordinating conjunction) creates a comma splice because both parts of the sentence are independent clauses.

Choice **B** is incorrect. A comma between *tonight* and *therefore* (without a coordinating conjunction) creates a comma splice because both parts of the sentence are independent clauses.

Choice **D** is incorrect. The semicolon and the comma are switched.

15. Choice **B** is correct. *Two of the following* lets you know that a list is coming, and a colon is the correct punctuation mark to introduce a list.

Choice **A** is incorrect. A comma is not the correct punctuation mark to introduce a list and leaves the list without definition.

Choice **C** is incorrect. A semicolon is used to separate independent thoughts and is not the correct punctuation mark to introduce a list.

Choice **D** is incorrect. The list of books is not a sentence on its own; using a period after *novels* is incorrect.

16. Choice **B** is correct. The em-dashes are used to set off the author's own comment (*if you really want to know*) because 1) the author is pausing to add this aside; and 2) the information contained in the clause is not essential to the meaning of the sentence.

Choice **A** is incorrect. The em-dash (—) is used for emphasis, as well as for separating nonrestrictive clauses. The punctuation should be consistent within a sentence. If you start a clause off with an em-dash, you should end it with an em-dash as well.

Choice **C** is incorrect. The punctuation should be consistent within a sentence. If you start a clause off with an em-dash, you should end it with an em-dash as well.

Choice **D** is incorrect. The absence of all punctuation makes this sentence very difficult to understand. The author's comment (*if you really want to know*) should be set off with em-dashes.

17. Choice **B** is correct. *Mr. Clayton* is correctly set off by a comma to indicate that he is the new candidate. Because this completes the thought of the first independent clause, it is followed by a semicolon to set the pause before the reader moves onto the related (but independent) second independent clause of the compound sentence.

Choice **A** is incorrect. With only one comma, it's unclear what role *Mr. Clayton* plays in the sentence. Is he the new candidate, or is he the person whom the speaker is addressing? Also, the placement of the comma between the independent clauses with no coordinating conjunction creates a comma splice.

Choice **C** is incorrect. *Mr. Clayton* belongs to the sentence before it, as it describes the new candidate. It should not be separated by a period.

Choice **D** is incorrect. The presence of a single comma is incorrect and makes the sentence unclear. Who is the candidate? Which clauses are subordinate? This punctuation makes it very difficult to discern the meaning of the sentence.

18. Choice **A** is correct. *Whose* and *yours* are possessive pronouns, so no apostrophe is needed in either case. *Eric's* is possessive, so it should have an apostrophe.

Choice **B** is incorrect. *Yours* should never have an apostrophe. Possessive pronouns do not require apostrophes, even when they are plural.

Choice **C** is incorrect. The possessive pronoun of *who* is *whose*, not *who's*, and *yours* should never have an apostrophe. Possessive pronouns do not require apostrophes, even when they are plural.

Choice **D** is incorrect. The possessive pronoun of *who* is *whose*, not *who's*. However, possessive versions of names (like *Eric*) should always have an apostrophe (*Eric's*).

19. Choice **A** is correct. Del's two direct quotes should be punctuated with quotation marks.

    Choice **B** is incorrect. Without quotation marks, the reader can't tell that *May I ride with you?* is a direct quote from Del.

    Choice **C** is incorrect. *Asked Del* is a tag that tells you who is speaking; it is not part of the quotation. You should be careful to make sure that each part of the quote has the necessary opening and closing quotation marks.

    Choice **D** is incorrect. The question mark is part of Del's quote, so it should be included inside the ending quotation mark.

20. Choice **B** is correct. Stories and other smaller parts of a larger work should be placed in quotation marks.

    Choice **A** is incorrect. A book is considered a complete work in itself, so it should be italicized or underlined.

    Choice **C** is incorrect. A movie is considered a complete work in itself, so it should be italicized or underlined.

    Choice **D** is incorrect. A newspaper is a larger work containing smaller pieces (articles), so it should be italicized or underlined.

21. Choice **C** is correct. The adjective phrase, the coequal nouns, and the number-word adjective phrase should all be hyphenated.

    Choice **A** is incorrect. *Well-known* and *singer-songwriter* are hyphenated correctly, but *three-hour* should also have a hyphen because it is a number-word adjective.

    Choice **B** is incorrect. *Well* and *known* work together as a single adjective , and because the adjective phrase comes before the noun, it

should contain a hyphen. Additionally, *singer* and *songwriter* should be hyphenated because they are coequal nouns working together to describe a single person.

    Choice **D** is incorrect. The adjective phrase *well-known* should be hyphenated because they work together as a single adjective and come before the noun they modify. The number-word adjective *three-hour* should also be hyphenated.

22. Choice **D** is correct. *Five* and *pieces* are separate words and not joined together as an adjective. Therefore, they should not be connected with a hyphen.

    Choice **A** is incorrect. All numbers between 21 and 99 should contain hyphens when they're written as words.

    Choice **B** is incorrect. Fractions that are written as words should be hyphenated.

    Choice **C** is incorrect. Number-word adjective phrases should always contain hyphens.

23. Choice **A** is correct. The parentheses are used to set off additional information (the former name of Belize) that is not necessary to the sentence's meaning.

    Choice **B** is incorrect. *Central American country of* does not interrupt the sentence, and if it were removed, crucial information about where the country is located would be missing.

    Choice **C** is incorrect. The information inside the parentheses is not extra information, and if it were removed, you wouldn't be able to tell what kind of report the speaker is writing.

    Choice **D** is incorrect. The information inside the parentheses is not extra information, and if it were removed, you would not know which country the report covers.

24. Choice **D** is correct. *Got* is the past tense of *to get*, and because the event happened last night (and is not still happening), a past tense is correct.

Choice **A** is incorrect. *Last night* tells you that the event is in the past. *Has gotten* is the present perfect tense, which is not correct in this sentence.

Choice **B** is incorrect. *Gotten* is the past participle of *to get*, but it is not correct here because past participles should always be preceded by *has/have/had*.

Choice **C** is incorrect. *Last night* tells you that the event is in the past, but *will get* is future tense.

25. Choice **B** is correct. *So he could photograph the basketball game* is the past tense, so this tells you that you are looking for another past tense verb for consistency. *Brought* is the correct past tense form of the verb *to bring*.

    Choice **A** is incorrect. *Brang* is not a word, and it is not a correct form of the verb *to bring*.

    Choice **C** is incorrect. Because *So he could photograph the basketball game* is in the past tense, the simple perfect tense (*bring*) does not fit in this sentence.

    Choice **D** is incorrect. *Brung* is not a word, and *had brung* is not a correct form of the verb *to bring*.

26. Choice **B** is correct. Because the sentence starts with the past tense, you should make sure that all of the other verbs in the sentence are consistent. *Sunbathe* is the present tense and does not fit in with the rest of the sentence; it should be *sunbathed*.

    Choice **A** is incorrect. *Last year* indicates that the vacation happened in the past, and *vacationed* is the correct past tense verb.

    Choice **C** is incorrect. The verb *explored* is in the correct past tense.

    Choice **D** is incorrect. *Couldn't* is the past tense, which matches the rest of the sentence.

27. Choice **C** is correct. Although *was* can indicate passive voice in some cases, here it's used as an active verb because it describes the speaker,

not a third person. Additionally, *my sister took me to the public library* is now written in the active voice—the sister is performing the action directly.

Choice **A** is incorrect. *I was taken* is written in the passive voice.

Choice **B** is incorrect. The introductory clause *Before learning to read* appears to be modifying *my sister*. This incorrectly changes the meaning of the original sentence, even though the writer removed the passive tense.

Choice **D** is incorrect. *Was taken* and *by my sister* are both passive phrases.

28. Choice **B** is correct. *Maya was hoping* contains a passive verb phrase because there is an additional verb separating the subject (*Maya*) and the active verb (*hoping*).

    Choice **A** is incorrect. *Maya hoped* contains an active verb phrase, not a passive verb phrase.

    Choice **C** is incorrect. *Maya is hoping* contains a future tense verb, not a passive verb phrase.

    Choice **D** is incorrect. *Maya has hoped* contains a past perfect tense verb, not a passive verb phrase.

29. Choice **D** is correct. *Has been* is a singular verb and agrees with the singular pronoun *neither*, which is the subject of the sentence.

    Choice **A** is incorrect. *Have been* suggests that the subjects are plural; and although *boys* is plural, *neither* is the subject of the sentence and is a singular pronoun, which means that the sentence talks about the boys individually.

    Choice **B** is incorrect. This choice is missing the past participle. This sentence would read *Neither of the boys were to basketball camp*. The boys *were* doing what? This choice leaves you hanging. It also suggests a plural subject, which doesn't match the actual, singular subject (*neither*).

Choice **C** is incorrect. *Is been* is not a correct form of the verb *to be*, so it cannot be correct in this sentence.

30. Choice **A** is correct. *Christian and Jennifer* is a plural subject, so *are* is correct. *Next Saturday* indicates that the event will happen in the future, but they *are trying* now, so the present form of the verb is needed.

    Choice **B** is incorrect. *Is* is singular, but *Christian and Jennifer* is a plural subject.

    Choice **C** is incorrect. Because you know that the event has not yet taken place (the introductory phrase *next Saturday* indicates that the event will happen in the future), the past tense verb *tried* can be eliminated.

    Choice **D** is incorrect. Because the introductory phrase *next Saturday* indicates that the event has not yet taken place, the past tense verb *have tried* can be eliminated.

31. Choice **D** is correct. *Some* means more than one customer, which agrees with the plural verb *have complained*.

    Choice **A** is incorrect. The verb *have complained* suggests that the number of customers is plural, so the singular pronoun *one* cannot be correct.

    Choice **B** is incorrect. The verb *have complained* suggests that the number of customers is plural, so the singular pronoun *neither* cannot be correct.

    Choice **C** is incorrect. The verb *have complained* suggests that the number of customers is plural, so the singular pronoun *each* cannot be correct.

32. Choice **C** is correct. The verb *is* is singular, and it does not agree with the plural subject *forms*.

    Choice **A** is incorrect. *Are* agrees with the plural *forms*.

Choice **B** is incorrect. The verb *is* agrees with the singular *form*.

Choice **D** is incorrect. The verb *are* agrees with the plural *people*.

33. Choice **A** is correct. The underlined pronoun is acting as the subject of the sentence along with Alicia, so the nominative case pronoun *I* is needed.

    Choice **B** is incorrect. The conjunction *either . . . or* means that Sam and William treated separately, and therefore singularly, so the singular pronoun *his* is correct.

    Choice **C** is incorrect. *I* is used correctly as a nominative case pronoun in the subject of the sentence, naming the speaker along with *she*.

    Choice **D** is incorrect. *Her* is the correct objective case pronoun because it follows the action verb *let*.

34. Choice **B** is correct. Both *he* and *I* are the correct nominative case pronouns in the subject of this sentence.

    Choice **A** is incorrect. *He* is the correct nominative case pronoun, but *me* is an objective case pronoun. Because these make up the subject of the sentence, both pronouns need to be in the nominative case. *Me* should be *I*.

    Choice **C** is incorrect. *Him* and *me* are objective case pronouns, but they are acting as the subjects of the sentence. Pronouns that act as subjects must be in the nominative case.

    Choice **D** is incorrect. *Him* is objective and *I* is nominative. Because these make up the subject of the sentence, both pronouns need to be in the nominative case.

35. Choice **D** is correct. The nominative case pronoun *I* and the objective case pronoun *us* are used correctly in this sentence.

    Choice **A** is incorrect. *Me* is an objective case pronoun, but in this sentence it is acting as the subject, which requires a nominative case pronoun. Also, *we* is a nominative case pronoun, but in this sentence it is the object of the preposition *of*, which requires an objective case pronoun.

Choice **B** is incorrect. *Me* is an objective case pronoun, but in this sentence it is acting as the subject, which requires a nominative case pronoun.

Choice **C** is incorrect. In the second sentence, *we* is a nominative case pronoun, but in this sentence it is the object of the preposition *of*, which requires an objective case pronoun.

36. Choice **B** is correct. *Set*, which means *to put* or *to place*, is the most accurate description of Marcus leaving the bags of groceries on the counter.

Choice **A** is incorrect. In sentences like this, you should look at the meanings of the words you're filling in. *Sat* means *rested*; is that the meaning you want? *Set*, which means *to put* or *to place*, is a more accurate description of Marcus leaving the bags of groceries on the counter. *Rested* is close, but would you normally say that he *rested* something on the counter, or that he *put* something on the counter?

Choice **C** is incorrect. *Sit* is a present tense verb, while the sentence reveals that the action took place 15 minutes in the past. A past tense verb is needed.

Choice **D** is incorrect. In sentences like this, you should look at the meanings of the words you're filling in. *Sat* means *rested*; is that the meaning you want? *Set*, which means *to put* or *to place*, is a more accurate description of Marcus leaving the bags of groceries on the counter. *Rested* is close, but would you normally say that he *rested* something on the counter, or that he *put* something on the counter?

37. Choice **C** is correct. Both the word choice (*rises*) and the contraction *it's* are correct.

Choice **A** is incorrect. Because *raise* is a verb easily confused with *rise*, you need to look closely at the word's meaning. To *raise* means to *move up*. Does the sun *move up*, or does it *go up*? In this case, *rise* is the more accurate option.

Choice **B** is incorrect. Because *raise* is a verb easily confused with *rise*, you need to look closely at the word's meaning. To *raise* means to *move up*. Does the sun *move up*, or does it *go up*? In this case, *rise* is the more accurate option. Additionally, the possessive pronoun *its* is incorrect in this sentence. *Its* should be *it's*, the contraction of *it is*.

Choice **D** is incorrect. Additionally, the possessive pronoun *its* is incorrect in this sentence. *Its* should be *it's*, the contraction of *it is*.

38. Choice **D** is correct. The adverb w*ell* modifies *ran*, and the superlative modifier *best* tells you how Kyle's score compares to Julian's and any other runners' who aren't mentioned by name.

Choice **A** is incorrect. In the first blank, you're seeking a word to modify the verb *ran*—in other words, an adverb. *Good* is an adjective, so you can eliminate this choice. Also, *better* is a comparative adverb that compares two items. However, the word *overall* suggests that there were more scores than Kyle's and Julian's, so you need a different modifier that compares more than two scores. In this case, that would be the superlative adverb, *best*.

Choice **B** is incorrect. In the first blank, you're seeking a word to modify the verb *ran*—in other words, an adverb. *Good* is an adjective, so you can eliminate this choice.

Choice **C** is incorrect. *Well* is an adverb that correctly modifies the verb *ran*. *Better* is a comparative adverb that compares two items, but the word *overall* suggests that there were more scores than Kyle's and Julian's. A different modifier is needed that compares more than two scores. In this case, that would be the superlative adverb, *best*.

39. Choice **C** is correct. In the introductory clause it is clear that *we* are driving the car. The pause at the comma lets you know that the two ideas are separate (that we were driving the car AND that the deer ran across the road in front of the car). This sentence is the clearest of the choices.

Choice **A** is incorrect. Because *a deer* directly follows *Driving along the country road*, it sounds like the deer is driving the car. This is an amusing image, but it makes for an incorrect and unclear sentence.

Choice **B** is incorrect. The way this sentence is written, it's unclear who is driving the car. Any scenario that could end with the deer driving the car should be eliminated as an incorrect sentence.

Choice **D** is incorrect. This sentence manages to make it sound like the people are running and the deer is driving. It is very unclear and needs to be rewritten.

40. Choice **A** is correct. *Among* means that more than two people will be involved; the sentence tells you that there are five people. For the second blank, look at the clues around the blank: *there won't be . . . pieces left over*. You know there will be no pieces left, but hopefully you also noticed that the sentence already contains *won't*. Another negative word like *no* would create a double negative, which indicates that *any* is correct.

Choice **B** is incorrect. *Among* matches *five people*, but *no* creates a double negative with *won't*.

Choice **C** is incorrect. The preposition *between* is incorrect because it divides into two, and you already know from the sentence that you're dealing with five people.

Choice **D** is incorrect. The preposition *between* is incorrect because it divides into two, and you already know from the sentence that you're dealing with five people. Also, the word *no* creates an incorrect double negative with *won't*.

41. Choice **D** is correct. The sentence tells you that the action took place yesterday, so the past tense verb *led* is correct. Also, *site* refers to a physical location and has the correct meaning in this sentence: *I led the campers to the [place] we had chosen by the river*.

Choice **A** is incorrect. *Lead* is the simple present tense of the verb. However, the sentence tells you that the action took place yesterday, so the present tense is incorrect. For *cite/site*, you should look at the meaning of each word and determine which fits best. *Cite* means to refer to something, while *site* refers to a physical location. In the context of this sentence, *cite* is not the correct word because it does not have the correct meaning.

Choice **B** is incorrect. *Lead* is the simple present tense of the verb. However, the sentence tells you that the action took place yesterday, so the present tense is incorrect.

Choice **C** is incorrect. The past-tense *led* is correct. However, *cite* means to refer to something, while *site* refers to a physical location. In the context of this sentence, *cite* is not the correct word because it does not have the correct meaning.

42. Choice **A** is correct. The noun *past* completes the prepositional phrase; and the verb *meet* creates the action in the sentence.

Choice **B** is incorrect. Look closely at the sentence. *Meat* means flesh. Does it make sense that you will "[flesh] at the coffeehouse at 10:00 A.M."? *Meat* is a noun, but you need a verb to complete the sentence.

Choice **C** is incorrect. *In the _____* is a prepositional phrase, so you're looking for a noun to fill in the blank as the object of the preposition. *Passed* is a verb, so it is incorrect here.

Choice **D** is incorrect. *Passed* is a verb, not a noun, so it cannot complete the prepositional phrase. Also, *meat* is a noun, but a verb is needed to complete the sentence.

43. Choice **D** is correct. *Plainly* is the correct adverb to modify *see*, and a *break* (or disruption) in the pipe sounds more realistic than a *brake* (or a device/object) in the pipe.

Choice **A** is incorrect. *Planely* is not a real word, and without a valid definition, you can't tell how the word should fit into the sentence. Also, if you think about the meaning of the word *brake*, the word doesn't seem to fit into the sentence either: *. . . there has been a [device for slowing] in the water pipe.*

Choice **B** is incorrect. *Planely* is not a real word, and without a valid definition, you can't tell how the word should fit into the sentence. *Break*, when used as a noun, means *a disruption*. This is the correct meaning for this sentence.

Choice **C** is incorrect. The adverb *plainly* (or obviously) has the correct meaning for this sentence. However, if you think about the meaning of the word *brake*, the word doesn't seem to fit into the sentence: *. . . there has been a [device for slowing] in the water pipe.*

44. Choice **C** is correct. The conjunction *whether* works with the verb *to choose* (it sets up Teresa's alternatives of choosing the organization or not choosing the organization), and the future tense of *choose* aligns with *Teresa will.*

Choice **A** is incorrect. This is another question where you should look at the definitions of two easily confused words. *Weather,* a noun, is an atmospheric state. *Whether,* a conjunction, is meant to introduce alternatives. In the context of this sentence, the conjunction *whether* has the correct meaning.

Choice **B** is incorrect. In addition to *weather* not having the correct meaning for this sentence, *chose* is incorrect as well. The sentence is in future tense (*Teresa will*), so the past-tense verb *chose* is not consistent with the rest of the sentence.

Choice **D** is incorrect. This usage of *whether* is correct, but the past-tense verb *chose* is not consistent with the rest of the sentence in future tense.

45. Choice **D** is correct. When you read the sentence, you can see that you need a verb in each blank. *Lose* is a verb, and so is *wear*; both have the correct meanings to complete this sentence.

Choice **A** is incorrect. *Loose* is either an adjective that means *free* or *not tight*, or a verb that means *to set free*. In this sentence, you need a verb that goes with the subject, *jacket*. It is not likely that you'd be setting a team jacket free, so you should look for another verb that better fits the meaning of the sentence.

Choice **B** is incorrect. The verb *lose* is correct in this sentence ("Did you [fail to keep] the team jacket?"), but the second part of the sentence calls for a verb as well. *Where* is an adverb that describes place.

Choice **C** is incorrect. *Loss* is a noun, while you already know from reading the sentence that you need a verb. However, *wear* is the correct verb form of the easily confused word in the second blank.

46. Choice **B** is correct. Both *know* and *won* are verbs. When you insert them into the sentence, the thought is complete and makes sense: *Do you know if Serena Williams won the tournament?*

Choice **A** is incorrect. From the context of the sentence, you can tell that you need a verb (alongside the subject *you*) and then another verb (what act did Serena Williams perform?). *Know* is a verb, but *one* is a noun, making it an incorrect choice for the second blank.

Choice **C** is incorrect. *No* is a versatile word that can be several different parts of speech (noun, adverb, adjective), but it is never a verb. *One* is also not a verb; it's a noun meaning *single*. Neither word fits the sentence.

Choice **D** is incorrect. *No* is a versatile word that can be several different parts of speech (noun, adverb, adjective), but it is never a verb. *Won* is a verb and has the correct meaning to complete this sentence.

47. Choice **C** is correct. When you see the words *temporarily delayed*, you can already infer that the judges have postponed the competition to a future date. Therefore, *until later* at the end of the sentence repeats information you already know and is therefore redundant.

Choice **A** is incorrect. This sentence is straightforward; nothing is repeated.

Choice **B** is incorrect. This sentence does have two modifiers that describe *well* (*very* and *in school*), but they do not compete by expressing the same idea.

Choice **D** is incorrect. Because you see two subjects (Liz and Lauren) as well as the word *both*, you might assume that this is redundant. However, *both* is an important compound pronoun that tells you that each woman performed the action in the sentence and is not redundant.

48. Choice **A** is correct. "There's no time like the present" is an exact phrase you've undoubtedly heard hundreds (if not thousands!) of times in your life. If you read or hear a sentence that automatically sounds like you ve heard it before in that exact form, it is very likely a cliché.

Choice **B** is incorrect. *Just keep trying* may be a common idea, but as a specific phrase it isn t necessarily a cliché. The idea may be a cliché, but this particular phrase is not.

Choice **C** is incorrect. This sentence is a statement of how the speaker is feeling. Again, this might be a common feeling or sentiment, but a cliché is a specific phrase that has been used over and over.

Choice **D** is incorrect. This sentence is more of a statement of a common feeling than a specific phrase or sentence that you've heard before.

49. Choice **C** is correct. Both the first and second sentences are told in the third person.

Choice **A** is incorrect. This choice starts with a third-person narration (*The history of English is . . .*), then moves into the second person (*You could mark . . .*).

Choice **B** is incorrect. This choice starts with the second person (*You can say that . . .*), but then switches over to the first person (*I know the . . .*).

Choice **D** is incorrect. The first-person (*I learned that . . .*) quickly shifts to the second-person (*you begin . . .*) in the same sentence.

50. Choice **D** is correct. The colon after *We write for a variety of purposes* tells you that you're reading a list. Each item in the list starts with the infinitive phrase *to + verb*, making each item parallel to the others.

Choice **A** is incorrect. The colon after *We write for a variety of purposes* tells you that you're reading a list. If the list were parallel, all items would be presented in the same way. *In expressing our feelings* is not an infinitive phrase that uses *to*, like the other list items are.

Choice **B** is incorrect. The list starts with the infinitive preposition *to*, but then each list item is written in a different way: simple verb phrase (*convey information*), noun (*persuasion*), and transitive verb phrase (*giving pleasure*).

Choice **C** is incorrect. If the list were parallel, all items would be presented in the same way, but each list item is written in a different way: a noun (*an expression of our feelings*), a transitive verb (*conveying information*), and an infinitive phrase (*to give pleasure*).

1 ▶ CAPITALIZATION

Words have a longer life than deeds.

—PINDAR, Greek poet (522 B.C.E.–443 B.C.E.)

LESSON SUMMARY

Capitalization goes beyond the first word of a sentence. This chapter covers the finer points of capitalization by breaking them down into two segments: general rules and specific rules.

Start by seeing just how much you already know about the proper use of capital letters. On the next page, you see the same passage written twice. The first column, called **Problem**, contains some capitalization, but there are some words that still need to be capitalized, and others that are capitalized but shouldn't be! Circle those letters you think should be capitalized, and underline those letters that are incorrectly capitalized, in the **Problem** column, and then check yourself against the **Solution** column.

Problem

The Metropolitan museum of art in New York city is home to thousands of rare and priceless works of art. From primitive Ancient Art to modern classics of painting and photography, these grand stone walls on the city's upper east side trace the history of Art itself. Visitors can walk through a replica of an Egyptian temple covered in scrolls of hieroglyphics, only to find themselves touring ancient greece, rome, and africa next. Paintings by renaissance masters such as Leonardo da Vinci are mere feet from the bold, modern work of Vincent van Gogh and Jackson Pollock. And it's not just traditional painting and sculpture on display—the collections of historical clothing (from French revolution-era dresses to modern Alexander McQueen Designs), musical instruments, and ancient texts round out the Museum's diverse offerings.

Solution

The Metropolitan Museum of Art in New York City is home to thousands of rare and priceless works of art. From primitive ancient art to modern classics of painting and photography, these grand stone walls on the city's Upper East Side trace the history of art itself. Visitors can walk through a replica of an Egyptian temple covered in scrolls of hieroglyphics, only to find themselves touring ancient Greece, Rome, and Africa next. Paintings by Renaissance masters such as Leonardo da Vinci are mere feet from the bold, modern work of Vincent van Gogh and Jackson Pollock. And it's not just traditional painting and sculpture on display—the collections of historical clothing (from French Revolution-era dresses to modern Alexander McQueen designs), musical instruments, and ancient texts round out the museum's diverse offerings.

How did you do? As you progress through the lesson, try to identify the specific rules that you missed.

General Capitalization Rules

This table summarizes general capitalization rules. Rules relating to specific categories of proper nouns are addressed in the next section.

CAPITALIZATION RULES	
RULE	**EXAMPLE**
Capitalize the first word of a sentence. If the first word is a number, write it as a word.	**T**his is the first word of the sentence. **T**hree of us worked the early shift.
Capitalize the pronoun *I* or the contraction *I'm*, and the abbreviations B.C. or A.D.	The group left when **I** asked them to go. The manuscript was dated A.D. 501.
Capitalize the first word of a quotation. Do not capitalize the first word of a partial quotation.	I said, "**W**hat's the name of your dog?" He called me "**t**he worst excuse for a student" he had ever seen.

Here is an example of a dialogue that illustrates these rules. (A note about paragraphing in dialogue: Each time a speaker finishes, begin a new paragraph for the next speaker's dialogue.)

"**G**ood afternoon," said the personal trainer as **I** walked into the gym.

"**G**ood afternoon!" **I** replied, excited to get started. "**Y**ou must be Ms. Milner. **I**'m Jennifer Burnett. **I**t's very nice to meet you."

"**T**ell me about your current workout routine, Jennifer. **I**'m eager to put together a brand-new exercise program for you."

I smiled and said, "**I**t's so nice to be working with you. **I** heard you were a '**t**rue fitness guru.'"

Practice

Check your ability to apply these rules in the following practice questions. Choose the correctly capitalized option from each of the following sets. Answers to each set of questions can be found at the end of the lesson.

1. a. the movie terrified me at first. after a few minutes, i began to calm down.
   b. The movie terrified me at first. after a few minutes, I began to calm down.
   c. The movie terrified me at first. After a few minutes, I began to calm down.

2. a. "what are you doing?" my supervisor asked. "trying to finish the memo I've been writing," i replied.
   b. "What are you doing?" my supervisor asked. "Trying to finish the memo I've been writing," I replied.
   c. "What are you doing?" My supervisor asked. "Trying to finish the memo I've been writing," I replied.

3. a. the book noted that Henry VIII reigned from A.D. 1509–1547.
  b. The book noted that henry VIII reigned from A.D. 1509–1547.
  c. The book noted that Henry VIII reigned from A.D. 1509–1547.

4. a. After the game is over, I want to watch the interviews with the players.
  b. after the game is over, I want to watch the interviews with the players.
  c. After the game is over, i want to watch the interviews with the players.

Proper Nouns and Proper Adjectives

All proper nouns and proper adjectives—ones that name a specific person, place, or thing—must be capitalized, but remembering which nouns and adjectives are proper can be difficult. The tables that follow lay out the most common categories of proper nouns and adjectives. Each section begins with a table that illustrates five to seven related rules, followed by several practice exercises.

PROPER NOUNS, PART ONE	
CATEGORY OF PROPER NOUNS	EXAMPLES
days of the week	Friday, Saturday
months	January, February
holidays	Christmas, Halloween
historical events, periods, documents	Civil War (historical event), Dark Ages (historical period), Declaration of Independence (document)
special events, calendar events	Pebble Beach Fall Classic, Renaissance Festival, Green River Days (special events); Labor Day, Father's Day (calendar events)
names of people and places	John Doe, United States

Practice

Using these rules, choose the correctly capitalized version of each of the following pairs.

5. a. Chaucer was one of the foremost poets from the Middle ages.
  b. Chaucer was one of the foremost poets from the Middle Ages.

6. a. The Martins will begin their summer with a weeklong Memorial Day celebration at a beautiful lakeside hotel.
  b. The Martins will begin their summer with a weeklong Memorial day celebration at a beautiful Lakeside hotel.

7. a. The u.s. constitution contains the bill of rights.
  b. The U.S. Constitution contains the Bill of Rights.

8. a. Judy has two Uncles who fought in world war II.
  b. Judy has two uncles who fought in World War II.

PROPER NOUNS, PART TWO	
CATEGORY OF PROPER NOUNS	EXAMPLES
names of structures and buildings	Washington Memorial, Empire State Building
names of trains, ships, aircraft, and other modes of transportation	*Queen Elizabeth, Discovery,* Sioux Lines, TransWorld Airlines
names of products	Corn King hams, Dodge Intrepid
names of officials	Mayor Daley, President Clinton
works of art and literature	*Black Elk Speaks* (book), "Mending Wall" (poem), *Mona Lisa* (painting)
ethnic groups, races, languages, nationalities	Asian American, Caucasian, French, Indian

Practice

Choose the correctly capitalized version of each of the following pairs.

9. **a.** Shakespeare's *comedy of errors* is one of his easiest plays to read.
   b. Shakespeare's *Comedy of Errors* is one of his easiest plays to read.

10. **a.** We caught a Vanguard Airlines flight to Orlando.
    b. We caught a Vanguard airlines flight to Orlando.

11. **a.** The Talmud is a guide to the teachings of judaism.
    b. The Talmud is a guide to the teachings of Judaism.

12. **a.** Paul has an editing job with Meredith Publishing.
    b. Paul has an Editing job with Meredith Publishing.

13. **a.** The University of Michigan has an excellent business school.
    b. The university of Michigan has an excellent business school.

14. **a.** Dr. Gallagher researched her book at the Library of Congress.
    b. Dr. Gallagher researched her book at the Library of congress.

PROPER NOUNS, PART THREE	
CATEGORY OF PROPER NOUNS	EXAMPLES
cities, states, and governmental units	Des Moines, Iowa; Barrow, Alaska; Republic of South Africa
streets, highways, and roads	Grand Avenue, Interstate 29, Deadwood Road
landmarks and geographical locations	Continental Divide, Grand Canyon
public areas and bodies of water	Superior Forest, Missouri River
institutions, organizations, and businesses	Dartmouth College, Lions Club, Dodge Trucks

Practice

Choose the correctly capitalized version of each of the following pairs.

15. a. New York City's Sixth Avenue is also called the Avenue of the Americas.
b. New York city's sixth avenue is also called the Avenue of the Americas.

16. a. Near a body of water called firth and forth, you can see Edinburgh, Scotland.
b. Near a body of water called Firth and Forth, you can see Edinburgh, Scotland.

17. a. There is an incredible view of the Pacific ocean from Big Sur, California.
b. There is an incredible view of the Pacific Ocean from Big Sur, California.

18. a. Mount Everest, which is in the middle of the Himalayas, is the highest mountain in the world.
b. Mount Everest, which is in the middle of the Himalayas, is the highest mountain in the World.

19. a. I have traveled on the Garden state Parkway, a main highway in New Jersey.
b. I have traveled on the Garden State Parkway, a main highway in New Jersey.

Proper Adjectives

Proper adjectives are adjectives—that is, words that modify nouns—formed from a proper noun, often the name of a place. For instance, the proper noun *Canada* becomes the proper adjective *Canadian* when it modifies another noun, as in *Canadian bacon*. Note that the noun is not capitalized unless it is a proper noun in its own right.

Examples:
English **m**uffin, **P**olish **s**ausage, **J**apanese **y**en

Practice

Choose the correctly capitalized version of each of the following pairs.

20. a. Some residents of ireland still speak the Gaelic Language.
b. Some residents of Ireland still speak the Gaelic language.

21. a. Frida Kahlo, a Mexican artist, painted many self-portraits.
b. Frida Kahlo, a mexican artist, painted many self-portraits.

22. a. My Irish ancestors immigrated to the United States in 1853.
b. My irish ancestors immigrated to the United States in 1853.

23. a. I will never attempt to swim the English channel.

  b. I will never attempt to swim the English Channel.

24. a. The new Ethiopian Restaurant was getting rave reviews.

  b. The new Ethiopian restaurant was getting rave reviews.

When NOT to Capitalize

Putting capital letters where they don't belong is as bad as leaving them out where they do belong. Watch for these capitalization traps.

- Avoid unnecessarily capitalizing compass directions; however, direction words that refer to a specific area of the country should be capitalized.
  Examples:
  We headed **w**est after the Depression.
  The future of the country was cultivated in the **W**est.
- Avoid unnecessarily capitalizing the words referring to family members. Capitalize them only when they are used as names. If a possessive adjective (*my, our, your, his, her, their*) comes before the word referring to a family member, the family word is not capitalized.
  Examples:
  When **U**ncle Harry visited last winter, none of my other **u**ncles came to see him.
  After my **m**other called me for lunch, **F**ather served the entree.
- Avoid unnecessarily capitalizing the seasons of the year or parts of the academic year.
  Example:
  If the university offers History of Education 405 in the **s**pring **s**emester, Horace can graduate in May.
- Avoid unnecessarily capitalizing school subjects. They should be capitalized only if they are part of the name of a specific course.

Examples:
  I try to avoid **m**ath courses because I'm not very good at them.
  Betsy is taking **A**lgebra II and **T**rigonometry I next semester.
- Avoid unnecessarily capitalizing words modified by proper adjectives.
  Examples:
  Polish **s**ausage, not Polish Sausage
  Mexican **r**estaurant, not Mexican Restaurant

Practice
Choose the correctly capitalized version of each of the following pairs.

25. a. Digging the Canal through Panama took many years.

  b. Digging the canal through Panama took many years.

26. a. The Smoky Mountains are in the Southeastern part of the country.

  b. The Smoky Mountains are in the southeastern part of the country.

27. a. Nicholi Milani does more business in the East than in the West.

  b. Nicholi Milani does more business in the east than in the west.

28. a. My least favorite subject in school is history, although I have to admit I enjoyed taking European History I last semester.

  b. My least favorite subject in school is History, although I have to admit I enjoyed taking European History I last semester.

29. a. Marianne had never been as far East as Columbus, Ohio.

  b. Marianne had never been as far east as Columbus, Ohio.

Answers

1. c.	**16.** b.
2. b.	**17.** b.
3. c.	**18.** a.
4. a.	**19.** b.
5. b.	**20.** b.
6. a.	**21.** a.
7. b.	**22.** a.
8. b.	**23.** b.
9. b.	**24.** b.
10. a.	**25.** b.
11. b.	**26.** b.
12. a.	**27.** a.
13. a.	**28.** a.
14. a.	**29.** b.
15. a.	

TIP

Find the wedding notices in your local newspaper. Examine the capitalization used in the writing. How many of the rules you learned today can you find represented in a single wedding notice?

PERIODS, QUESTION MARKS, AND EXCLAMATION POINTS

No iron can pierce the heart with such force as a period put just at the right place.

—Isaac Babel, Russian journalist (1894–1940)

LESSON SUMMARY

End punctuation is as essential to writing as road signs are to drivers. This chapter shows which end marks to use and where.

The exercise that follows reviews Lesson 1, Capitalization, and gives you an opportunity to see what you already know about periods and end marks. Correct the capitalization in the **Problem** column on the next page, adding periods, question marks, and exclamation points where you think they should go. Check your answers with the **Solution** column as you go.

Problem

"Watch out," Henrietta yelled, as a car sped past me on the street. After the danger had passed, she began to lecture me. "You could have been killed. You need to watch more carefully before you try to cross the street," she admonished. "Do you want to get hurt because you weren't careful."

She was right—I had been texting rather than paying attention to the traffic But now I would be more careful. My brush with disaster made me wonder about how many people might be doing the same thing. How many accidents had been caused in my town alone because people were texting or talking on the phone when they should have been paying attention to the road. I began researching the issue, and found out some alarming statistics about the number of traffic accidents caused by distracted driving and/or walking. Too many. Not everyone is lucky enough to have a friend like Henrietta looking out for him or her, so my advice to everyone is this: Watch out.

Solution

"Watch out!" Henrietta yelled, as a car sped past me on the street. After the danger had passed, she began to lecture me. "You could have been killed! You need to watch more carefully before you try to cross the street," she admonished. "Do you want to get hurt because you weren't careful?"

She was right—I had been texting rather than paying attention to the traffic. But now I would be more careful. My brush with disaster made me wonder about how many people might be doing the same thing. How many accidents had been caused in my town alone because people were texting or talking on the phone when they should have been paying attention to the road? I began researching the issue, and found out some alarming statistics about the number of traffic accidents caused by distracted driving and/or walking. Too many! Not everyone is lucky enough to have a friend like Henrietta looking out for him or her, so my advice to everyone is this: Watch out.

Rules for Using Periods

- Use a period after an initial and after every part of an abbreviation, unless the abbreviation is initials for a U.S. state (NY, FL), has become an acronym (an abbreviation that is pronounced as a word, such as NASA) or a widely recognized name (TV, FBI, CD). Titles—Mr., Ms., Dr., and so on—are also abbreviations that use periods. If the abbreviation comes at the end of a sentence, only one period is needed.
  Examples:
  The tour leaves on **Mon., Jan. 1, at 3 P.M.**
  The book was written by **C.S.** Lewis.
  A.J. Mandelli researched brain function for the **FBI.**
- Use a period as a decimal between numbers and between dollars and cents.

Examples:
A gallon equals **3.875** liters.
The new textbook costs **$54.75.**
Only **5.6%** of our consumers spend over **$100.00** per month on our products.

- Use a period at the end of a sentence that makes a statement.
  Examples:
  Henry Kissinger served under two U.S. presidents.
  Wilson will lecture in the forum after school today.
  Many consider P.T. Barnum the best salesman ever to have walked the earth.
- Use a period at the end of a sentence that makes a request, gives an instruction, or states a command.
  Examples:
  Empty the kitchen trash before you take the garbage out.
  Turn right at the first stop light, and then go to the second house on the left.

- Use a period at the end of a sentence that asks an indirect question.

  Examples:

  My neighbor asked if we had seen his cat. (The direct question was, "Have you seen my cat?")

  Quentin wanted to know how we had arrived at that answer. (The direct question was "How did you arrive at that answer?")

Practice

Choose the correctly written version from each of the following sets of sentences. You will find the answers to each set of questions at the end of the lesson.

1. a. The train passed through Rockford, IL., on its way to St. Joseph, MO.
   b. The train passed through Rockford, IL, on its way to St Joseph, MO.
   c. The train passed through Rockford, IL, on its way to St. Joseph, MO.

2. a. Ms Cory Ames, Dr Matthew Olson, and H.J. Lane went to Chicago, IL..
   b. Ms Cory Ames, Dr Matthew Olson, and HJ Lane went to Chicago, IL.
   c. Ms. Cory Ames, Dr. Matthew Olson, and H.J. Lane went to Chicago, IL.

3. a. At the age of 15, Justin measured 5 ft. 11 in. tall. Now, at 17, he has grown to 6 ft. 3 in.
   b. At the age of 15, Justin measured 5 ft. 11 in. tall.. Now, at 17, he has grown to 6 ft. 3 in..
   c. At the age of 15, Justin measured 5 ft 11 in tall. Now, at 17, he has grown to 6 ft 3 in.

4. a. Bob asked if the price of the CD was $13.98?
   b. Bob asked if the price of the CD was $13.98.
   c. Bob asked if the price of the CD was $1398¢.

5. a. Tie your shoe. Before you trip and break a leg.
   b. Tie your shoe before you trip and break a leg.
   c. Tie your shoe before you trip and break a leg

6. a. Mr and Mrs Fletcher visited 10 cities in 20 days.
   b. Mr. and Mrs. Fletcher visited 10 cities in 20 days.
   c. Mr and Mrs. Fletcher visited 10 cities in 20 days.

7. a. Mayor and Mrs. Dorian will address the city council at 8:00 P.M.
   b. Mayor and Mrs Dorian will address the city council at 8:00 P.M.
   c. Mayor and Mrs. Dorian will address the city council at 8:00 P.M.

8. a. Oh, all right. Tell me your riddle.
   b. Oh. all right. Tell me your riddle.
   c. Oh, all right Tell me your riddle.

Rules for Using Question Marks and Exclamation Points

- Use a question mark after a word or group of words that asks a question, even if it is not a complete sentence.

  Examples:

  What did you do last night?

  Will you put out the trash?

  Okay?

  May we go to the movies after we've finished our homework?

  Are we?

- Use an exclamation point after a sentence that expresses strong feeling.

  Examples:

  Look out for that car!

  I just can't stand the smell in here!

A word of caution about using exclamation points to show strong feeling: Exclamation points are a little bit like salt on food. Most people like a little bit. Nobody likes too much.

- Use an exclamation point after an interjection—a word or phrase expressing strong feeling—when it is written as a single sentence.

   Examples:

   Doggone it!

   Yikes!

- Use an exclamation point after a sentence that begins with a question word but doesn't ask a question.

   Examples:

   What a dunce I am!

   How marvelous of you to come!

Practice

Choose the correctly written version of each of the following sets of sentences.

9. a. Wow! That is an incredible view?

b. Wow? That is an incredible view!

c. Wow! That is an incredible view!

10. a. I can't believe how naïve I was!

b. I can't believe how naïve I was.

c. I can't believe how naïve I was?

11. a. The auditor asked me why I didn't save the receipts?

b. The auditor asked me why I didn't save the receipts.

c. The auditor asked me why I didn't save the receipts!

12. a. Can you tell me the seating capacity of this meeting room.

b. Can you tell me the seating capacity of this meeting room?

c. Can you tell me the seating capacity of this meeting room!

13. a. Unbelievable. I never thought she would go through with it!

b. Unbelievable? I never thought she would go through with it.

c. Unbelievable! I never thought she would go through with it!

14. a. Was Alexander the Great born in 350 B.C.E.

b. Was Alexander the great born in 350 B.C.E.?

c. Was Alexander the Great born in 350 B.C.E.?

15. a. Our group will meet at the library at 10:00 P.M. to research T.S. Eliot.

b. Our group will meet at the library at 10:00 PM to research T.S. Eliot.

c. Our group will meet at the library at 10:00 P.M. to research TS. Eliot.

16. a. Hannah asked how much the prom bid was. Kayla told her $50.00.

b. Hannah asked how much the prom bid was? Kayla told her $50.00?

c. Hannah asked how much the prom bid was? Kayla told her $50.00.

17. a. Wow. What a close call that was?

b. Wow! What a close call that was.

c. Wow! What a close call that was!

18. a. Those carpenters. Do you know how much they charged?

b. Those carpenters? Do you know how much they charged?

c. Those carpenters! Do you know how much they charged?

Answers

1. c.
2. c.
3. a.
4. b.
5. b.
6. b.
7. c.
8. a.
9. c.

10. a.
11. b.
12. b.
13. c.
14. c.
15. a.
16. a.
17. c.
18. c.

TIP

Take a few minutes to practice what you have learned today. If you are reading a book right now, look through a few of the pages until you find at least three examples of each type of end mark you learned about today. Are the end marks used according to the rules you used? If you're not currently reading a book, just grab one from the shelf at home or at work.

AVOIDING FAULTY SENTENCES

A sentence is made up of words; a statement is made in words....
Statements are made, words or sentences are used.

—JOHN LANGSHAW AUSTIN, British philosopher (1911–1960)

LESSON SUMMARY
How do we distinguish between complete sentences and sentence fragments, run-ons, and comma splices? Read this chapter to find out.

Begin your study of complete sentences by looking at the **Problem** paragraph that appears on the next page. Underline the groups of words that form complete sentences. See if you can distinguish them from the fragments, run-ons, and comma splices included in the paragraph. Then check your work against the **Solution** paragraph, also on the next page, where the complete sentences are underlined.

Problem

I never realized that making a pie would be so simple. I started out with a pound of apples that I'd picked at the local fruit orchard. I sliced and cored those apples; mixed them in a bowl with butter. Brown sugar. Cinnamon. Nutmeg, and a bit of orange juice. (That prevents the apples from turning brown.) To make the crust, I had already mixed butter, flour, and salt into a dough, then let it refrigerate for several hours. Once I had my apple mixture ready, I rolled out the crust dough, spread it in a pie pan, and added my apples. Then covered the pan with more crust. Baked it at 350 degrees for 45 minutes. After it cooled, I was finally able to try a piece. Delicious! Also much easier than I expected.

Solution

I never realized that making a pie would be so simple. I started out with a pound of apples that I'd picked at the local fruit orchard. I sliced and cored those apples; mixed them in a bowl with butter. Brown sugar. Cinnamon. Nutmeg, and a bit of orange juice. (That prevents the apples from turning brown.) To make the crust, I had already mixed butter, flour, and salt into a dough, then let it refrigerate for several hours. Once I had my apple mixture ready, I rolled out the crust dough, spread it in a pie pan, and added my apples. Then covered the pan with more crust. Baked it at 350 degrees for 45 minutes. After it cooled, I was finally able to try a piece. Delicious! Also, much easier than I expected.

Complete Sentences

A complete sentence is a group of words that meets **all** three of the following criteria:

1. It has a verb (a word or phrase that explains an action, such as *want, run, take, give,* or a state of being, such as *am, is, are, was, were, be*). Many sentences have more than one verb. The verbs in the following sentences are highlighted for you.

   Examples:

   Bob and Alexandra both **want** a promotion. (action verb)

   Yurika **drafted** a memo and **sent** it to the sales department. (action verbs)

   Herbert and Tan **are** the chief operators in this department. (state of being verb)

2. It has a subject (someone or something that performs the action or serves as the main focus of the sentence). As with verbs, many sentences have more than one subject.

   Examples:

   Bob and **Alexandra** both want a promotion.

   Yurika drafted a memo and sent it to the sales department.

   Herbert and **Tan** are the chief operators in this department.

3. It expresses a complete thought. In other words, the group of words has a completed meaning. Sometimes, a group of words has both a subject and a verb but still does not express a complete thought. Look at the following examples. The subjects and verbs are highlighted to make them easier to identify.

Complete sentences (also called **independent clauses**):

   I left an hour earlier than usual.

   Our **team finished** its year-end evaluation.

   Roger tried to explain his position.

Sentence fragments (also called **dependent clauses**):

   If **I left** an hour earlier than usual.

   When our **team finished** its year-end evaluation.

   Whenever **Roger tried** to explain his position.

Sentence Fragments

In the last set of examples, you may have noticed that each fragment is longer than the similar complete sentence. The groups of words are otherwise the same, except the fragments have an extra word at the beginning. These words are called *subordinating conjunctions*. If a group of words that would normally be a complete sentence is preceded by a subordinating conjunction, you need something more to complete the thought. These *subordinate* or *dependent clauses* need something more to complete their meaning; therefore, they *depend* on an *independent clause*, a group of words that by itself could form a complete sentence. Examine how the fragments have been rewritten here to express a complete thought.

> If I left an hour earlier than usual, I would be able to avoid rush hour.
>
> When our team finished its year-end evaluation, we all took the next day off.
>
> Whenever Roger tried to explain his position, he misquoted the facts.

These words can be used as subordinating conjunctions:

after	once	until
although	since	when
as	than	whenever
because	that	where
before	though	wherever
if	unless	while

Sometimes, a subordinating conjunction is a phrase rather than a single word:

as if we didn't already know
as though she had always lived in the town
as long as they can still be heard
as soon as I can finish my work
even though you aren't quite ready
in order to proceed more carefully
so that all of us understand exactly

Subordinate clauses are only one type of sentence fragment. For each of the following questions, choose the group of words that forms a complete sentence. See if you notice any similarities among the groups of words that are fragments.

1. a. We are ready for next week.
   b. Washing the car.

2. a. Seeing the plane arrive.
   b. Heather's family rushed to the gate.

3. a. Broken after years of use.
   b. The receptionist finally got a new phone.

4. a. We saw Andrea sitting all by herself.
   b. Imagining what Florida was like in March.

The complete sentences are 1. A, 2. B, 3. B, and 4. A. The fragments are simply phrases. They do not contain a subject or a verb. If you combine the two sets of words, both will be part of a complete sentence. See how this is done in the following examples. With some of the sentences, all you need is a comma. With others, you must add extra words to incorporate the phrase into the rest of the sentence.

1. We are ready for the next task, which is washing the car.
2. Seeing the plane arrive, Heather's family rushed to the gate.
3. Since the phone was broken after years of use, the receptionist finally got a new one.
4. We saw Andrea sitting all by herself, imagining what Florida was like in March.

Now look at the sentences below. In each set, one of the options is a complete sentence, and the other is a fragment. Mark the letter of the complete sentence. See if you notice any similarities among the fragments.

1. a. About the way he combs his hair.
   b. I've noticed something strange.

2. a. My aunt is a respiratory therapist.
   b. A person who helps people rebuild their lungs and circulatory system.

3. a. Benjamin saw a piece of key lime pie.
   b. His favorite type of desert.

4. a. And tried to sell popcorn and candy.
   b. We went door to door.

5. a. During the rest of the afternoon.
   b. Everything went smoothly.

6. a. Icy roads and hazardous weather.
   b. We couldn't make the deadline.

7. a. In the parking ramp near our building.
   b. I was fortunate to find a parking spot.

8. a. And saw the picture of our company's new owner.
   b. We read the morning paper.

9. a. We traveled through the desert all night.
   b. Without seeing a single car or building.

10. a. We walked all over downtown.
    b. And applied for part-time jobs at theaters.

The complete sentences are 1. B, 2. A, 3. A, 4. B, 5. B, 6. B, 7. B, 8. B, 9. A, and 10. A.

Most of the fragments are phrases that can easily be incorporated into a complete sentence using the independent clause with which they are paired. Try to do this yourself. Compare your sentences with the versions that follow.

Look at sentences 1, 5, 7, and 9. The fragments in these sentences were nothing more than phrases separated from the independent clauses. All you need to do is add the fragment to the complete sentence in a spot where it fits. No punctuation or additional words are needed.

1. I've noticed something very strange about the way he combs his hair.
5. Everything went smoothly during the rest of the afternoon.
7. I was fortunate to find a spot in the parking ramp near our building.
9. We traveled through the desert all night without seeing a single car or building.

Now examine sentences 2 and 3. These fragments are phrases that explain or further identify something in the complete sentence. Such phrases are called *appositive* phrases. All you need to do is place a comma after the word being explained or identified, and then add the appositive phrase.

2. My aunt is a respiratory therapist, a person who helps people rebuild their lungs and respiratory system.
3. Benjamin saw key lime pie, his favorite type of dessert.

Take a look at sentences 4, 8, and 10. In these sentences, the fragment is a verb (action) separated from the independent clause or the complete sentence. All that is required is to add the fragment to the sentence.

4. We went door to door and tried to sell popcorn and candy.
8. We read the morning paper and saw the picture of our company's new owner.
10. We walked all over downtown and applied for part-time jobs at theaters.

Finally, look at the remaining sentence, 6. In this sentence, extra words are needed to add the fragment to the sentence.

6. We couldn't make the deadline because of the icy roads and hazardous weather.

Run-On Sentences

An *independent clause* is a group of words that could be a complete sentence all by itself. A *run-on sentence* is one in which independent clauses have been run together without punctuation (a period, semicolon, or comma).

Examples:
> Lynn moved from Minneapolis her job was transferred.
>
> The concert seemed unending it lasted almost until midnight.
>
> We got some gas then we headed off to Omaha.

All three examples can be corrected quite easily in one of three ways:

1. By adding a period and a capital letter.

> Lynn moved from Minneapolis. Her job was transferred.
>
> The concert seemed unending. It lasted almost until midnight.
>
> We got some gas. Then we headed off to Omaha.

2. By adding a comma and a conjunction (*and, but, or, for, nor, yet, so*). Sometimes, you have to change the order of the words.

> Lynn's job was transferred, so she moved from Minneapolis.
>
> The concert seemed unending, for it lasted almost until midnight.
>
> We got some gas, and then we headed off to Omaha.

3. By turning one of the independent clauses into a dependent clause. To do this, you need to add a subordinating conjunction where it fits in the sentence. This can usually be done in two different ways: by rewording the clauses or by using different subordinating conjunctions. Remember the list of subordinating conjunction you saw earlier in this lesson?

> Lynn moved from Minneapolis because her job was transferred.
>
> When her job was transferred, Lynn moved from Minneapolis.
>
> Since the concert lasted almost until midnight, it seemed unending.
>
> The concert seemed unending because it lasted until almost midnight.
>
> After we got some gas, we headed off to Omaha.
>
> We headed off to Omaha after we got some gas.

Practice

Choose the complete sentence. Watch for fragments as well as run-ons. Answers are at the end of the lesson.

1. a. The puppy chewed on everything. And ruined my favorite shoes.
   b. The puppy chewed on everything and ruined my favorite shoes.

2. a. Julie is a loyal friend. She helps whenever she is needed.
   b. Julie is a loyal friend she helps whenever she is needed.

3. a. Paula bought a new car in February she picked it up only last week.
   b. Paula bought a new car in February. She picked it up only last week.

4. a. Lisa lost five pounds. After only one week on the new diet.

b. Lisa lost five pounds after only one week on the new diet.

5. a. You can register for the class in the office on the second floor.

b. You can register for the class. In the office on the second floor.

6. a. Samantha needs a few more days to finish the report it is more involved than she anticipated.

b. Samantha needs a few more days to finish the report. It is more involved than she anticipated.

7. a. My sister's new friend Lisa came for dinner. And she brought her mom's famous chocolate cream pie for dessert.

b. My sister's new friend Lisa came for dinner, and she brought her mom's famous chocolate cream pie for dessert.

8. a. Tanya completed the form she gave it to the receptionist.

b. Tanya completed the form, and she gave it to the receptionist.

9. a. Louis was eager to see the dentist his toothache was getting worse.

b. Louis was eager to see the dentist. His toothache was getting worse.

10. a. Jenny looked for a bank that offered better interest rates.

b. Jenny looked for a bank. Offered better interest rates.

Comma Splices

A *comma splice* is a special type of run-on sentence in which a comma is used in place of a semicolon to join two independent clauses without a conjunction. A comma splice can be corrected by putting a semicolon in place of the comma, or by adding a conjunction after the comma.

Wrong:

Henry lives across the street, he has been there for 25 years.

Correct:

Henry lives across the street; he has been there for 25 years.

Henry lives across the street, and he has been there for 25 years.

Wrong:

Mary heads the search committee, John is the recorder.

Correct:

Mary heads the search committee; John is the recorder.

Mary heads the search committee, and John is the recorder.

Wrong:

Sid gave demonstrations all summer long, he returned in the fall.

Correct:

Sid gave demonstrations all summer long; he returned in the fall.

Sid gave demonstrations all summer long, but he returned in the fall.

Practice

Here is an opportunity to apply what you have learned about complete sentences, fragments, run-ons, and comma splices. In each of the following numbered items, decide whether the group of words is a correctly written sentence or sentences (S), a fragment (F), a run-on sentence (ROS), or a comma splice (CS). Write the label next to each number, and then check your work against the answer key at the end of the lesson. You may recognize some of these sentences from the opening example paragraph. By now, you know how to correct the ones that were not complete sentences.

11. Dr. Anders left detailed care instructions for the patient. A personal friend of his.

12. The night before, someone from Publisher's Clearinghouse had called. To tell me that I would be receiving a prize package worth potentially millions of dollars.

13. I was so excited because unlike the other offers, this really sounded legitimate, it sounded to me as though I might really win something this time.

14. I hastily opened the mailbox. Hoping to find the promised envelope.

15. There it was. The promised letter.

16. Because I couldn't wait to open it to read its contents.

17. The officer responded to the call, he received it at 8:10 P.M.

18. Emily posted the last transaction it was time to close the books for the day.

19. Our new computer system is still not working properly.

20. Even though a computer repair man had looked at the system and deemed it in proper working order.

Rewrite the fragments, run-ons, and comma splices as complete sentences in the following space.

———————————————————————

———————————————————————

———————————————————————

———————————————————————

———————————————————————

———————————————————————

———————————————————————

———————————————————————

———————————————————————

———————————————————————

———————————————————————

———————————————————————

———————————————————————

———————————————————————

———————————————————————

———————————————————————

———————————————————————

———————————————————————

Answers

1. b.		**11.** F	
2. a.		**12.** F	
3. b.		**13.** CS	
4. b.		**14.** F	
5. a.		**15.** F	
6. b.		**16.** F	
7. b.		**17.** CS	
8. b.		**18.** ROS	
9. b.		**19.** S	
10. a.		**20.** F	

TIP

Go back to the paragraph at the beginning of the lesson. Revise it to eliminate the sentence fragments, comma splices, and run-on sentences. As you read the morning paper or written material at work, look for sentence faults. If you find none, look for complete sentences that could be combined. Chances are, you'll find plenty of those in a newspaper. You can also find plenty of sentence faults, especially fragments, in advertisements. Practice writing complete sentences in any written work you are assigned.

 ▶ COMMAS AND SENTENCE PARTS

The writer who neglects punctuation, or mispunctuates, is liable to be misunderstood. . . . For the want of merely a comma, it often occurs that an axiom appears a paradox, or that a sarcasm is converted into a sermonoid.

—EDGAR ALLAN POE, American poet (1809–1849)

LESSON SUMMARY
Commas, one form of internal punctuation, play an important role in many sentences. In this lesson, learn how they highlight specific parts of a sentence in order to make them cohesive with the rest of the sentence.

During this lesson, you will learn how to use commas in relationship to sentence parts. As you progress through this lesson, remember what you learned about sentences and sentence faults in Lesson 3. Before you begin this lesson, see how much you already know about commas and sentence parts. Insert commas where you think they should be in the **Problem** version of the sentences that appear on the next page. Check your answers against the corrected version of the sentences in the **Solution** section that follows.

Problem

After several years at the company Marcus decided it was time to ask for a raise. Always a good worker he had a strong record of coming to work on time working well with other members of his team and solving problems creatively. He was unsure of where to start so he began by making a list of both his accomplishments in his time at the company as well as his strengths as an employee. After he had finished his list feeling more confident than ever he e-mailed his boss to set up a meeting to discuss the reasons why he deserved a pay raise. Before the meeting he rehearsed what he was going to say. Ultimately his boss was impressed with his list and she agreed with his reasons. After all his hard work Marcus got his raise.

Solution

After several years at the company, Marcus decided it was time to ask for a raise. Always a good worker, he had a strong record of coming to work on time, working well with other members of his team, and solving problems creatively. He was unsure of where to start, so he began by making a list of his accomplishments in his time at the company as well as his strengths as an employee. After he had finished his list, feeling more confident than ever, he e-mailed his boss to set up a meeting to discuss the reasons why he deserved a pay raise. Before the meeting, he rehearsed what he was going to say. Ultimately, his boss was impressed with his list, and she agreed with his reasons. After all his hard work, he got his raise.

Commas Following Introductory Words, Phrases, and Clauses

Use a comma to set off introductory words, phrases, and clauses from the main part of a sentence. The comma keeps a reader from accidentally attaching the introductory portion to the main part of the sentence and having to go back and reread the sentence. In other words, commas following introductory elements will save the reader time and reduce the chances of misinterpretation. Examine the following examples to see how introductory words, phrases, and clauses are set off with commas.

Words:
> Disappointed, we left the movie before it ended.
> Annoyed, the manager stomped back into the storeroom.
> Amazed, Captain Holland dismissed the rest of the troops.

Phrases:
> Expecting the worst, we liquidated most of our inventory.
> Badly injured in the accident, the president was gone for two months.
> Reluctant to make matters any worse, the doctor called in a specialist.

Clauses:
> If we plan carefully for the grand opening, we can increase sales.
> While we were eating lunch, an important fax came.
> Because we left before the meeting ended, we were not eligible to win a door prize.

Remember the fragment section of Lesson 3? Part of it dealt with subordinate or dependent clauses. Subordinate or dependent clauses are what you see in the last set of previous examples. The first part of each sentence, the subordinate or dependent clause, is followed by a comma. The two parts of each of these sentences could very easily be reversed and the sentence would still make sense. However, if you reverse the sentence parts, making the independent clause the first clause in the sentence, you would NOT need a comma.

Subordinate clauses *after* the independent clause:

We can increase sales if we plan carefully for the grand opening.

An important fax came while we were eating lunch.

We were not eligible to win a door prize because we left before the meeting ended.

Practice

Choose the correctly written sentence from each of the following pairs. Answers are provided at the end of the lesson.

1. **a.** Content for the first time in his life, Bryce returned to school.
   b. Content for the first time in his life Bryce returned to school.

2. **a.** After eating the train conductor finished his scheduled route and headed back to the train yard.
   b. After eating, the train conductor finished his scheduled route and headed back to the train yard.

3. **a.** I will never forget this moment, as long as I live.
   b. I will never forget this moment as long as I live.

4. **a.** By the time we finally made up our minds, the contract had been awarded to someone else.
   b. By the time we finally made up our minds the contract had been awarded to someone else.

5. **a.** Indignant, Mr. Caster left the restaurant without leaving a tip.
   b. Indignant Mr. Caster left the restaurant without leaving a tip.

6. **a.** Wayne was delighted when he found out he'd been awarded the leading role in the show.
   b. Wayne was delighted, when he found out he'd been awarded the leading role in the show.

7. **a.** By designing the program ourselves, we saved a great deal of expense.
   b. By designing the program ourselves we saved a great deal of expense.

8. **a.** Weeping Wanda gently wiped her eyes while adsorbed in her favorite opera.
   b. Weeping, Wanda gently wiped her eyes while adsorbed in her favorite opera.

9. **a.** Dripping with water from head to toe, Angie climbed the bank of the river.
   b. Dripping with water from head to toe Angie climbed the bank of the river.

10. **a.** The company honored its oldest employee at the annual meeting.
   b. The company honored its oldest employee, at the annual meeting.

Commas help a reader know which words belong together. Add commas to the following sentences to help make their meaning clear.

1. Inside the house was clean and tastefully decorated.
2. After running the greyhounds settled back into their boxes.
3. Alone at night time seems endless.
4. As he watched the game slowly came to an end.

You should have marked the sentences like this:

1. Inside, the house was clean and tastefully decorated.
2. After running, the greyhounds settled back into their boxes.
3. Alone at night, time seems endless.
4. As he watched, the game slowly came to an end.

Commas with Appositives

An *appositive* is a word or group of words that immediately follows a noun or pronoun. The appositive makes the noun or pronoun clearer or more definite by explaining or identifying it. Look at the following examples. The appositives and appositive phrases have been highlighted.

Examples:
Rachel Stein won the first prize, **an expense-paid vacation to the Bahamas**.
New Orleans, **home of the Saints**, is one of my favorite cities.
One of the most inspiring motivators in college basketball is Dr. Tom Davis, **coach of the Iowa Hawkeyes**.

Sometimes, a proper name that identifies or further explains will follow a noun or pronoun. Although this is also a type of appositive, it is not set off by commas.

Examples:
My sister **Deb** lives four hours away.
The noted novelist **Barbara Kingsolver** writes about the South and Southwest.

Place commas where they are needed in the following sentences.

1. Ms. Mason the bank manager scheduled a meeting with new employees.
2. MP3 players devices virtually unheard of a decade ago are very common today.
3. Maggie loves to take long walks on the nature trail an oasis of calm.
4. Health care coverage a major consideration for everyone has steadily worsened over the years.
5. The poem was written by Sylvia Plath a very accomplished poet.
6. My friend Cynthia threw me a surprise party last year.

You should have marked the sentences like this:

1. Ms. Mason, the bank manager, scheduled a meeting with new employees.
2. MP3 players, devices virtually unheard of a decade ago, are very common today.
3. Maggie loves to take long walks on the nature trail, an oasis of calm.
4. Health care coverage, a major consideration for everyone, has steadily worsened over the years.
5. The poem was written by Sylvia Plath, a very accomplished poet.
6. My friend Cynthia threw me a surprise party last year. (no comma needed)

Commas and Nonrestrictive Clauses

In some sentences, a clause cannot be omitted without changing the basic meaning of the sentences. Omitting such a clause changes the meaning of the sentence or makes it untrue. Such a clause is called an *essential* or *restrictive* clause.

Example:

All drivers **who have had a drunk driving conviction** should have their licenses revoked.
All drivers should have their licenses revoked.

The highlighted clause is essential because the meaning of the sentence is changed drastically if the clause is removed from the sentence. A restrictive clause is not set off with commas.

However, a *nonessential* or *nonrestrictive* clause must be set off by commas. A clause is nonrestrictive if it simply adds information that is not essential to the basic meaning of the sentence. If a nonrestrictive clause is removed, the basic meaning of the sentence is not changed.

Example:

My father, **who is still farming**, is 74 years old.
My father is 74 years old.

The highlighted clause is nonrestrictive. If it is removed from the sentence, the basic meaning of the sentence is not changed. Nonrestrictive clauses usually begin with one of these subordinating conjunctions: *who, whom, whose, which,* or *that.* (Technically, the proper subordinating conjunction for a restrictive clause is *that,* while nonrestrictive clauses use *which,* but in practice, many writers ignore this distinction.)

Practice

Each of the following sentences contains a subordinate clause. These are highlighted for you. If the clause is restrictive, or essential, write (**a**) in the box at the right. If the clause is nonrestrictive, or nonessential, put (**b**) in the box and set the clause off with commas. Answers are at the end of the lesson.

11. Cheryl **my college roommate** sent me a postcard from Mexico. ☐
   a. restrictive
   b. nonrestrictive

12. My grandfather **who was born in Berlin** speaks with a German accent. ☐
   a. restrictive
   b. nonrestrictive

13. James **who is very shy** had a great deal of trouble with his first speech. ☐
   a. restrictive
   b. nonrestrictive

14. All employees **who have put in more than 10 hours of overtime this week** may take this Friday off. ☐
   a. restrictive
   b. nonrestrictive

15. People **who are born on February 29** grow old more slowly than the rest of us. ☐
   a. restrictive
   b. nonrestrictive

16. Animals **that have backbones** are called vertebrates. ☐
   a. restrictive
   b. nonrestrictive

17. Nicotine **which is present in tobacco products** is a powerful poison. ☐
   a. restrictive
   b. nonrestrictive

18. Many Scandinavian names end with -*sen* or -*son* **both of which mean *son of.*** ☐
   a. restrictive
   b. nonrestrictive

19. We live on Fleur Drive **which is right next to the airport.** ☐
   a. restrictive
   b. nonrestrictive

20. Mrs. Olson is not a teacher **who takes homework lightly.** ☐
   a. restrictive
   b. nonrestrictive

Review

This next exercise reviews everything you have learned so far. This passage contains no commas, end marks, or capitalization. Use what you have learned to add capitalization, end marks, and commas to make sense of the **Problem** version of the passage. Check your work against the **Solution** version that follows.

Problem

if you're ever in washington dc in april be sure to catch the annual national cherry blossom festival since 1935 tourists have been flocking to our nations capital to see the extravaganza of white blossoms

originally a gift from tokyo mayor yukio ozaki the original cherry trees in washington dc were meant to strengthen the relationship between the united states and japan the first cherry trees were planted on the banks of the potomac river in 1912 by first lady helen herron taft and viscountess chinda the wife of the japanese ambassador In exchange the us sent japan a gift of flowering dogwood trees the trees grew in popularity until local civics groups established the first official cherry blossom festival in 1935

the modern version of the festival hosts hundreds of thousands of visitors and includes an ever-growing lineup of music sporting events parades art and history exhibits and cultural events every year the festival ends with celebratory fireworks

Solution

If you're ever in Washington, D.C. in April, be sure to catch the annual National Cherry Blossom Festival. Since 1935, tourists have been flocking to our nation's capital to see the extravaganza of white blossoms.

Originally a gift from Tokyo mayor Yukio Ozaki, the original cherry trees in Washington, D.C. were meant to strengthen the relationship between the U.S. and Japan. The first cherry trees were planted on the banks of the Potomac River in 1912, by First Lady Helen Herron Taft and Viscountess Chinda, the wife of the Japanese ambassador. In exchange, the U.S. sent Japan a gift of flowering dogwood trees. The trees grew in popularity, until local civics groups established the first official Cherry Blossom Festival in 1935.

The modern version of the festival hosts hundreds of thousands of visitors and includes an ever-growing lineup of music, sporting events, parades, art and history exhibits, and cultural events. Every year, the festival ends with celebratory fireworks.

Answers

1. a.

2. b.

3. b.

4. a.

5. a.

6. a.

7. a.

8. b.

9. a.

10. a.

11. N. Cheryl, my college roommate, sent me a postcard from Mexico.

12. N. My grandfather, who was born in Berlin, speaks with a German accent.

13. N. James, who is very shy, had a great deal of trouble with his first speech.

14. R. No commas are needed.

15. R. No commas are needed.

16. R. No commas are needed.

17. N. Nicotine, which is present in tobacco products, is a powerful poison.

18. N. Many Scandinavian names end with *-son* or *-sen*, both of which mean *son of*.

19. N. We live on Fleur Drive, which is right next to the airport.

20. R. No commas are needed.

TIP

As you learned in this lesson, omitting commas before introductory elements or wrongly placing commas around restrictive clauses can lead to humorous misreadings. Write some sentences of your own that are hard to read without commas, like this: "As they ate the horse moved closer." Then correct them by adding commas.

5 ▶ COMMAS THAT SEPARATE

Proper punctuation is both the sign and the cause of clear thinking.
—LYNNE TRUSS, British writer and journalist (1955–)

LESSON SUMMARY
Besides setting off sentence parts, commas are used in many other situations. This lesson reviews the many instances in which you should use commas to separate sentence elements.

ommas are used to separate or clarify relationships between sentence parts to make the meaning of a sentence clear and easy to grasp. In this lesson, you'll learn how to use commas to separate independent clauses, items in a series, items in a date or address, two or more adjectives preceding a noun, and contrasting elements and words that interrupt the flow of thought in a sentence. The last section of the lesson explains how to use commas in the greetings and closings of a friendly letter.

Begin by seeing how much you already know about commas that separate. Add commas where you think they are needed to the **Problem** column on the next page. Check your answers against the corrected version in the **Solution** column. Try to identify the rules that apply to those you missed as you go through the lesson.

Problem

Dear Ellen

Thanks so much for your email! It was great to hear from you. I'm glad to hear that Paulie Andrew and Melissa are doing so well in school and that you're really liking your new job.

Things here are busy busy busy as usual! We just moved into the new house a couple of weeks ago, and we've finally managed to unpack everything. Our new mailing address is 540 Stuyvesant Circle St. Clair WI 55555.

We've also adopted a new border collie Frankie adding to our little menagerie: Brownie (cat). Mr. Butters (cat). Sophie (Boston Terrier). Timmy (turtle) and Washington and Lincoln (goldfish). Things get pretty crazy, but all the animals get along—and we can't imagine the house without them!

I'd love to get together and have coffee when you have time. Maybe we could meet at Java Joint downtown? I've also heard good things about some newer places: Bella's Café Backstage Deli and Flora's Bakery. Either way I'm looking forward to seeing you and catching up on everything else.

Best

Carrie

Solution

Dear Ellen,

Thanks so much for your email! It was great to hear from you. I'm glad to hear that Paulie, Andrew, and Melissa are doing so well in school, and that you're really liking your new job.

Things here are busy, busy, busy as usual! We just moved into the new house a couple of weeks ago, and we've finally managed to unpack everything. Our new mailing address is 540 Stuyvesant Circle, St. Clair, WI 55555.

We've also adopted a new border collie, Frankie, adding to our little menagerie: Brownie (cat), Mr. Butters (cat), Sophie (Boston Terrier), Timmy (turtle), and Washington and Lincoln (goldfish). Things get pretty crazy, but all the animals get along—and we can't imagine the house without them!

I'd love to get together and have coffee when you have time. Maybe we could meet at Java Joint, downtown? I've also heard good things about some newer places: Bella's Café, Backstage Deli, and Flora's Bakery. Either way, I'm looking forward to seeing you and catching up on everything else.

Best,

Carrie

Commas with Independent Clauses Joined by a Conjunction

As you may recall from Lesson 3, an *independent clause* is a group of words that could stand alone as a complete sentence. A *conjunction* is a joining word: *and, but, or, for, nor, so,* or *yet.* Sometimes, a writer will combine two or more independent clauses to form a compound sentence. If a conjunction joins the clauses, place a comma after the first clause. The commas and conjunctions are highlighted in the following examples.

Examples:

> I went to bed early last night, **so** I felt rested this morning.
>
> The city's economic situation has improved, **but** there are still neighborhoods where many people depend on the generosity of others in order to live.
>
> Susan worked through lunch, **and** now she is able to leave the office early.

If independent clauses are joined *without* a conjunction, they are separated by a semicolon instead of a comma.

Examples:

I went to bed early last night; I felt rested this morning.

The city's economic situation has improved; however, there are still neighborhoods where many people depend on the generosity of others in order to live.

Susan worked through lunch; now she is able to leave the office early.

Practice

Use commas and semicolons to correctly punctuate the following sentences. Answers are at the end of the lesson.

1. You can safely view an eclipse through the viewing glass of a welding helmet or you can look through a piece of overexposed film.

2. Jack my cat will lounge lazily in the bay window most of the afternoon soaking up the warmth of the sun.

3. The young calf put its head over the fence and it licked my hand.

4. Icebergs in the Antarctic are flat and smooth but those in the Arctic are rough.

5. Only resort members are allowed to enter the pool area please have your membership pin visible at all times.

6. I like Sam he likes me for we are best of friends.

7. The inventory is valued at one million dollars but it's not enough to cover our debt.

8. If you know of anyone with data processing experience encourage him or her to apply for this new position.

Commas to Separate Items in a Series

Commas are used to separate items in lists of similar words, phrases, or clauses to make the material easier for a reader to understand. The last item in a series is also usually preceded by a conjunction. Strictly speaking, no comma is needed before the conjunction. (However, many writers—some test writers included—prefer to use a comma before the final conjunction to avoid confusion.)

Examples:

Al, Jane, Herbert, **and** Willis all applied for the promotion.

The old Tempo's engine squealed loudly, shook violently, **and** came to a halt.

The instructions clearly showed how to assemble the equipment, how to load the software, **and** how to boot the system.

If each item in the series is separated by a conjunction, no commas are needed.

Example:

Billie **and** Charles **and** Cameron performed at the company Christmas party.

Commas to Separate Items in a Date or an Address

When giving a complete date in the format *month-day-year*, put a comma on either side of the year. When giving a date that is only a month and year, no comma is needed.

Use a comma to separate each element of an address, such as the street address, city, state, and country. A comma is also used after the state or country if the sentence continues after the address.

Examples:

We moved from Fayetteville, North Carolina, on May 16, 2005.

Since November 1994, Terry has lived at 654 36th Street, Lincoln, Nebraska.

Dwana attended Drake University in Des Moines, Iowa, both fall 2004 and spring 2005.

Practice

Add commas and end marks where they are needed to the following sentences. Use not only what you are learning in this lesson, but also what you learned in Lesson 4. Answers appear at the end of the lesson.

9. For safety reasons make sure the tires are properly inflated you should check the oil too.

10. The homegrown philosopher who lives next door at 251 Acorn Street Libertyville Kansas claims to know exactly who invented the wheel sliced bread and kissing.

11. On May 4 2006 Richard celebrated his birthday in grand style he turned 61.

12. Looking for a solution to the printing problem Karissa asked an older employee questioned the supervisor and finally consulted the printer manual.

13. Baruch brought a pasta salad to the potluck Shannon brought peanuts mints and pretzels.

Commas to Separate Adjectives

Use commas to separate two or more equally important adjectives.

Examples:

Alex avoided the **friendly, talkative, pleasant** boy sitting next to him at school.

The carpenter repaired the floor with **dark, aged, oak** flooring.

The reporter spoke with several **intense, talented** high school athletes.

Pay close attention to the last sentence. You'll notice that the words *several* and *high school* are also adjectives modifying *athletes*. Not all adjectives modifying the same word are equally important. Only those of equal importance are separated with a comma. If you apply one or both of these tests, you can easily tell whether a comma is needed:

■ Change the order of the adjectives. If the sentence reads just as clearly, separate the adjectives with a comma. If the sentence becomes unclear or sounds awkward, do not use a comma. The first two example sentences make sense even if the position of the adjectives is changed. The last example sentence makes no sense if you change the order of any of the adjectives other than *intense* and *talented*. Therefore, those are the only adjectives separated by a comma.

✓ Alex avoided the **talkative, friendly, pleasant** boy sitting next to him at school.

✓ The carpenter repaired the floor with **aged, dark, oak** flooring.

X The reporter spoke with **intense, several, talented, high school** athletes.

- A second, equally effective test is to place *and* between the adjectives. If the sentence still reads well, then use commas between the adjectives. If the sentence sounds unclear or awkward, do not use commas. Again, this works with the first two example sentences, but in the last sentence, *and* makes sense only between *intense* and *talented*. Where do commas go in the following sentences?

> We bought an **antique wrought iron** daybed.
> The envelope contained **three crisp clean brand-new one hundred** dollar bills.

You should have punctuated the sentences like this:

> We bought an **antique, wrought iron** daybed.
> The envelope contained **three crisp, clean, brand-new one hundred** dollar bills.

Commas to Separate Other Elements of a Sentence

- Use commas to separate contrasting or opposing elements in a sentence. The comma functions as a signal to the reader: What follows is an opposite idea. It makes the idea easier for the reader to grasp.
  Examples:
  > We searched the entire house, **but found nothing**.
  > We need strong intellects, **not strong bodies,** to resolve this problem.
  > The racers ran slowly at first, **quickly at the end**.
  > We expected to meet the president, **not a White House aide**.

- Use commas to separate words or phrases that interrupt the flow of thought in a sentence.
  Examples:
  > The deadline, **it seemed clear,** simply could not be met.
  > We came to rely, **however,** on the kindness and generosity of the neighbors.
  > The alternative route, **we discovered,** was faster than the original route.

- Whenever the name of the person being addressed is included in a sentence, it should be set off by commas.
  Examples:
  > **Dave,** we wanted you to look at this layout before we sent it to printing.
  > We wanted you to look at this layout, **Dave,** before we sent it to printing.
  > We wanted you to look at this layout before we sent it to printing, **Dave**.

- Mild exclamations included in a sentence are also set off with commas.
  Examples:
  > **Well,** that was certainly a pleasant surprise.
  > **Yes,** I'll call you as soon as we get the information.
  > **Heavens,** that was a long-winded speaker.

- Use a comma after the greeting and closing of a personal or friendly letter.
  Examples:
  > Dear Uncle Jon,
  > Sincerely,
  > Yours truly,

Practice

Choose the correctly punctuated version of each of the following sets of sentences. Keep in mind what you learned about commas in the previous lesson.

14. a. Oscar's grocery list included bread, milk, toothpaste, soap, dog food, and a fly swatter.
   b. Oscar's grocery list, included bread, milk, toothpaste, soap, dog food and a fly swatter.
   c. Oscar's, grocery list included bread, milk, toothpaste, soap, dog food, and a fly swatter.

15. a. My daughter loved the museum, my son, on the other hand, was bored out of his mind.
   b. My daughter loved the museum; my son, on the other hand, was bored out of his mind.
   c. My daughter loved the museum, my son, on the other hand was bored out of his mind.

16. a. Well, Marcus, I hope that Lisa left you a number where she can be reached.
   b. Well, Marcus I hope that Lisa left you a number where she can be reached.
   c. Well Marcus, I hope that Lisa left you a number where she can be reached.

17. a. When I go to my yoga class, I need to bring comfortable clothes a yoga mat and a bottle of water.
   b. When I go to my yoga class I need to bring comfortable clothes, a yoga mat, and a bottle of water.
   c. When I go to my yoga class, I need to bring comfortable clothes, a yoga mat, and a bottle of water.

18. a. The restaurant I believe is located at 112 West Orange Street, Philadelphia, Pennsylvania.
   b. The restaurant, I believe, is located at 112 West Orange Street, Philadelphia, Pennsylvania.
   c. The restaurant, I believe, is located at 112, West Orange Street, Philadelphia, Pennsylvania.

19. a. Ben, and Trace, and Samuel are all excellent athletes students and musicians they play in a rock band together.
   b. Ben and Trace and Samuel are all excellent athletes, students, and musicians, they play in a rock band together.
   c. Ben and Trace and Samuel are all excellent athletes, students, and musicians; they play in a rock band together.

20. a. I'm afraid, Mr. Dobbs, that you lack the qualifications for this job but we have another that might interest you.
   b. I'm afraid Mr. Dobbs, that you lack the qualifications for this job, but we have another that might interest you.
   c. I'm afraid, Mr. Dobbs, that you lack the qualifications for this job, but we have another that might interest you.

21. a. Usually, at the company picnic we play badminton, Frisbee golf, volleyball, and horseshoes.
   b. Usually, at the company picnic, we play badminton Frisbee golf, volleyball and horseshoes.
   c. Usually at the company picnic, we play badminton, Frisbee, golf, volleyball, and horseshoes.

22. a. We will advertise our biggest sale of the decade on June 21, 1997, the 25th anniversary of our Grand Opening sale.

b. We will advertise our biggest sale of the decade on June 21 1997, the 25th anniversary of our Grand Opening sale.

c. We will advertise our biggest sale of the decade on June 21, 1997 the 25th anniversary of our Grand Opening sale.

23. a. Exhausted by the heat, rather than the exertion, Ming collapsed under a tall shady oak tree.

b. Exhausted by the heat rather than the exertion, Ming collapsed under a tall, shady oak tree.

c. Exhausted by the heat, rather than the exertion, Ming collapsed under a tall, shady oak tree.

Answers

1. You can safely view an eclipse through the viewing glass of a welding helmet, or you can look through a piece of overexposed film.

2. Jack, my cat, will lounge lazily in the bay window most of the afternoon, soaking up the warmth of the sun.

3. The young calf put its head over the fence, and it licked my hand.

4. Icebergs in the Antarctic are flat and smooth, but those in the Arctic are rough.

5. Only resort members are allowed to enter the pool area; please have your membership pin visible at all times.

6. I like Sam; he likes me, for we are best of friends.

7. The inventory is valued at one million dollars, but it's not enough to cover our debt.

8. If you know of anyone with data processing experience, encourage him or her to apply for this new position.

9. For safety reasons, make sure the tires are properly inflated; you should check the oil, too.

10. The homegrown philosopher, who lives next door at 251 Acorn Street, Libertyville, Kansas, claims to know exactly who invented the wheel, sliced bread, and kissing.

11. On May 4, 2006, Richard celebrated his birthday in grand style; he turned 61.

12. Looking for a solution to the printing problem, Karissa asked an older employee, questioned the supervisor, and finally consulted the printer manual.

13. Baruch brought a pasta salad to the potluck. Shannon brought peanuts, mints, and pretzels.

14. a.

15. b.

16. a.

17. c.

18. b.	**21.** c.
19. c.	**22.** a.
20. c.	**23.** c.

TIP

As you read the newspaper, a book, or written materials at work, take special note of the commas you see. Try to remember why a comma might be used in each of the situations. Since commas are one of the most frequently misused punctuation marks, look for places where other writers have misused them.

6 ▶ SEMICOLONS AND COLONS

Sometimes you get a glimpse of a semicolon coming, a few lines farther on, and it is like climbing a steep path through woods and seeing a wooden bench just at a bend in the road ahead, a place where you can expect to sit for a moment, catching your breath.

—LEWIS THOMAS, English scientist (1913–1993)

LESSON SUMMARY

Is it the colon that links and the semicolon that introduces? Or is it the other way around? You will learn exactly which does what in this lesson.

You learned to use semicolons to separate independent clauses in Lesson 3. In this lesson, you'll review that use of semicolons, as well as the use of some of the other punctuation marks you have studied so far. You will learn how to use semicolons with conjunctive adverbs and when to separate items in a series with semicolons. You will also learn to use colons in business communications and other settings.

Begin by seeing how much you know. Insert semicolons and colons where you think they are needed in the **Problem** column on the following page. Check your answers against the correct version in the **Solution** column on the right as you go.

Problem

Dear community member

This spring, Memorial Library has an exciting slate of events planned for all ages. Come one, come all!

As part of the Awesome Authors reading series, the library will be hosting the following writers Priscilla Jones, author of *Making It Count*, Chuck Meyers, author of *Financial Insanity* Marybeth Miller and Cindy Chang, authors of *Flashpoint How a Dark Horse Changed the 2012 Election* and Jim Friedrich, author of *Bartonville: A Local History*. All readings will take place in the Eleanor Starkey Reading Room, please check our Events calendar for dates and times.

Kids of all ages are welcome to join us for the Family Flicks series. This year's movies will include *Jungle Story Stephanie Spangle and the Magic Marbles The Mermaid King* and *Middle School Blues*, which will be accompanied by a Q&A with Haley Santiago, author of the original book. All movies will be shown in the Memorial Media room please check our Events calendar for dates and times.

The library will also continue its successful "The Things You Know" series of classes, which will include the following topics pasta-making, basic accounting, decoupage crafts, first aid, and more! Space will be available on a first-come, first served basis, please register at least one week prior to the start date of your chosen class. RSVPs should be sent to Programs Coordinator Liz Langdon at Langdon@memoriallibrary.com. Please check our Events calendar for dates and times.

We're looking forward to a busy spring! For more information please contact our Programs office. Warm wishes,

The Memorial Library Staff

Semicolons

There are three different cases in which a semicolon is used to separate independent clauses. (See Lesson 3 if you've forgotten what an independent clause is.)

Solution

Dear community member:

This spring, Memorial Library has an exciting slate of events planned for all ages. Come one, come all!

As part of the Awesome Authors reading series, the library will be hosting the following writers: Priscilla Jones, author of *Making It Count*; Chuck Meyers, author of Financial Insanity; Marybeth Miller and Cindy Chang, authors of *Flashpoint: How a Dark Horse Changed the 2012 Election*; and Jim Friedrich, author of *Bartonville: A Local History*. All readings will take place in the Eleanor Starkey Reading Room; please check our Events calendar for dates and times. Kids of all ages are welcome to join us for the Family Flicks series. This year's movies will include *Jungle Story*; *Stephanie Spangle and the Magic Marbles*; *The Mermaid King*; and *Middle School Blues*, which will be accompanied by a Q&A with Haley Santiago, author of the original book. All movies will be shown in the Memorial Media room; please check our Events calendar for dates and times.

The library will also continue its successful "The Things You Know" series of classes, which will include the following topics: pasta-making, basic accounting, decoupage crafts, first aid, and more! Space will be available on a first-come, first served basis; please register at least one week prior to the start date of your chosen class. RSVPs should be sent to Programs Coordinator Liz Langdon at Langdon@memoriallibrary.com. Please check our Events calendar for dates and times.

We're looking forward to a busy spring! For more information, please contact our Programs office. Warm wishes,

The Memorial Library Staff

■ Use a semicolon to separate independent clauses joined without a conjunction. This rule may seem familiar to you because it was also included in the last lesson.
Examples:
Three doctors began the research project; only one completed it.

Discard the packaging; save the paperwork for accounting.

The hour is over; it's time to stop working.

- Use a semicolon to separate independent clauses that contain commas even if the clauses are joined by a conjunction. The semicolon helps the reader see where the break in thought occurs.

Example:

The team needed new equipment, updated training manuals, and better professional advice; but since none of this was provided, they performed as poorly as they had in the previous competition.

- Use a semicolon to separate independent clauses connected with a conjunctive adverb. A *conjunctive adverb* is an adverb that joins independent clauses. Conjunctive adverbs are punctuated differently from regular conjunctions. The first independent clause is followed by a semicolon; the conjunctive adverb is followed by a comma.

Examples:

Our copy of the central warehouse catalogue arrived after the budget deadline; **consequently,** our requests are late.

In the book *An American Childhood,* Annie Dillard recounts her experiences as a child; **furthermore,** she questions and speculates about the meaning of life.

Here is a complete list of words used as conjunctive adverbs.

accordingly	instead
besides	moreover
consequently	nevertheless
furthermore	otherwise
hence	therefore
however	thus

Many people confuse subordinating conjunctions, such as *because, though, until,* and *while,* with the conjunctive adverbs previously mentioned. The difference is important. A clause beginning with a subordinating conjunction is only a subordinate clause; it can't stand alone as a sentence. A clause with a conjunctive adverb is an *independent clause,* which should be separated from another independent clause with a period and capital letter or with a semicolon.

Here's a trick to determine whether the word that begins a clause is a conjunctive adverb. If you can move the word around within the clause, it's a conjunctive adverb. If you can't, it's probably a subordinating conjunction. For example, here are two main clauses:

My paycheck was delayed. I couldn't pay my rent on time.

Here are two ways of joining those two main clauses:

My paycheck was delayed; therefore, I couldn't pay my rent on time.

I couldn't pay my rent on time because my paycheck was delayed.

Check whether the first version uses a conjunctive adverb. Can you move *therefore* around in its clause? Yes, you could say, "I couldn't, therefore, pay my rent on time." So *therefore* is a conjunctive adverb.

Use the same test to see whether *because* is a conjunctive adverb that should come after a semicolon. Can you move *because* around in its clause: "My paycheck because was delayed"? No. So *because* is a subordinating conjunction, and the clause it introduces is not a main clause.

There's one more way a semicolon is used to separate:

- Use a semicolon to separate items in a series if the items contain commas. Unlike items in a series separated by commas, a semicolon is used even when there is a conjunction.

Examples:

The dates we are considering for our annual party are **Thursday, June 5; Saturday, June 7; Sunday, June 8; or Monday, June 9**.

When we go to the lake, I am sure to take a pizza pan, a popcorn popper, and pancake **griddle; fishing** tackle, life jackets, and ski **equipment; and** puzzles, cards, board games, and my guitar.

The expansion committee is considering locations in Columbus, **Ohio; Orange, California; Minton, Tennessee; and Jacksonville, Florida**.

Practice

Practice what you've learned by adding semicolons where they are needed in the following sentences. You will find the answers at the end of this lesson.

1. I need a break I've been working for five hours straight.

2. The storm was torrential it hammered the small town with high winds and heavy rain.

3. We had no problem meeting the deadline however, we were still able to find ways of streamlining production.

4. It was a typical Saturday afternoon of washing clothes vacuuming and mopping the floors changing all the bed sheets and grocery shopping.

5. Paige left some of the confidential documents sitting on her desk at work consequently, she worried about their safety all night long.

Colons

Colons That Introduce

- Use a colon to introduce a list of items, as long as the part before the colon is already a complete sentence.

Examples:

These people were cast in the play: Andrea, Horatio, Thom, Alley, and Benito.

We packed these items for the trip: cameras, dress clothes, scuba equipment, and beach wear.

- Do not use a colon if the list of items complements a verb; in other words, if it completes the meaning begun by the verb. Look at the previous sample sentences rewritten in such a way that a colon is not necessary.

Examples:

The people cast in the play were Kristin, Horatio, Thom, Alley, and Benito.

For our trip, we packed cameras, dress clothes, scuba equipment, and beach wear.

- Use a colon to introduce a formal quotation.

Example:

John F. Kennedy ended the speech with these notable words: "Ask not what your country can do for you. Ask what you can do for your country."

- Use a colon to emphasize a word, phrase, or clause that adds particular emphasis to the main body of a sentence. Again, the part before the colon should already be a complete sentence.

Examples:

The financial problems our company has been experiencing have been caused by one thing: poor planning.

We were missing a vital piece of information: how the basic product design differed from last year's model.

Colons That Show a Subordinate Relationship

Use a colon to show a subordinate relationship in the following cases:

- Between two sentences when the second explains the first.

  Examples:

  > Brenton shouted and threw his fists in the air: He had just set a new world record.
  >
  > Nicole put the check into her scrapbook rather than cashing it: It was the first check she had ever earned.
  >
  > Scott ignored the phone: He knew it was a salesman for whom he had no time.

- Between the title and the subtitle of a book.

  Examples:

  > *Internet Starter Kit: A Complete Guide to Cyberspace*
  >
  > *Beyond 2000: A Futuristic View of Time*
  >
  > *O Death, Where Is Thy Sting: Tales from the Other Side*

- Between volume and page number or between chapter and verse.

  Examples:

  > *World Book Encyclopedia* V: 128
  >
  > *New Age Journal of Medicine* IX: 23
  >
  > John 3:16
  >
  > Genesis 1:1
  >
  > Psalms 23:2

- Between hour and minute.

  Examples:

  > 12:53 A.M.
  >
  > 2:10 P.M.

- After the greeting of a business letter. You learned that commas are used after greetings in personal or friendly letters. A colon signals the reader that what is to follow is a business matter, something to be taken seriously. This is particularly true if you include the position, but not the name of the person to whom the letter is addressed. However, even in a business letter, the closing is followed by a comma.

  Examples:

  > Dear Mr. Strange:
  >
  > > Cordially,
  >
  > Dear Operations Manager:
  >
  > > Respectfully submitted,

Practice

Choose the correctly punctuated version in each of the following sets of sentences. You will find the correct answers at the end of the lesson.

6. **a.** The next bus that leaves for Las Vegas, Nevada, from Bakersfield, California, is at 6:45 A.M.

   b. The next bus that leaves for Las Vegas, Nevada from Bakersfield, California is at 6:45 A.M.

   c. The next bus that leaves for Las Vegas Nevada, from Bakersfield California, is at 6:45 A.M.

7. **a.** Margo said she completed the application, however the last two sections were still blank.

   b. Margo said she completed the application; however the last two sections were still blank.

   c. Margo said she completed the application; however, the last two sections were still blank.

8. **a.** When I go to the employee retreat I'll need a tennis racket, a bathing suit, a pair of sneakers, and a towel.

   b. When I go to the employee retreat, I'll need a tennis racket, a bathing suit, a pair of sneakers, and a towel.

   c. When I go to the employee retreat, I'll need: a tennis racket, a bathing suit, a pair of sneakers, and a towel.

9. a. Dear Aunt Sally:

It was so nice to see you at the family picnic yesterday.

b. Dear Aunt Sally,

It was so nice to see you at the family picnic yesterday.

c. Dear Aunt Sally;

It was so nice to see you at the family picnic yesterday.

10. a. Matthew made certain the essential items were packed for the weekend hike into Big Bear: a tent and stakes; sleeping bag; a working compass; extra food and water; a first-aid kit; a map, pencil, and paper; a flashlight with batteries and an extra bulb; insect repellant; and waterproof matches.

b. Matthew made certain the essential items were packed for the weekend hike into Big Bear, a tent and stakes, sleeping bag, a working compass, extra food and water, a first-aid kit, a map, pencil, and paper, a flashlight with batteries and an extra bulb, insect repellant, and waterproof matches.

c. Matthew made certain the essential items were packed for the weekend hike into Big Bear; a tent and stakes, sleeping bag, a working compass, extra food and water; a first-aid kit, a map, pencil, and paper, a flashlight with batteries and an extra bulb; insect repellant, and waterproof matches.

11. a. We agreed to plant tulips, a cheerful and colorful flower; daisies, a simple yet lovely crowd favorite; lavender, a delicate flowering herb; and ivy, a low-maintenance ground cover.

b. We agreed to plant tulips, a cheerful and colorful flower: daisies, a simple yet lovely crowd favorite: lavender, a delicate flowering herb: and ivy, a low-maintenance ground cover.

c. We agreed to plant tulips a cheerful and colorful flower, daisies a simple yet lovely crowd favorite, lavender a delicate flowering herb, and ivy, a low-maintenance ground cover.

12. a. The students learned the following information from the museum guide: the artist's name; the artist's date of birth; the artist's credentials; and the artist's general style.

b. The students learned the following information from the museum guide the artist's name, the artist's date of birth, the artist's credentials, and the artist's general style.

c. The students learned the following information from the museum guide: the artist's name, the artist's date of birth, the artist's credentials, and the artist's general style.

Answers

1. I need a break; I've been working for five hours straight.

2. The storm was torrential; it hammered the small town with high winds and heavy rain.

3. We had no problem meeting the deadline; however, we were still able to find ways of streamlining production.

4. It was a typical Saturday afternoon of washing clothes; vacuuming and mopping the floors; changing all the bed sheets; and grocery shopping.

5. Paige left some of the confidential documents sitting on her desk at work; consequently, she worried about their safety all night long.

6. a.

7. c.

8. b.

9. b.

10. a.

11. a.

12. c.

TIP

Take a look at some of the letters or communications you have received or written recently. Examine the punctuation. Did the author use end marks, commas, semicolons, and colons correctly? If not, correct them. It will be good practice.

LESSON

7 ▶ APOSTROPHES AND DASHES

Many writers profess great exactness in punctuation, who never yet made a point.

—GEORGE PRENTICE, newspaper editor (1802–1807)

LESSON SUMMARY

This lesson will put you in control of tricky apostrophes (') and dashes (—), two of the most commonly misused marks of punctuation.

Apostrophes communicate important information in written language. Dashes, when used sparingly, add emphasis. Before you begin the lesson, see how much you already know. Add apostrophes—and one pair of dashes—where you think they belong in the **Problem** column on the following page. Check your answers with the **Solution** column.

Problem

Last nights premiere of *The Haunting of Amherst* was a star studded event, drawing famous faces and fashionistas galore. 200 300 people attended the premiere of the movie, which is generating Oscar buzz. Actress Randi Phillips star of *The Haunting of Amherst* beamed on the red carpet, clad in a stunning gown by well known designer Arturo Bruno. Her costar, singer actor Marcus L. Hoffman, brought an entourage with him, and his three daughters all joined him on the red carpet. Other Hollywood luminaries on the red carpet included Charles Mason, the movies director; Ashley Kirkland, star of the ABC sitcom *The Ashley Chronicles*; and supermodel Philomena Chang, fresh off *Fashion Monthlys* September cover.

Solution

Last night's premiere of *The Haunting of Amherst* was a star-studded event, drawing famous faces and fashionistas galore. 200–300 people attended the premiere of the movie, which is generating Oscar buzz. Actress Randi Phillips—star of *The Haunting of Amherst*—beamed on the red carpet, clad in a stunning gown by well-known designer Arturo Bruno. Her costar, singer-actor Marcus L. Hoffman, brought an entourage with him, and his three daughters all joined him on the red carpet. Other Hollywood luminaries on the red carpet included Charles Mason, the movie's director; Ashley Kirkland, star of the ABC sitcom *The Ashley Chronicles*; and supermodel Philomena Chang, fresh off *Fashion Monthly's* September cover.

Apostrophes

To Show Possession

Use an apostrophe to show possession. The highlighted words in each of the following examples are *possessive adjectives*: They show to whom or what a noun belongs.

SINGULAR NOUNS (ADD -'S)	PLURAL NOUNDS ENDING IN -S (ADD ')	PLURAL NOUNS NOT ENDING IN -S (ADD -'S)
boy's toy (The toy is the **boy's**.)	**boys'** bicycles (The bicycles are the **boys'**.)	**men's** schedules (The schedules are the **men's**.)
child's play	**kids'** bedrooms	**children's** opinions
lady's coat	**ladies'** skirts	**women's** department
dentist's aide	**players'** representative	**people's** choice

Apostrophes are *not* used to form plurals. When you're thinking of putting an apostrophe in a noun that ends in *-s,* ask yourself whether you're merely showing that there's more than one thing. If so, there's no apostrophe.

Examples:

There are a lot of **potatoes** in the refrigerator.
Cut out the **potatoes'** eyes.

You can avoid putting apostrophes in words that are merely plurals by trying this formula: *The _____ of the _____,* as in *the eyes of the potatoes.* If the words don't fit in that formula, the noun doesn't take an apostrophe.

Here are some special cases for the use of apostrophes to show possession.

- When there is more than one word in the possessive adjective—for example, with a compound noun, a business or institution, or jointly possessed items—add the apostrophe *-s* to the last word of the compound.
  Examples:
    someone **else's** problem
    mother-in-**law's** visit
    board of **directors'** policy
    Pope John Paul **II's** death
    Proctor and **Gamble's** product
    Wayne and **Judy's** log cabin
- Words showing periods of time or amounts of money need apostrophes when used as possessive adjectives.
  Examples:
    day's pay, **month's** vacation, **morning's** work
    two **cents'** worth, **dollar's** worth
- A singular noun that ends in *-s* still takes apostrophe *-s.*
  Examples:
    Roger **Maris's** batting record
    Lotus's personal organizer

- When a possessive pronoun (*mine, ours, yours, his, hers, theirs*) is used, no apostrophe is needed.
  Examples:
    The idea is **theirs**.
    The flight plan is **ours**.
    This manual must be **yours**.

Practice

From each set that follows, choose the option in which apostrophes are used correctly. You will find the answers to each set of questions at the end of the lesson.

1. a. The students' weekly lunch special was supposed to include a piece of fruit and a drink.
   b. The student's weekly lunch special was supposed to include a piece of fruit and a drink.

2. a. Employees reward's differ from an owners'.
   b. Employees' rewards differ from an owner's.

3. a. Elaine has worked three years as a physicians assistant.
   b. Elaine has worked three years as a physician's assistant.

4. a. The puppies tail wagged eagerly when he saw Jason approach.
   b. The puppy's tail wagged eagerly when he saw Jason approach.

5. a. The companies' sales force has doubled in recent years, and the credit is your's.
   b. The company's sales force has doubled in recent years, and the credit is yours.

6. a. Her's is the most ambitious plan I have seen yet.
   b. Hers is the most ambitious plan I have seen yet.

7. a. The city's mayor commended the surfers' heroic efforts to rescue two swimmers caught in a dangerous rip tide.
  b. The cities mayor commended the surfers' heroic efforts to rescue two swimmers caught in a dangerous rip tide.

8. a. Pat and Janice's proposal requires a month's work.
  b. Pat's and Janice's proposal requires a months' work.

9. a. The computer supply store's top-selling printer is the companies latest model.
  b. The computer supply store's top-selling printer is the company's latest model.

10. a. Ms. Jones's boutique sells the same products as Mr. Smith's.
  b. Ms. Jones boutique sells the same products as Mr. Smiths.

To Show Omission

Use an apostrophe to show that letters or numbers have been omitted.

Examples:
Morton **doesn't** (does not) live here anymore.
The officer **couldn't** (could not) give me a speeding ticket.
Who's (who is) on first?
I just **can't** (cannot) understand this memo.
My first car was a **'67** (1967) Chevy.
Grandpa tells stories about life in the **'40s** (1940s).

Em–Dashes

An *em-dash* is a specialized punctuation mark reserved for only a few situations. However, many writers use it incorrectly in place of other marks. Em-dashes call attention to themselves—A careful writer uses them sparingly. Em-dashes are very effective if used correctly, but they lose their impact if overused.

Remember to distinguish an em-dash from a hyphen when typing. An em-dash is **three** hyphens.

- Use an em-dash to mark a sudden break in thought or to insert a comment.
  Examples:
  Here is your sandwich and your—Look out for that bee!
  I remember the day—what middle-aged person doesn't—that President Kennedy was shot.
  John is sorry—we all are—about your unfortunate accident.
- Use an em-dash to emphasize explanatory material.
  Examples:
  Knowing yourself—your thoughts, values, and dreams—is the most important knowledge.
  "The writer is by nature a dreamer—a conscious dreamer."—*Carson McCullers*
  We spend our summers in Canada—Ontario, to be precise.
- Use an em-dash to indicate omitted letters or words.
  Examples:
  "Oh, d—, I can't believe I forgot to mail that package!"
  "Hello?—Yes, I can hear you just fine.—Of course—I think I can.—Good!—I'll see you later.—"
- Use an em-dash to connect a beginning phrase to the rest of the sentence.
  Examples:
  Honesty, integrity, tenacity—these are marks of motivated salespeople.
  Nashville, Tennessee; Olympia, Washington; Oceola, Iowa—these are the prospective locations.

Practice

Choose the option in which em-dashes and other punctuation are used correctly in each of the following sets.

11. a. Beth's new car—a sleek sedan—has an outstanding extended warranty.
b. Beths' new car—a sleek sedan—has an outstanding extended warranty.

12. a. Her preference—just in case anyone asks, is to find an inexpensive Italian restaurant for dinner.
b. Her preference—just in case anyone asks—is to find an inexpensive Italian restaurant for dinner.

13. a. Mr. Jackson can be such an annoying, I suppose I should be careful about what I say.
b. Mr. Jackson can be such an annoying—I suppose I should be careful about what I say.

14. a. New York, Chicago, Atlanta—these are the cities on her itinerary.
b. New York, Chicago, Atlanta: These are the cities on her itinerary.

15. a. I've managed to misplace that d— memo that I wrote—Oh, it's right on my desk.
b. I've managed to misplace that d— memo that I wrote, Oh it's right on my desk.

Practice and Review

Check yourself with these sample test questions. These extremely difficult questions cover much of what you have learned about punctuation so far. Look at the items carefully. Which of the following options is punctuated correctly?

16. a. Although it may seem strange, my partners purpose in interviewing Dr. E.S. Sanders Jr., was to eliminate him as a suspect in the crime.
b. Although it may seem strange my partner's purpose in interviewing Dr. E.S. Sanders, Jr. was to eliminate him, as a suspect in the crime.
c. Although it may seem strange, my partner's purpose in interviewing Dr. E.S. Sanders, Jr., was to eliminate him as a suspect in the crime.
d. Although it may seem strange, my partner's purpose in interviewing Dr. E.S. Sanders, Jr. was to eliminate him, as a suspect in the crime.

17. a. After colliding with a vehicle at the intersection of Grand, and Forest Ms. Anderson saw a dark hooded figure reach through the window, grab a small parcel and run north on Forest.
b. After colliding with a vehicle at the intersection of Grand, and Forest, Ms. Anderson saw a dark hooded figure reach through the window, grab a small parcel, and run north on Forest.
c. After colliding with a vehicle at the intersection of Grand and Forest Ms. Anderson saw a dark, hooded figure reach through the window, grab a small parcel and run north on Forest.
d. After colliding with a vehicle at the intersection of Grand and Forest, Ms. Anderson saw a dark, hooded figure reach through the window, grab a small parcel, and run north on Forest.

18. a. When we interviewed each of the boys and the fathers, we determined that the men's stories did not match up with the boy's versions.

b. When we interviewed each of the boys and the fathers, we determined that the men's stories did not match up with the boys' versions.

c. When we interviewed each of the boys and the fathers, we determined that the mens' stories did not match up with the boys' versions.

d. When we interviewed each of the boy's and the father's, we determined that the men's stories did not match up with the boys' versions.

19. a. Nathans' college resume includes many outstanding achievements: academics, athletics, volunteer hours, and work experience—making him an excellent candidate for most colleges.

b. Nathan's college resume includes many outstanding achievements—academics, athletics, volunteer hours, and work experience—making him an excellent candidate for most colleges.

c. Nathans' college resume includes many outstanding achievements—academics, athletics, volunteer hours, and work experience; making him an excellent candidate for most colleges.

d. Nathan's college resume includes many outstanding achievements, academics, athletics, volunteer hours, and work experience, making him an excellent candidate for most colleges.

20. a. James Autry, Stephen Covey, Madeline Hunter—these authors are responsible for my management style, a combination of Autry's personnel philosophy, Covey's process for prioritizing, and Hunter's organizational principles.

b. James Autry, Stephen Covey, Madeline Hunter. These authors are responsible for my management style, a combination of Autry's personnel philosophy, Covey's process for prioritizing and Hunter's organizational principles.

c. James Autry, Stephen Covey, Madeline Hunter—these authors are responsible for my management style, a combination of Autrys personnel philosophy, Coveys process for prioritizing and Hunters organizational principles.

d. James Autry, Stephen Covey, Madeline Hunter: These authors are responsible for my management style; a combination of Autry's personnel philosophy; Covey's process for prioritizing; and Hunter's organizational principles.

Answers

1. a.	**11.** a.
2. b.	**12.** b.
3. b.	**13.** b.
4. b.	**14.** a.
5. b.	**15.** a.
6. b.	**16.** c.
7. a.	**17.** d.
8. a.	**18.** b.
9. b.	**19.** b.
10. a.	**20.** a.

TIP

Few people fully understand the rules of apostrophes and dashes. Advertisers are notorious for misusing both types of punctuation. Pay special attention to billboards and advertisements in newspapers and magazines. Look for places where apostrophes and em-dashes were used correctly. Notice places where they were omitted or added when they shouldn't have been. If your job produces promotional material, examine some of your own literature to see if apostrophes and dashes have been used correctly.

QUOTATION MARKS

I often quote myself. It adds spice to my conversation.
—GEORGE BERNARD SHAW, Irish playwright (1856–1950)

LESSON SUMMARY
This lesson covers rules regarding the use of quotation marks, both double and single. Although these marks are most often found in dialogue, they are important in other writing situations as well.

Begin this lesson by seeing how much you already know about quotation marks. Insert them where you think they belong in the sentences in the **Problem** column on the following page. Some sentences will also need end marks and commas. Check your answers against the corrected versions of the sentences in the **Solution** column.

Problem

A local man is hailed as a survivor this morning, after enduring a bear attack on McDuff Mountain yesterday afternoon.

Felix Quintana was hiking familiar trails on Sunday when he encountered a small bear raiding a campsite. Quintana suffered minor injuries to his arms and legs before he was able to break away and call for help.

Quintana, an experienced hiker for more than 30 years, has never encountered anything like this before. You learn what to do, but in the moment, your mind just goes blank. I'm so thankful that I'm still here.

McDuff Mountain park ranger Phyllis Majeski reports that bear sightings are rare on the mountain; bear attacks are even rarer. In my 15 years here, I've never heard of this kind of aggression from our small bear population. But this is a good reminder that we need to be careful at all times when we're out in these woods.

Per state policy, the bear (who is approximately a year old) was located and taken into custody by Animal Control. According to Animal Control spokeswoman Arlene Stevens, his official status is pending review. The bear's fate will be determined next week.

Despite his close call, Quintana has no plans to abandon his future hiking plans. I don't want to let this scare me into staying home he said I just hope that everyone is more vigilant, even when you think you're alone out there.

Solution

A local man is hailed as a survivor this morning, after enduring a bear attack on McDuff Mountain yesterday afternoon.

Felix Quintana was hiking familiar trails on Sunday when he encountered a small bear raiding a campsite. Quintana suffered minor injuries to his arms and legs before he was able to break away and call for help.

Quintana, an experienced hiker for more than 30 years, has never encountered anything like this before. "You learn what to do, but in the moment, your mind just goes blank. I'm so thankful that I'm still here."

McDuff Mountain park ranger Phyllis Majeski reports that bear sightings are rare on the mountain; bear attacks are even rarer. "In my 15 years here, I've never heard of this kind of aggression from our small bear population. But this is a good reminder that we need to be careful at all times when we're out in these woods."

Per state policy, the bear (who is approximately a year old) was located and taken into custody by Animal Control. According to Animal Control spokeswoman Arlene Stevens, his official status is "pending review." The bear's fate will be determined next week.

Despite his close call, Quintana has no plans to abandon his future hiking plans. "I don't want to let this scare me into staying home," he said. "I just hope that everyone is more vigilant, even when you think you're alone out there."

Quotation Marks with Direct Quotations

■ Use quotation marks to set off a direct quotation or thought within a sentence or paragraph. This includes quotations that are signed, etched, inscribed, carved, and so on.

Examples:

Mr. Hurley called our prototype "a model of pure genius."

I was certain he had said, "Campbells will accept delivery on Tuesday."

"When will help arrive?" I wondered.

The sign clearly read, "No trespassing."

"Happy and Fulfilled," the headstone read.

- Do *not* use quotation marks for paraphrases or indirect quotations.

  Examples:

  I was sure Campbells had wanted a Tuesday delivery.

  I wondered when help would arrive.

  The sign said that trespassing and hunting were not allowed.

- Use single quotation marks to set off a quotation within a quotation.

  Examples:

  "I distinctly heard her say, 'The store opens at nine,'" said Gene.

  The speaker continued, "I am ever mindful of Franklin Roosevelt's famous words, 'We have nothing to fear but fear itself.' But fear is a terrible thing."

  My speech teacher asked, "Does anyone in this room remember the way Jim Nabors used to say, 'Golly'?"

A Word about Dialogue

Correctly punctuating dialogue means understanding how to use quotation marks, commas, and end marks. Take a close look at the sentences in the following dialogue sample. They include the basic dialogue structures. The words quoted are called *quotations*, and the words explaining who said the quotations are called *tags*. In this sample, the tags are highlighted.

1. **Horace said,** "I'm really thirsty. Let's grab something to drink."
2. "I'm thirsty, but I don't have any cash. Do you have some?" **Nancy replied.**
3. "I don't get it," **Horace answered.** "You're the manager with the high-paying job."
4. "Well," **Nancy replied,** "credit cards are all I ever use."

Quoted words are always surrounded by quotation marks. Place quotation marks before a group of quoted words and again at the end.

Tags are punctuated differently depending upon where they appear in the sentence. Whenever the tag follows a quotation and the quotation is a sentence that would normally be punctuated with a period, use a comma at the end of the quotation. The period comes at the end of the tag. However, if the quotation is a sentence that would normally be followed with a question mark or an exclamation point, insert the question mark or exclamation point at the end of the quotation. Place a period after the tag. (See sentence 2 in the previous column.)

"I'm really thirsty. Let's grab something to drink," said Alvina.

"I'm really thirsty. Do you want to grab something to drink?" asked Alvina.

"I'm really thirsty. Hold it—a vending machine!" exclaimed Alvina.

Sometimes, the tag precedes the quotation. When this happens, place a comma after the tag. Put quotation marks around the quoted words, capitalize the first word of the quotation, and punctuate the sentence as you would normally. (See sentence 1.)

Sometimes, the tag interrupts the quotation. If both the first and second parts of the quotation are complete sentences, the first part of the quotation is punctuated in the same way as a quotation with the tag at the end. In other words, the period follows the tag. The rest of the quotation is punctuated in the same way as a quotation preceded by a tag. (See sentence 3.)

When the tag interrupts the quotation and the sentence, the words preceding the tag begin the thought, and the words following the tag complete the thought. Place quotation marks around the quoted words and follow the first part of the quotation with a comma. Place a comma after the tag (not a period, since the sentence is not completed). Place quotation marks around the last part of the quotation, but do NOT capitalize the first letter of the quotation. It is not the beginning of a sentence. Punctuate the rest of the sentence as you would normally. (See sentence 4.)

NOTE: All the punctuation, except the punctuation marks following the tags, is **inside** the quotation marks.

Dialogue at a Glance

- Tag following the quotation mark:
    "_____," said Rose.
    "_____?" asked Rose.
    "_____!" exclaimed Rose.
- Tag preceding quotation:
    Iris said, "_____."
    Iris asked, "_____?"
    Iris exclaimed, "_____!"
- Tag between two sentences of a quotation:
    "_____," said Lily. "_____."
    "_____?" asked Lily. "_____?" *or*
    "_____!" exclaimed Lily. "_____!".
- Tag interrupting a quotation and a sentence:
    "_____," said Daisy, "_____."
    "_____," asked Daisy, "_____?"
    "_____," exclaimed Daisy, "_____!"

Other Uses of Quotation Marks

- Use quotation marks to set off unfamiliar terms and nicknames. You will often see italics used in the same manner.
    Examples:
    None of us had heard of "chutney" before we read the article.
    He was dubbed "Sir Tagalong" by the other members of the staff.
    The Scrabble players disagreed over the term "ptu." (*or . . .* over the term *ptu.*)
- Use quotation marks to indicate irony or raised eyebrows. But avoid overusing quotation marks in this way; it doesn't work if you do it all the time.
    Examples:
    When we were camping, our "bathroom" was a thicket behind our tent.
    Our "guide" never mentioned the presence of poison ivy.
    The "fun" of surgery begins long before the operation commences.
- Use quotation marks to set off titles of certain items. Other titles should be underlined or italicized.

ENCLOSE IN QUOTATION MARKS	UNDERLINE OR ITALICIZE
name of a short story or chapter of a book	title of a novel
name of a TV episode	name of a TV series or movie
title of a short poem	title of a collection of poetry or an epic poem
headline of an article or title of a report	name of a magazine or newspaper
title of a song	title of a musical, play, or long musical composition
	name of a ship, plane, train, etc.

Punctuating within Quotation Marks

Here are the rules regarding the use of other punctuation marks and quotation marks.

- Question marks, exclamation points, and dashes go inside the quotation marks if they are part of the quotation. If they are not, place them outside the quotation marks.

  Examples:

  The doctor asked, "Can you feel any pain in this area**?"** [Part of the quotation]

  Have you read Nathaniel Hawthorne's "The Birthmark"**?** [Not part of the quotation]

  "I wish I'd never heard of—" Karen stopped abruptly as Nick walked in the room. [Part of the quotation]

  "Stage left," "stage right," "upstage," and "downstage"—I always confused these terms. [Not part of the quotation]

- Periods and commas go **inside** closing quotation marks.

  "Let's wait a few minutes**,**" suggested Doris, "before we leave."

- Colons and semicolons go **outside** closing quotation marks.

  I can see only one challenge for the speaker of "The Road Less Traveled"**:** ambivalence.

  The critic called the latest sculpture an "abomination to sensitive eyes"**;** the artist was hurt.

Practice

Choose the correctly punctuated version in each of the following sets of sentences. Also, check for punctuation other than quotation marks.

1. **a.** "Have you ever read the story 'The Open Window' by O. Henry? asked Martha.
   b. "Have you ever read the story 'The Open Window' by O. Henry?" asked Martha.
   c. "Have you ever read the story "The Open Window" by O. Henry?" asked Martha.

2. **a.** It escapes me why Trent, a Barley Brothers clown who is touted an "expert," was not asked to speak at the NE Clown Association meeting tomorrow.
   b. It escapes me why Trent, "a Barley Brothers clown who is touted an expert," was not asked to speak at the NE Clown Association meeting tomorrow.
   c. It escapes me why Trent, a "Barley Brothers clown" who is touted an expert, was not asked to speak at the NE Clown Association meeting tomorrow.

3. **a.** After reading a review of Toy Story, I wanted to see the movie.
   b. After reading a review of *Toy Story*, I wanted to see the movie.
   c. After reading a review of "Toy Story," I wanted to see the movie.

4. **a.** Leaving five minutes early on Friday was our "reward."
   b. Leaving five minutes early on Friday was our "reward".
   c. Leaving five minutes early on Friday was our 'reward.'

5. a. "Firewall," "bandwidth," "URL"—these are some of the technical terms you'll learn in this class.
 b. "Firewall," "bandwidth," "URL—" these are some of the technical terms you'll learn in this class.
 c. "Firewall", "bandwidth", "URL'—these are some of the technical terms you'll learn in this class.

6. a. If you read my article Budget Play in this morning's *Register,* you'll understand why I'm so cynical about Washington politicians.
 b. If you read my article "Budget Play" in this morning's "Register", you'll understand why I'm so cynical about Washington politicians.
 c. If you read my article "Budget Play" in this morning's *Register*, you'll understand why I'm so cynical about Washington politicians.

7. a. "Never have I seen anything quite like today's performance," remarked Coach Smith.
 b. "Never have I seen anything quite like today's performance", remarked Coach Smith.
 c. "Never have I seen anything quite like today's performance.", remarked Coach Smith.

8. a. "I wonder why Dad names all of his cats Bob?" said Chris.
 b. "I wonder why Dad names all of his cats Bob." said Chris.
 c. "I wonder why Dad names all of his cats Bob," said Chris.

9. a. The officer asked us whether we had seen the accident.
 b. The officer asked us whether we had seen the accident?
 c. The officer asked us, "Whether we had seen the accident."

10. a. The police officer asked the suspect, "where were you on October twenty-eighth at four in the afternoon?"
 b. The police officer asked the suspect, "Where were you on October twenty-eighth at four in the afternoon?"
 c. The police officer asked the suspect, "Where were you on October twenty-eighth at four in the afternoon?".

Answers

1. b.
2. a.
3. b.
4. a.
5. a.
6. c.
7. a.
8. c.
9. a.
10. b.

TIP

Look for examples of quotation marks in anything you read. When you find them, check to see if they've been used correctly.

"DESIGNER" PUNCTUATION

My attitude toward punctuation is that it ought to be as conventional as possible. The game of golf would lose a good deal if croquet mallets and billiard cues were allowed on the putting green. . . .

—ERNEST HEMINGWAY, American novelist (1899–1961)

LESSON SUMMARY

This lesson covers some of the less commonly used punctuation marks, including hyphens, parentheses, brackets, ellipses, and diagonal slashes. While these marks aren't necessary all that often, when they *are* necessary, it's important to use them correctly.

The punctuation marks covered in this lesson—hyphens, parentheses, brackets, ellipses, and diagonals—are not often used in regular writing. However, they serve very specific purposes. Knowing and understanding their functions gives a writer an advantage in communicating ideas. Most of these rules are so specialized that only a few people know them, but see how much you know by inserting these "designer" punctuation marks into the **Problem** column on the next page, and check your answers against the corrected passage in the **solution** column. The last part of the lesson discusses using numbers in written text.

Problem

To prepare for your camping trip, please consider the following advice. For starters, the weather may be sunny and warm when you leave your house, don't take that for granted! Always pack for the worst case weather scenario. In the winter, make sure you have warm gloves, thermal underclothes, and a parka. In the summer, make sure you have a rain poncho and a sweater just in case there are chilly nights in addition to lightweight clothes in case the temperatures rise during the day. No matter what the weather, it's always a good idea to wear solid, waterproof boots available at your local sporting goods store. A proper indoor outdoor sleeping bag will help keep you warm at night.

For food, be sure to pack high-protein snacks that don't require refrigeration, granola bars, trail mix, and or dried fruit. Always make sure to have clean water available if you can't carry a lot of bottled water with you, you can find water purification tablets also available at sporting goods stores. And perhaps the most important part of all be sure to pack a well-stocked first-aid kit to handle any scrapes, cuts, and bruises you may accumulate along the way. And always, always! have items in your kit to alert people nearby if you have an emergency, including flashlights, matches, and a whistle.

Solution

To prepare for your camping trip, please consider the following advice. For starters, the weather may be sunny and warm when you leave your house...don't take that for granted! Always pack for the worst-case weather scenario. In the winter, make sure you have warm gloves, underclothes, and a parka. In the summer, make sure you have a rain poncho and a sweater (just in case there are chilly nights) in addition to lightweight clothes (in case the temperatures rise during the day). No matter what the weather, it's always a good idea to wear solid, waterproof boots (available at your local sporting goods store). A proper indoor/outdoor sleeping bag will help keep you warm at night.

For food, be sure to pack high-protein snacks that don't require refrigeration (granola bars, trail mix, and/or dried fruit). Always make sure to have clean water available—if you can't carry a lot of bottled water with you, you can find water purification tablets (also available at sporting goods stores). And—perhaps the most important part of all—be sure to pack a well-stocked first-aid kit to handle any scrapes, cuts, and bruises you may accumulate along the way. And always (always!) have items in your kit to alert people nearby if you have an emergency, including flashlights, matches, and a whistle.

Hyphens

The main purpose of a hyphen (-) is to join words in creating compound nouns or adjectives. Hyphens signal words that work together for a single purpose.

Compound nouns may be written as a single word, as two words, or as a hyphenated word. Whenever you are in doubt, consult an up-to-date dictionary. Since language changes constantly, these words also evolve. A compound noun written as two words may come to be written as a hyphenated word and eventually become a single word. For example, the word *semicolon* began as two separate words: *semi colon*. In the late 1950s, dictionaries began listing it as a hyphenated word: *semi-colon*. A recent dictionary will list it as a single word: *semicolon*.

SINGLE-WORD COMPOUND NOUNS	TWO-WORD COMPOUND NOUNS	HYPHENATED COMPOUND NOUNS
tablecloth	parking lot	jack-in-the-box
horsefly	couch potato	brother-in-law
textbook	floppy disk	money-maker
catwalk		city-state
bedroom		well-being
		merry-go-round

- Use a hyphen to join two coequal nouns working together as one.

  Shannon is a **teacher-poet**.

  Pete Rose was a **player-coach** for the Cincinnati Reds.

  Kevin Costner has joined the ranks of well-known **actor-directors**.

- Use a hyphen to join multiword compound nouns.

  fly-by-night, stick-in-the-mud, good-for-nothing, three-year-old

- Use a hyphen to join two or more words that function as a single adjective *preceding* the noun.

  The hikers saw a **run-down** cabin in the clearing.

  Much has been written about the **Kennedy-Nixon** debates.

  An **ill-trained** police officer is more of a menace than protector.

  The company employed a **high-powered** consultant.

  A **soft-spoken** answer to the angry accusation ended the disagreement.

  His **off-the-wall** remarks keep our meetings lively and interesting.

  The parties finally agreed after three months of **hard-nosed** negotiations.

  A **French-Canadian** bicyclist won the **three-week** race.

- If the words functioning as a single adjective *follow* the noun, they are not hyphenated.

  The cabin the hikers saw in the clearing was **run down**.

  A police officer who is **ill trained** is more of a menace than a protector.

  The consultant employed by the company was **high powered**.

  The parties finally agreed after three months of negotiations that were **hard nosed**.

- Use a hyphen to join prefixes such as *self, half, ex, all, great, post, pro,* and *vice,* or the suffix *elect,* to words.*

  Harry Truman unleashed the **all-powerful** atomic weapon.

  Abraham Lincoln was a **self-made** man.

  Keep your **half-baked** ideas to yourself.

  Simone spotted her **ex-husband** walking into the grocery store.

  My **great-grandfather** turns 102 next Wednesday.

  Many remember the **post-WWII** years with great fondness.

  The **secretary-elect** picked up all the records from the presiding secretary.

---

* Refer to a dictionary for common words to determine if they still use the hyphen or if they are closed up.

Conservatives consider the front-runner to be a **proabortion** candidate. (per Merriam-Webster)

You are almost **halfway** through this book. (per Merriam-Webster)

- Use a hyphen to avoid confusion or awkward spellings.

  The coach decided to **re-pair** [rather than *repair*] the debate partners.

  The neighbors decided to **re-cover** [rather than *recover*] their old sofa.

  The sculpture had a **bell-like** [rather than *belllike*] shape.

- Use a hyphen to join a capital letter to a word.

  The **U-joint** went out in our second car.

  The architect worked with nothing more than a **T-square**.

- Use a hyphen to write two-word numbers between 21 and 99 as words.

  twenty-six, thirty-three, sixty-four, seventy-two, ninety-nine

- Use a hyphen to join fractions written as words.

  three-fifths, five-sixteenths, five thirty-seconds

- Use a hyphen to join numbers to words used as a single adjective.

  three-yard pass, **eight-inch** steel, **two-word** sentence, **five-stroke** lead

NOTE: When a series of similar number-word adjectives is written in a sentence, use a hyphen/comma combination with all but the last item in the series.

Precut particle board comes in **two-, four-,** and **six-foot** squares.

Andy scored three touchdowns on **eight-, fourteen-,** and **two-yard** runs.

- Use a hyphen to join numbers and adjectives.

  fifty-four-year-old woman, **ten-dollar** profit, **two-thousand-acre** ranch, **twenty-minute** wait

- Use a hyphen to write the time of day as words.

  twelve-thirty, four-o'clock appointment, **six-fifteen** A.M., **one-fifty-five** in the morning

- Use a hyphen to separate a word between syllables at the end of a line. Here are a few guidelines for dividing words:
  - Never leave a single-letter syllable on a line.
  - Divide hyphenated words at the hyphen.
  - Never divide a one-syllable word.
  - Avoid dividing words that have fewer than six letters.
  - Avoid dividing the last word of a paragraph.
  - Avoid dividing a number.
  - Always check a dictionary if you are in doubt.

Parentheses

- Use parentheses to enclose explanatory material that interrupts the normal flow of the sentences and is only marginally related to the text.

  Thirty-sixth Street (**a party street if there ever was one**) is a fun place to live.

  Our neighbors threw a huge party on New Year's Eve. (**Fortunately, we were invited.**)

  Unfortunately, another set of neighbors (**who were not invited**) called the police to complain about the noise.

  We party-goers (**how were we to know?**) were completely surprised by the officers.

Notice the last three sentences. Each set of parentheses contains a complete sentence. If the parenthetical construction comes at the end of a sentence, it is punctuated as its own sentence within the parentheses. On the other hand, if it comes within another sentence, no capital letters or periods are necessary. However, if the parenthetical construction in the middle of another sentence is a sentence that would normally require a question mark or exclamation point, include that punctuation.

- Use parentheses to enclose information when accuracy is essential.

    The two sons of Richard Hannika (**Scott and William**) are sole heirs to his fortune.

    We hereby agree to sell the heirloom for sixty-three dollars (**$63.00**).

- Use parentheses to enclose letters or numbers marking a division.

    This lesson includes several little-used, often-misused punctuation marks: (**a**) hyphens, (**b**) parentheses, (**c**) brackets, (**d**) diagonals, and (**e**) ellipses.

    Your task consists of three steps: (**1**) locating information, (**2**) writing a report, and (**3**) delivering a presentation about your findings.

Brackets

- Use brackets to enclose parenthetical material within parentheses.

    Brandi planned to work as an aeronautic engineer (she completed an internship at National Aeronautics and Space Administration [**NASA**]) as soon as she completed her doctoral work.

- Use brackets to enclose words inserted into a quotation.

    "The next head nurse [**Shawna DeWitt**] will face the challenge of operating the floor with a reduced staff."

- Use brackets around the word *sic* to show that an error in a quotation was made by the original writer or speaker.

    "Unless we heel [**sic**] the nation's economic woes, social problems will continue to mount."

Ellipses

An ellipsis looks like periods, but it does not function as an end mark. Type three spaced periods to form an ellipsis. This mark indicates omitted material or a long pause.

- Use ellipses to show that quoted material has been omitted. If the omission comes at the end of a sentence, follow the ellipsis with a period.

    "Four-score and seven years ago . . . equal."

    "We hold these truths to be self-evident . . ."

- Use an ellipsis to indicate a pause or hesitation.

    And the winner for "Best Actor" is . . . Dustin Hoffman.

    I think that adds up to . . . exactly eighty-three dollars.

Diagonals

Much like the hyphen, a diagonal is a mark used to join words or numbers. The most frequent use of the diagonal is with the phrase *and/or*, which shows that the sentence refers to one or both of the words being joined.

    For breakfast, we can make bacon **and/or** French toast.

    Vinegar **and/or** egg whites added to plain water will make an excellent hair rinse that leaves hair soft and silky.

- Use a diagonal to separate numbers in a fraction.

    Normally, it takes us **3½** hours to sort the bulk mail at the end of the week.

    You'll need a **1⅝-inch** wrench for this nut.

- Use a diagonal to show line divisions in poetry.

    "Goodnight, goodnight, parting is such sweet sorrow / That I shall say good night 'till it be morrow. / Sleep dwell upon thine eyes and peace in thy breast! / Would I were sleep and peace so sweet to rest!"

- Use a diagonal to indicate *per* or *divided by*.

    The cars in the new fleet average over 25 **miles/ gallon**.

    Shares are calculated in this way: **net profit/ number of shareholders**.

Numbers

A few rules guide the use of numbers in writing. In journalistic writing, numbers are preferable to words because they are easier to identify and read. However, a number at the beginning of a sentence is always written as a word. In more formal writing, follow the conventions listed here.

- Use Arabic rather than Roman numerals: *1, 2, 3, 4* rather than *I, II, III, IV.*
- If a number can be written as one or two words, write it as a word. Otherwise, write the numeral: eight, twenty-six, 124, three hundred, 8,549, five million.
- Always write a number at the beginning of sentence as a word even if it is more than two words.

Practice

Add hyphens and parentheses where they are needed in the following sentences.

1. Cheryl's ex sister in law is a high powered attorney with twenty five years of experience.

2. Dr. Pratt was so concerned about the two year old girl's injury that he ordered an X ray.

3. Judy's well written essay impressed all twenty five judges.

4. For breakfast you may choose from the following options: a sausage and eggs, b a bagel with cream cheese, or c pancakes or waffles.

5. "The Trojan Horse was actually a cleverly plotted red herring decoy created by the Greeks to conceal soldiers waiting to attack the Trojans."

Add hyphens, parentheses, brackets, ellipses, and diagonals where they are needed in the following sentences.

6. Muhammad Ali one of the greatest boxers of our time wrote a poem describing himself as someone who could ". . . float like a butterflie sic, sting like a bee."

7. After the workshop, please 1 collect the completed forms 2 compile all the data and 3 leave your report in Mr. White's right hand drawer.

8. Prizes for the three week contest can be collected in the form of cash and or merchandise and approximately one third of our members will be eligible.

Answers

1. Cheryl's ex-sister-in-law is a high-powered attorney with twenty-five years of experience.
2. Dr. Pratt was so concerned about the two-year-old girl's injury that he ordered an X-ray.
3. Judy's well-written essay impressed all twenty-five judges.
4. For breakfast, you may choose from the following options: (a) sausage and eggs, (b) a bagel with cream cheese, or (c) pancakes or waffles.
5. "The Trojan Horse was actually a cleverly plotted red herring [decoy] created by the Greeks to conceal soldiers waiting to attack the Trojans."
6. Muhammad Ali (one of the greatest boxers of our time) wrote a poem describing himself as someone who could ". . . float like a butterflie [sic], sting like a bee."
7. After the workshop, please (1) collect the completed forms, (2) compile all the data, and (3) leave your report in Mr. White's right-hand drawer.
8. Prizes for the three-week contest can be collected in the form of cash and/or merchandise and approximately one-third of our members will be eligible.

TIP

Look for examples of the punctuation marks from this lesson as you read today. Since they are used less frequently than other marks, you probably won't see them as often. When you do, try to remember how the mark is used. Be especially aware of hyphens, parentheses, brackets, diagonals, and ellipses in advertising copy; check to see if they have been used correctly.

10 ▶ VERB TENSE

Language is fossil poetry.
—RALPH WALDO EMERSON, American poet (1803–1882)

LESSON SUMMARY

As the "movers and shakers" of language, verbs drive language and give it life. They are the energetic part of speech. Because they are so important, mistakes involving verbs really stand out. They can make or break the outcome of an exam, essay, or business letter. The next two lessons will help you learn how to avoid the most common errors involving these important words.

Writers use words to establish their credibility. Few things cast doubt on a writer's believability as much as misusing words—especially verbs. Incorrect verb forms call special attention to themselves and bring the writer's education and intelligence into question. Furthermore, exams often test your knowledge of how to use verbs and avoid errors involving verbs.

This lesson explains how to use verbs correctly and highlights a few of the most common mistakes writers make. See how many of the seven errors in verb usage you can find in the **Problem** version of the passage on the following page. In the **Solution** column, the paragraph is rewritten with the correct verb forms. As you go through the lesson, try to apply the rules you learn to these corrections.

Problem

When *Saturday Night Live* begun airing in 1975, it stars a small, ragtag bunch of comedians who look to create something different in the TV world: a late-night sketch comedy show with an edge. It is a hit at the time, and it made instant celebrities of original cast members like Dan Aykroyd, Jane Curtin, Bill Murray, Chevy Chase, and John Belushi. In more than 30 years, the show launches the careers of many who became household names, such as Eddie Murphy, Billy Crystal, Mike Myers, Chris Rock, and Tina Fey, who have all went on to successful movie and TV careers. And even the cast members who didn't goes on to become Hollywood superstars are still alumni of a long and proud comedy tradition.

Solution

When *Saturday Night Live* <u>began</u> airing in 1975, it <u>starred</u> a small, ragtag bunch of comedians who <u>were looking</u> to create something different in the TV world: a late-night sketch comedy show with an edge. It <u>was</u> a hit at the time, and it made instant celebrities of original cast members like Dan Aykroyd, Jane Curtin, Bill Murray, Chevy Chase, and John Belushi. In more than 30 years, the show <u>launched</u> the careers of many who became household names, such as Eddie Murphy, Billy Crystal, Mike Myers, Chris Rock, and Tina Fey, who have all <u>gone</u> on to successful movie and TV careers. And even the cast members who didn't <u>go</u> on to become Hollywood superstars are still alumni of a long and proud comedy tradition.

Principal Parts of Verbs

Verbs have three principal parts:

1. **Present**: the form of the verb that would complete the sentence, "Now, I _____."
2. **Past**: the form of the verb that would complete the sentence, "Yesterday, I _____."
3. **Past participle**: the form of the verb that would complete the sentence, "Often, I have _____."

For most verbs, it's easy to form the three principal parts if you know the present form. Take the verb *look*, for example. *Now, I look. Yesterday, I looked. Often, I have looked.* For regular verbs, the past and past-participle forms both add *-ed* to the present form. But English is full of irregular verbs that form the past and past participle in some other way. The following table shows the principal parts of several often misused verbs.

THREE PRINCIPAL PARTS OF VERBS		
PRESENT	**PAST**	**PAST PARTICIPLE***
do	did	done
go	went	gone
see	saw	seen
drink	drank	drunk
break	broke	broken
bring	brought	brought
choose	chose	chosen
know	knew	known
wear	wore	worn
write	wrote	written

* **Note:** Past participles must be preceded by the words *have, has,* or *had.*

Practice

Circle the correct form of the verb in each of the following sentences. The answers can be found at the end of the lesson.

1. Agnes (writes, wrote, written) in her diary every day last week.

2. Mr. Marks has not (do, did, done) a very good job of communicating with the staff.

3. Michael has (fly, flew, flown) countless times across the Atlantic.

4. Louise had already (speak, spoke, spoken) to the insurance agent several times.

5. They (give, gave, given) his little brother a hard time whenever they see him.

6. Has your department (go, went, gone) to lunch?

7. Jason (see, saw, seen) the car leaving the parking area.

8. The city has not yet (begin, began, begun) the new recycling program.

9. Olivia couldn't believe that she had actually (forget, forgot, forgotten) the key to her office again.

10. Jonathan was very nervous when he (take, took, taken) his place at the podium.

Consistent Verb Tense

The tense of a verb tells when an action occurs, occurred, or will occur. Verbs have three basic tenses: present, past, and future. It's important to keep verb tenses consistent as you write. A passage that begins in present tense should continue in present tense. If it begins in past tense, it should stay in past tense. Do not mix tenses.

Wrong:
> Dan **opened** the car door and **looks** for his briefcase.

Correct:
> Dan **opened** the car door and **looked** for his briefcase.

Wrong:
> When we **increase** maintenance services, we **reduced** repair costs.

Correct:
> When we **increase** maintenance services, we **reduce** repair costs.

However, sometimes a writer must show that an action occurred at another time regardless of the tense in which the passage was begun. To allow this, each of these three tenses has three subdivisions: progressive, perfect, and progressive perfect.

Present Tense Forms

Present tense shows action that happens now or action that happens routinely. The *present progressive* tense shows an action happening now. An auxiliary verb (*am, is,* or *are*) precedes the *-ing* form (progressive form) of the verb. The *present perfect* tense shows an action that began in the past and is now completed. An auxiliary verb (*have* or *has*) precedes the past participle form of the verb. The *present perfect progressive* tense also shows action that began in the past and is continuing in the present. Auxiliary verbs (*have been* or *has been*) precede the verb written in its progressive form.

PRESENT TENSE			
PRESENT	PROGRESSIVE	PERFECT	PERFECT PROGRESSIVE
shows action happening now	shows action continuing now	shows action that began in the past, is completed	shows action that began in the past, continues now
Activists *lobby* for change.	Activists *are lobbying* for change.	Activists *have lobbied* for change.	Activists *have been lobbying* for change.
Sulfur *pollutes* the air.	Sulfur *is polluting* the air.	Sulfur *has polluted* the air.	Sulfur *has been polluting* the air.

All the above present tense forms can be used together without constituting a shift in tense. Look at the following paragraph to see how this is done. The verbs are highlighted, and the brackets identify the tense.

I **am writing** [present progressive] to protest the condition of the Mississippi River, from which our city **draws** [present] its drinking water. For years, industrial waste **has polluted** [present perfect] its waters, and officials **pay** [present] little attention to the problem. People who live near the river **have been lobbying** [present perfect progressive] for protective legislation, but their efforts **have failed** [present perfect]. I **want** [present] safe water to drink.

Past Tense Forms

Past tense shows action that happened in the past. It uses the past form of the verb. The *past progressive* tense shows a continuing action in the past. An auxiliary verb (*was* or *were*) precedes the progressive (*-ing*) form of the verb. The *past perfect* tense shows an action completed in the past or completed before some other past action. The auxiliary verb *had* precedes the past participle form of the verb. The *past perfect progressive* tense shows continuing action that began in the past. The auxiliary verbs *had been* precede the progressive (*-ing*) form of the verb.

All of the following past tense forms can be used together in writing a passage without constituting a shift in tense. The paragraph on the next page illustrates how this is done. The verbs are highlighted for you, and the brackets identify the tense.

PAST TENSE			
PAST	PROGRESSIVE	PERFECT	PERFECT PROGRESSIVE
occurred in the past	continuing action in the past	completed prior to another action	continuing action started in the past
Local officials *spoke* to the management.	Local officials *were speaking* to the management.	Local officials *had spoken* to the management.	Local officials *had been speaking* to the management.
The reporter *covered* the meetings.	The reporter *was covering* the meetings.	The reporter *had covered* the meetings.	The reporter *had been covering* the meetings.

Last year, local officials **cited** [past] a manufacturing company in our county for improperly disposing of hazardous waste. The company **ignored** [past] the action and **continued** [past] to dump its waste as they **had been doing** [past perfect progressive]. They **had dumped** [past perfect] waste the same way for years and **planned** [past] to continue. Several months later, the residue **seeped** [past] into the drinking water supply. A local environmentalist, who **had been tracking** [past perfect progressive] the company's dumping procedures, alerted local officials. They fined the company $3,000 for damages, but the company **has** never **paid** [past perfect] the fine.

Future Tense Forms

Future tense shows action that has yet to happen. The auxiliary verbs *will, would,* or *shall* precede the present form of the verb. The *future progressive* tense shows continuing actions in the future. The auxiliary verb phrases *will be, shall be,* or *would be* precede the progressive form of the verb. The *future perfect* tense shows actions that will be completed at a certain time in the future. The auxiliary verb phrases *will have, would have,* or *will have been* precede the past participle form of the verb. The *future perfect progressive* tense shows continuing actions that will be completed at a certain time in the future. The verb phrases *will have been, would have been,* or *shall have been* precede the progressive form of the verb.

All the future tense forms on the following table can be used together in writing a paragraph. They do not constitute a shift in tense. The following paragraph illustrates how this is done. The verbs are highlighted for you, and the brackets identify the tense.

Starting next week, we **will reduce** [future] the money we spend on waste disposal. We **will do** [future] this because our public-relations costs have skyrocketed during the year. Since no one in the community **will sell** [future] land to us to use for waste disposal, we **will be relocating** [future progressive] in a new community with a better business environment. This move **would put** [future] over three hundred employees out of work. It **would reduce** [future] the amount of consumer dollars spent at local businesses.

By this time next year, nearly one thousand people **will have lost** [future perfect] their jobs. Your business leaders **will have been looking** [future perfect progressive] for ways to replace lost revenue. Furthermore, legislators **will be meddling** [future progressive] in our local affairs, and the news media **will have portrayed** [future perfect] us all as fools.

FUTURE TENSE			
FUTURE	**PROGRESSIVE**	**PERFECT**	**PERFECT PROGRESSIVE**
action that will happen	continuing action that will happen	action that will be completed by a certain time	continuing action that will be completed by a certain time
We *will begin* a letter-writing campaign.	Everyone *will be writing* letters.	By summer, we *will have written* reams of letters.	Legislators *will have been receiving* letters throughout the year.
Newspapers *will cover* this case.	Newspapers *will be covering* this case.	By summer, every newspaper *will have written* about this case.	Newspapers *will have been covering* the case throughout the year.

How Verb Tenses Convey Meaning

Managing verb tense carefully helps writers avoid the confusion that comes with thoughtless use. These examples illustrate how verb tense can completely change the meaning of a sentence.

Example:
> Beth discovered that Nick had left work and gone home.
>
> Beth discovered that Nick had left work and went home.

In the first sentence, because *gone* is the participle form, it goes with *had left* in the second part of the sentence. So Nick is the one who *had gone* home. In the second sentence, *went* is in the simple past tense like *discovered* in the first part of the sentence. So this time, it's Beth who *went* home.

Example:
> Cory told the officer that she had answered the phone and drank a can of soda pop.
>
> Cory told the officer that she had answered the phone and had drunk a can of soda pop.

In the first sentence, *drank* is in the same tense as *told*—they're both past tense. So Cory was drinking around the same time as she was telling. In the second sentence, *had drunk* matches *had answered,* so in this case, Cory was drinking around the time she answered the phone.

Have, *not* Of

When forming the various perfect tenses, people sometimes write *of* when they should write *have,* probably because they are writing what they hear. *I should've* (*should've* is a contraction of *should have*) sounds a lot like *I should of.* But the proper form in writing is *have,* not *of.*

Wrong:
> I **could of** seen the difference if I had looked more closely.

Correct:
> I **could have** seen the difference if I had looked more closely.

Wrong:
> The park ranger **should of** warned the campers about the bears.

Correct:
> The park ranger **should have** warned the campers about the bears.

Switching Verb Tenses

Sometimes, you have to switch from past tense to present to avoid implying an untruth.

Wrong:
> I met the new technician. He **was** very personable. [What happened? Did he die?]

Correct:
> I met the new technician. He **is** very personable.

Wrong:
> We went to the new Italian restaurant on Vine last night. The atmosphere **was** wonderful. [What happened? Did it burn down during the night?]

Correct:
> We went to the new Italian restaurant on Vine last night. The atmosphere **is** wonderful.

Even if a passage is written in past tense, a statement that continues to be true is written in present tense.

Examples:
> During Galileo's time, few people **believed** [past] that the Earth **revolves** [present] around the sun.
>
> The building engineer **explained** [past] to the plumber that the pipes **run** [present] parallel to the longest hallway in the building.

Subjunctive Mood

When Tevya in *Fiddler on the Roof* sings, "If I were a rich man," he uses the verb *were* to signal that he is, in fact, not a rich man. Normally, the verb *was* would be used with the subject *I*, but *were* serves a special purpose. This is called the subjunctive *were*. It indicates a condition that is contrary to fact.

Examples:
> If I **were** a cat, I could sleep all day long and never have to worry about work.
> If he **were** more attentive to details, he could be a copy editor.

Practice

Circle the correct verb form in each of the following sentences.

11. They (had won, won, win) five competitions before qualifying for Nationals.

12. By the time I get to Phoenix, he will (read, have read) my good-bye letter.

13. The scientist explained why Saturn (is, was) surrounded by rings.

14. I would ask for a transfer if I (was, were) you.

15. Just this past August, the interest rate (drops, dropped, had dropped) 2%.

16. The doctor took my pulse and (measures, measured) my blood pressure.

17. The president wishes he would (of, have) taken a stock option rather than a salary increase.

18. Boswick wishes he had ordered a bigger sweatshirt because his (is, was) too small.

19. Ms. Grey announced that the floor manager (is, was) responsible for work schedules.

20. We could cut transportation costs if the plant (was, were) closer to the retail outlets.

Answers

1. wrote
2. done
3. flown
4. spoken
5. give
6. gone
7. saw
8. begun
9. forgotten
10. took
11. had won
12. have read
13. is
14. were
15. dropped
16. measured
17. have
18. is
19. is
20. were

TIP

Listen carefully to people today. Do you hear common errors such as "I *could of* gone out if I had done my work"? Once you make it a habit to listen for verb choice errors, you'll realize how many people make them. Some mistakes are so accepted that they might not sound strange at first. The more sensitive you are to grammatical errors, the less likely you'll be to make them yourself—in both writing and speaking.

11 ▶ USING VERBS TO CREATE STRONG WRITING

If you make yourself understood, you're always speaking well.
—MOLIÈRE, French playwright (1622–1673)

LESSON SUMMARY

Capturing your reader's interest is your main goal in writing. In Lesson 11, learn how verbs can help you accelerate your writing abilities and liven up the tone of your work. Using strong verbs can help invigorate the way your message is delivered.

Few people bother to read uninteresting writing. Even if they read it, they may not absorb the message. This lesson discusses ways to use verbs that will make your writing lively and interesting for the reader. Read the two paragraphs on the next page. Which one seems livelier, more interesting? The paragraphs tell an identical story, but one of them uses verbs effectively to tell the story in such a way that it is more likely to be remembered. The sentences are presented one at a time, side by side, so you can make the comparison more easily.

PARAGRAPH 1	PARAGRAPH 2
The softball game played by my team last week was one of the best ever seen by me.	Last week's softball game was one of the most exciting ones I've ever played.
The bottom of the ninth inning was when I stepped up to the plate, with a score that was tied at 2-2 after the game-tying double that was hit by our first baseman.	In the bottom of the ninth inning, the score was tied at 2-2 after our first baseman hit a double to tie up the score.
Then it was my turn; with two outs left in the inning, I came to the plate.	Then it was my turn; with two outs left in the inning, I nervously stepped up to the plate.
The first pitch was the one I swung at, and was called a strike when I missed.	I swung at the first pitch, and missed. Strike one!
The second pitch, which was low, was also swung at by me. The call made by the umpire was "strike two."	The second pitch was low, but I swung at it anyway. Strike two!
There was worry as I was facing my last strike, as the ball was not hit by me, we would go into extra innings and the game might be lost.	If I got a hit, we would win; if I struck out, we would go into extra innings and might lose.
The last pitch, which was hit hard by me, was thrown down the middle of the plate by the pitcher.	The last pitch came right down the middle of the plate—I swung hard, and the bat connected with the ball.
The baserunning was done by me, as the ball was going over the fence.	I ran as hard as I could to get to first base, and saw that the ball had gone over the fence.
The homerun that had won the game was hit by by me!	I hit the game-winning homerun!

Active vs. Passive Voice

When the subject of a sentence performs the action of the verb, we say the sentence is active. Write using active verbs to make your writing more conversational and interesting. In a sentence with an active verb, the person or thing that performs the action is named before the verb, or the action word(s), in a sentence. This may sound confusing, but the following examples illustrate the difference. The italicized words show who is performing the action. The underlined words are verbs.

PASSIVE VERBS	ACTIVE VERBS
I <u>was taken</u> to my first horse show by my *grandfather*.	My *grandfather* <u>took</u> me to my first horse show.
I <u>was taught</u> to fish by my *mother* almost before I <u>was taught</u> to walk.	My *mother* <u>taught</u> me to fish almost before *I* <u>learned</u> to walk.

In each of the active verb sentences, the person performing the action is named first. If you look more closely at these examples, you'll notice that the active verb versions are shorter and clearer. They sound more like natural conversation. Strive for these qualities in your writing. The following table illustrates the difference between active and passive voice in several of the verb tenses you learned in Lesson 10.

Most writers prefer active voice to passive voice because it makes the writing lively and more dynamic. Generally, readers find active writing easier to read and remember. In this table and the one on page 90, you can see that active-voice sentences tend to be shorter than passive ones.

VERB TENSE	ACTIVE VOICE	PASSIVE VOICE
Present	The *clerk* <u>opens</u> the mail.	The mail <u>is opened</u> by the *clerk*.
Past	The *clerk* <u>opened</u> the mail.	The mail <u>was opened</u> by the *clerk*.
Future	The *clerk* <u>will open</u> the mail.	The mail <u>will be opened</u> by the *clerk*.
Present Perfect	The *clerk* <u>has opened</u> the mail.	The mail <u>has been opened</u> by the *clerk*.
Past Perfect	The *clerk* <u>had opened</u> the mail.	The mail <u>had been opened</u> by the *clerk*.
Future Perfect	The *clerk* <u>will have opened</u> the mail.	The mail <u>will have been opened</u> by the *clerk*.

Practice

Choose the sentence written in active voice from each of the following sets. The answers to each set of questions can be found at the end of the lesson.

1. a. Holly and Ryan played Monopoly all afternoon.
  b. Monopoly was played by Holly and Ryan all afternoon.

2. a. Next October, the new wing of the library will be open.
  b. Next October, the new wing of the library will open.

3. a. Three new members were introduced by the committee.
  b. The committee introduced three new members.

4. a. The shrubs will be planted by the gardener.
  b. The gardener will plant the shrubs.

5. a. I brought Kevin to school every day for the past month.
  b. Kevin was brought to school every day for the past month by me.

6. a. The company barbecue is often planned by the accounting department.
  b. The accounting department often plans the company barbecue.

7. a. Every summer, thousands of tourists will visit the island.
  b. Every summer, the island will be visited by thousands of tourists.

When to Use Passive Voice

In addition to lacking life, the passive voice can also signal an unwillingness to take responsibility for actions or an intention to discourage questioning. The following sentence illustrates this:

It has been recommended that twenty workers be laid off within the next three months.

The passive voice here is intended to make a definite statement of fact, one that will not be questioned. It leaves no loose ends. Dictators often write and speak in passive voice. A thoughtful person will see past the passive voice and ask questions anyway. Who is recommending this action? Why? Who will be doing the laying off? How will workers be chosen?

Passive voice is not always bad, however. Sometimes, though rarely, it actually works better than active voice. The following are situations in which passive voice is preferable to active voice.

1. **When the object is more important than the agent of action (the doer)**
   Sometimes, in scientific writing, the object is the focus rather than the doer. The following paragraph is written in both passive and active voice, respectively. The first paragraph is more appropriate in this case because the operation, not the doctor, is the focus of the action. The passage cannot be written in active voice without placing the emphasis on the doer, the doctor. Therefore, passive voice is the better choice in this instance.

Passive voice:
   The three-inch incision is made right above the pubic bone. Plastic clips are used to clamp off blood vessels and minimize bleeding. The skin is folded back and secured with clamps. Next, the stomach muscle is cut at a 15-degree angle, right top to bottom left.

Active voice:
   The doctor makes a three-inch incision right above the pubic bone. He uses plastic clips to clamp off the blood vessels and minimize bleeding. He folds back the skin and secures it with clamps. Next, he cuts the stomach muscle at a 15-degree angle, right top to bottom left.

2. **When the agent of action (doer) is unknown or secret**
   Sometimes, a newswriter will protect a source by writing, "It was reported that . . ." In other instances, perhaps no one knows who perpetrated an action: "First State Bank was robbed . . ."

3. **When passive voice results in shorter sentences without detracting from the meaning**
   Generally, active voice is shorter and more concise than passive voice. However, there are a few exceptions. Examine the examples in the following table. If using passive voice saves time and trouble, in addition to resulting in a shorter sentence, use it.

ACTIVE	PASSIVE
The designers of the study told the interviewer to give interviewees an electric shock each time they smiled.	The interviewer was told to give the interviewees an electric shock each time they smiled.
The police apprehended Axtell, the detectives interrogated him, and the grand jury indicted him.	Axtell was apprehended, interrogated, and indicted.

Other Life-Draining Verb Constructions

If thought is a train, then verbs are the wheels that carry the cargo along. The thought will move more quickly if it is transported by many big, strong wheels. Here are some constructions to avoid as well as suggestions for choosing bigger, better verbs.

Using State-of-Being Verbs

State-of-being verbs are all the forms of *be*: *am, is, are, was, were,* and so on. State-of-being verbs don't do as much as action verbs to move meaning. In our train-of-thought analogy, state-of-being verbs are very tiny wheels, incapable of moving big thoughts quickly or easily. If you have only trivial things to say, by all means, use state-of-being verbs. If your ideas are more complex or interesting, they will require bigger and better verbs.

Look at the following paragraphs. In the first version, most of the verbs are state-of-being verbs. In the second version, action verbs make the paragraph more interesting.

State-of-being verbs:

The class was outside during noon recess. The sunshine was bright. Earlier in the day, there was rain, but later, the weather was pleasant. The breeze was slight; the newly fallen leaves were in motion. Across the street from the school was an ice cream truck. It was what the children were looking at longingly.

Action verbs:

The class played outside during noon recess. The sun shone brightly. Earlier in the day, rain had fallen, but later, pleasant weather arrived. A slight breeze blew the newly fallen leaves. The children looked longingly at the ice cream truck across the street.

Turning Verbs into Nouns

Naturally, if you take the wheels off the train of thought and put them on a flatbed as cargo, the train will not move. Look at the following two sentences. In the first one, several verbs have been turned into nouns to make the writing sound intellectual. This "verbification" actually makes the writing more difficult to read. The second sentence communicates the same information with the same amount of sophistication, but turning the nouns back into verbs makes it easier to read. Verb forms are highlighted to make them easier to identify.

The customer service division **is** now **conducting an assessment** of its system for the reaction to consumer concerns and the development of new products.

The customer service division **is assessing** its system for **reacting** to consumer concerns and **developing** new products.

Adding Unnecessary Auxiliary Verbs

Generally, if you don't need an auxiliary verb (*have, had, is, are, was, were, will, would,* and so on) to carry meaning (see Lesson 10), don't use one.

UNNECESSARY AUXILIARY VERBS	CORRECTED VERSION
After lunch, we *would meet* in the lounge.	After lunch, we *met* in the lounge.
The temperature *was rising* steadily.	The temperature *rose* steadily.
Every morning, the doors *will open* at 8:00.	Every morning, the doors *open* at 8:00.

Starting with *There* or *It*

Many sentences unnecessarily begin with *there is/are/was/were* or with *it is/was*. Usually, all those words do is postpone the beginning of the actual thought. The following sentences illustrate how these life-draining words can be removed from your writing.

UNNECESSARY *THERE* OR *IT*	CORRECTED VERSION
There are three people who are authorized to use this machinery.	Three people are authorized to use this machinery.
There is one good way to handle this problem: to ignore it.	One good way to handle this problem is to ignore it.
It was a perfect evening for a rocket launch.	The evening was perfect for a rocket launch.
There were several people standing in line waiting for the bus.	Several people stood in line waiting for the bus.

Use Lively, Interesting Verbs

If you want to move thought efficiently, work for precision and look for verbs that create an image in the reader's mind. Compare the following sentences to see this principle in action.

DULL	LIVELY
At my barbershop, someone does your nails and your shoes while your hair is being cut.	At my barbershop, someone manicures your nails and shines your shoes as your hair is cut.
Violent cartoons are harmful to children's emotional development and sense of reality.	Violent cartoons stunt children's emotional development and distort their sense of reality.

Practice

Choose the best sentence from each set. Keep in mind what you have learned about verbs in this lesson.

8. a. Incredibly useful feedback was given by the committee members about the proposed fund-raiser.
   b. The committee members gave incredibly useful feedback about the proposed fund-raiser.

9. a. The campsite was set up by the group of scouts quickly and then they went to the mess tent for lunch.
   b. The group of scouts swiftly set up camp, then headed to the mess tent for lunch.

10. a. Those who hire customer service representatives think that an excellent phone manner is more important than previous work experience.
  b. Those responsible for the hiring of customer service representatives have a greater consideration for the manner in which applicants speak on the phone than they do for the work experience they bring to the job.

11. a. There are three rules that you should follow when you play this game.
  b. You should follow three rules when you play this game.

12. a. There are several options we have to choose from: fish, chicken, steak, or pasta.
  b. Several choices are offered: fish, chicken, steak, or pasta.

13. a. Jack ran fast to the store; trying get there before they closed.
  b. Jack raced to get to the store before it closed.

14. a. The applicant must have excellent programming skills.
  b. It is necessary for the applicant to have excellent programming skills.

Answers

1. a.
2. b.
3. b.
4. b.
5. a.
6. b.
7. a.
8. b.
9. b.
10. a.
11. b.
12. b.
13. b.
14. a.

TIP

As you read newspapers, magazines, textbooks, or other materials today, look for examples of sentences in active voice and in passive voice. Try converting some passive voice sentences into active voice and vice versa. Which version is more effective?

12 ▶ SUBJECT-VERB AGREEMENT

Grasp the subject, the words will follow.

—CATO THE ELDER, Roman orator and politician
(234–149 B.C.E.)

LESSON SUMMARY

Without thinking about it, you usually make sure your subjects and verbs agree, both in speaking and in writing. Only a few situations cause difficulty in subject-verb agreement. This lesson will show you how to deal with those few situations in your writing.

When a subject in a clause—the person or thing doing the action—matches the verb in number, we say the subject and verb *agree*. Most native English speakers have little trouble matching subjects with the correct verbs. A few grammatical constructions pose most of the problems. This lesson explains the concept of subject-verb agreement and provides practice in those problem areas. Test your knowledge by underlying instances of incorrect subject-verb agreement in the **Problem** column on the next page. Check your answers wit the **Solution** column.

Problem

Students who wants to join the university's Engineering program needs to meet a number of criteria. Each student should have taken Introductory Engineering Principles in his or her freshman years, as well as all of the following classes: Calculus I or II, Chemistry I, and Physics I. A prospective Engineering students should have at least a 3.0 grade point average in these classes. These students should also plan to take Chemistry II and Physics II in their sophomore or junior years (a class which may be taken after entry into the Engineering program). Once admitted into the program, students should be prepared to choose an engineering specialty and work closely with a faculty member in that department until graduation.

Solution

Students who <u>want</u> to join the university's Engineering program <u>need</u> to meet a number of criteria. Each student should have taken Introductory Engineering Principles in his or her freshman <u>year</u>, as well as all of the following classes: Calculus I or II, Chemistry I, and Physics I. A prospective Engineering <u>student</u> should have at least a 3.0 grade point average in these classes. These students should also plan to take Chemistry II and Physics II in their sophomore or junior years (<u>classes</u> which may be taken after entry into the Engineering program). Once admitted into the program, students should be prepared to choose an engineering specialty and work closely with a faculty member in that department until graduation.

Agreement between Noun Subjects and Verbs

In written language, a subject must agree with its verb in number. In other words, if a subject is singular, the verb must be singular. If the subject is plural, the verb must be plural. If you are unsure whether a verb is singular or plural, apply this simple test. Fill in the blanks in the two sentences that follow with the matching form of the verb. The verb form that best completes the first sentence is singular. The verb form that best completes the second sentence is plural.

Singular

One person _____.

Plural

Two people _____.

Look at these examples using the verbs *speak, do,* and *was.* Try it yourself with any verb that confuses you. Unlike nouns, verbs ending in *-s* are usually singular.

SINGULAR	PLURAL
One person <u>speaks</u>.	Two people <u>speak</u>.
One person <u>does</u>.	Two people <u>do</u>.
One person <u>was</u>.	Two people <u>were</u>.

Special Problems
Doesn't/Don't and Wasn't/Weren't

Some people have particular trouble with *doesn't/don't* (contractions for *does not* and *do not*) and with w*asn't/ weren't* (contractions for *was not* and *were not*). *Doesn't* and *wasn't* are singular; *don't* and *weren't* are plural. If you say the whole phrase instead of the contraction, you'll usually get the right form.

Phrases Following the Subject

Pay careful attention to the subject in a sentence. Do not allow a phrase following it to mislead you into using a verb that does not agree with the subject. The subjects and verbs are highlighted in the following examples.

> **One** of the print orders **is** missing.
> The software **designs** by Liu Chen **are** complex and colorful.
> A **handbook** with thorough instructions **comes** with this product.
> The **president**, along with her three executive assistants, **leaves** for the conference tomorrow.

Special Singular Subjects

Some nouns are singular even though they end in *-s*. Despite the plural form, they require a singular verb because we think of them as a single thing. Most of the nouns in the following list are singular. Some can be either singular or plural, depending on their use in the sentence.

measles	mathematics
mumps	civics
news	athletics
checkers	sports
marbles (the game)	politics
physics	statistics
economics	

Here are some examples of how these words work in sentences.

> The **news is** on at 6:00.
> **Checkers is** my favorite game.
> **Sports is** a healthy way to reduce stress.
> Low-impact **sports are** recommended for older adults.

Words stating a single amount or a time require a singular verb. Examine a sentence carefully to see if the amount or time is considered a single measure.

> Two dollars **is** the price of that small replacement part. [single amount]
> Two dollars **are** lying on my dresser.
> Three hours **was** required to complete this simulation. [single measure]
> Three hours of each day **were** spent rehearsing.
> Three-quarters of her time **is** spent writing.

Practice

Circle the correct verb in each of the following sentences. The answers to each set of questions can be found at the end of the lesson.

1. When the clown (performs, perform), the children in the audience (laughs, laugh).

2. This chocolate chip cookie with walnuts (is, are) absolutely delicious, and so (is, are) the brownies.

3. That pair of scissors (is, are) sharp; we should (handles, handle) it carefully.

4. Luigi (speaks, speak) English, but his parents (speaks, speak) Italian.

5. The bakery (wasn't, weren't) open on Sunday afternoon.

6. The new tenants (doesn't, don't) pay their rent on time.

7. Spaghetti and meatballs (is, are) a popular menu choice at Italian restaurants, as (is, are) macaroni and cheese.

8. The box office (doesn't, don't) sell tickets until the week before the show.

9. The office was closed yesterday because the heat (wasn't, weren't) working.

10. Marly (doesn't, don't) know if the neighbors (is, are) on vacation.

11. The milk, along with the eggs, (is, are) added to the batter before baking.

12. These statistics (is, are) not at all what we expected.

13. Statistics (was, were) a required course at my university.

14. One of the students (is, are) looking for the stack of books that (was, were) misplaced.

15. Half of the banana (was, were) eaten.

16. Half of the bananas (was, were) eaten.

Agreement between Pronoun Subjects and Verbs

Pronoun subjects present a problem for even the most sophisticated speakers of English. Some pronouns are always singular; others are always plural. A handful of pronouns can be either singular or plural.

Singular Pronouns

These pronouns are always singular.

each	anyone	nobody
either	everybody	one
neither	everyone	somebody
anybody	no one	someone

The first three pronouns are the ones most likely to be misused. You can avoid a mismatch by mentally adding the word *one* after the pronoun and removing the other words between the pronoun and the verb. Look at the following examples to see how this is done.

Each of the men wants his own car.
Each *one* wants his own car.
Either of the salesclerks knows where the sale merchandise is located.
Either *one* knows where the sale merchandise is located.

QUESTION FORM	STATEMENT FORM
(Is, Are) some of the customers noticing the difference?	Some of the customers **are** noticing the difference.
(Has, Have) either of the shipments arrived?	Either [one] of the shipments **has** arrived.
(Does, Do) each of the terminals have a printer?	Each [one] of the terminals **does** have a printer.

These sentences may sound awkward because so many speakers misuse these pronouns, and you have probably become accustomed to hearing them used incorrectly. Despite that, the substitution trick (*one* for the words following the pronoun) will help you avoid this mistake.

Watch Out for Questions

With questions beginning with *has* or *have*, remember that *has* is singular while *have* is plural. Pay special attention to the verb-subject combination in a question. In fact, the correct verb is easier to identify if you turn the question into a statement.

Plural Pronouns

These pronouns are always plural and require a plural verb.

both	many
few	several

Singular/Plural Pronouns

The following pronouns can be either singular or plural. The words or prepositional phrases following them determine whether they are singular or plural. If the phrase following the pronoun contains a plural noun or pronoun, the verb must be plural. If the phrase following the pronoun contains a singular noun or pronoun, the verb must be singular. See how this is done in the sentences following the list of pronouns. The key words are highlighted.

all	none
any	some
most	

SINGULAR	PLURAL
All of the **work is** finished.	**All** of the **jobs are** finished.
Is any of the **pizza** left?	**Are any** of the **pieces** of pizza left?
Most of the **grass has** turned brown.	**Most** of the **blades** of grass **have** turned brown.
None of the **time was** wasted.	**None** of the **minutes were** wasted.
Some of the **fruit was** spoiled.	**Some** of the **apples were** spoiled.

Practice

Circle the correct verb in each of the following sentences. Answers are at the end of the lesson.

17. Each of the soccer players (receive, receives) a new uniform this season.

18. Each of the letters (makes, make) a strong case for changing the policy.

19. All of the pieces of art (was, were) signed by their creators.

20. All of the recommendations (has, have) been made.

21. Either of these software programs (is, are) suitable for my staff.

22. (Was, Were) any of the parts missing?

23. (Has, Have) either of the owners expressed an interest in selling the property?

24. (Do, Does) some of the employees get bonuses?

25. Neither of our largest accounts (needs, need) to be serviced at this time.

26. Both of the applicants (seems, seem) qualified.

27. A woman in one of my classes (works, work) at the Civic Center box office.

28. None of our resources (goes, go) to outside consultants.

29. Many students from the school's band (perform, performs) in the Thanksgiving Day Parade.

30. Each of these prescriptions (causes, cause) bloating and irritability.

31. (Have, Has) either of them ever arrived on time?

Special Sentence Structures

Compound Subjects

- If two nouns or pronouns are joined by *and*, they require a plural verb.

    He and she **want** to buy a new house.
    Jack and Jill **want** to buy a new house.

- If two singular nouns or pronouns are joined by *or* or *nor*, they require a singular verb. Think of them as two separate sentences and you'll never make a mistake in agreement.

    Jack or Jill **wants** to buy a new house.
    Jack **wants** to buy a new house.
    Jill **wants** to buy a new house.

- Singular and plural subjects joined by *or* or *nor* require a verb that agrees with the subject closest to the verb.

    Neither management nor the **employees like** the new agreement.
    Neither the employees nor the **management likes** the new agreement.

Make Sure You Find the Subject

Verbs agree with the subject, not the complement, of a sentence. The verb, a form of *be*, links the subject and the complement, but usually, the subject comes first and the complement comes after the verb.

Taxes were the main challenge facing the financial department.
The main **challenge** facing the financial department **was** taxes.
A serious **problem** for most automobile commuters **is** traffic jams.
Traffic jams are a serious problem for most automobile commuters.

Questions and Sentences Beginning with There or Here

When a sentence asks a question or begins with the words *there* or *here*, the subject follows the verb. Locate the subject of the sentence and make certain the verb matches it. In the following examples, the subjects and verbs are highlighted in the corrected forms.

WRONG	CORRECTED
What is the conditions of the contract?	What **are** the **conditions** of the contract?
Why is her reports always so disorganized?	Why **are** her **reports** always so disorganized?
Here's the records you requested.	Here **are** the **records** you requested.
There is four people seeking this promotion.	There **are** four **people** seeking this promotion.

Inverted Sentences

Inverted sentences also contain subjects that follow, rather than precede, the verbs. Locate the subject in the sentence and make certain the verb agrees with it. In the following example sentences, the subjects and verbs in the corrected sentences are highlighted.

WRONG	CORRECT
Beside the front desk stands three new vending machines.	Beside the front desk **stand** three new vending **machines**.
Suddenly, out of the thicket comes three large bucks.	Suddenly, out of the thicket **come** three large **bucks**.
Along with our highest recommendation goes our best wishes in your new job.	Along with our highest recommendation **go** our best **wishes** in your new job.

Practice

Circle the correct verb in each of the following sentences. Answers are at the end of the lesson.

32. Every other day, either Bert or Ernie (takes, take) out the trash.

33. Neither the style nor the color (matches, match) what we currently have.

34. Due to unavoidable conflicts in the school calendar, neither the Fall Fest nor the charity bowl (fall, falls) in October, in time for homecoming.

35. Either the manager or the associates (orders, order) the merchandise.

36. (Is, Are) the men's wear or the women's wear department on the ground floor?

37. Mr. Jefson's passion (is, are) economics.

38. (Was, Were) there any furniture sets left over after the sale?

39. There (aren't, isn't) two people I can name that enjoyed the performance, despite the hype about the starring lineup.

40. Unfortunately, neither we nor they (swim, swims) well.

41. Off into the horizon (runs, run) the herd of buffalo.

Answers

1. performs, laugh
2. is, are
3. is, handle
4. speaks, speak
5. wasn't
6. don't
7. is, is
8. doesn't
9. wasn't
10. doesn't, are
11. is
12. are
13. was
14. is, was
15. was
16. were
17. receives
18. makes
19. were
20. have
21. is
22. Were
23. Has
24. Do
25. needs
26. seem
27. works
28. go
29. perform
30. causes
31. Has
32. takes
33. matches
34. falls
35. order
36. Is
37. is
38. Were
39. aren't
40. swim
41. runs

TIP

Listen to people as they speak. Do they use verbs correctly? Do they use the correct tense? Do the subjects and verbs match? It's probably not a good idea to correct your family, friends, and coworkers, but you can give yourself some good practice by listening for mistakes.

13 ▶ USING PRONOUNS

The words of the world want to make sentences.
—GASTON BACHELARD, French philosopher (1884–1962)

LESSON SUMMARY
Pronouns are so often *misused* in speech that many people don't know how to avoid pronoun errors in writing. This lesson shows you how to avoid the most common ones.

 *pronoun* is a word used in place of a noun. This lesson explains the basic principles of pronoun use and highlights the most common pronoun problems: agreement, case, noun-pronoun pairs, incomplete constructions, ambiguous pronoun references, and reflexive pronouns. See what you already know by underlying the incorrect pronoun usage in the **Problem** column on the next page, and check your answers against the **Solution** column.

Problem

Dear Mr. Hotchkiss,

I am pleased to let you know that the eWidget project have been a great success so far. We began with five team members on the product development committee (Alan from Marketing, Maryanne from Sales, me and Andrew from Creative Services, and Ginny from Product Design). Back on February 16, Ginny she presented his plans, specifications, and schedule for our company's new product, eWidget. Andrew and Maryanne followed up with some research them had done on the consumer market and sales for previous initiatives, and presented they're findings to the group on March 24. After we all agreed that eWidget would fill a gap in the market, Alan determined what kind of marketing campaign we would need to give them a successful public launch, and I created sample advertising mockups with different types of art who we could use in the campaign. Throughout the process, Ginny kept us updated on what was happening with the eWidget itself, which was already in the early stages of production. As of the last committee meeting, its ready to launch on March 1 of next year.

Sincerely,
Jeff

Solution

Dear Mr. Hotchkiss,

I am pleased to let you know that the eWidget project <u>has</u> been a great success so far. We began with five team members on the product development committee (Alan from Marketing, Maryanne from Sales, me and Andrew from Creative Services, and Ginny from Product Design). Back on February 16, <u>Ginny</u> <u>presented</u> <u>her</u> plans, specifications, and schedule for the eWidget. Andrew and Maryanne followed up with some research <u>they</u> had done on the consumer market and sales for previous initiatives, and presented <u>their</u> findings to the group on March 24. After we all agreed that eWidget would fill a gap in the market, Alan determined what kind of marketing campaign we would need to give <u>it</u> a successful public launch, and I created sample advertising mockups with different types of art <u>that</u> we could use in the campaign. Throughout the process, Ginny kept us updated on what was happening with the eWidget itself, which was already in the early stages of production. As of the last committee meeting, <u>it's</u> ready to launch on March 1 of next year.

Sincerely,
Jeff

Pronouns and Antecedents

The noun represented by a pronoun is called its *antecedent*. The prefix *ante-* means *to come before*. Usually, the antecedent comes before the pronoun in a sentence. In the following examples, the pronouns are italicized and the antecedents (the words the pronouns represent) are underlined.

The government <u>workers</u> received *their* paychecks.
<u>Jane</u> thought *she* saw the missing <u>boy</u> and reported *him* to the police.
The shift <u>supervisor</u> hates these <u>accidents</u> because *he* thinks *they* can be easily avoided.

A pronoun must match the number of its antecedent. In other words, if the antecedent is singular, the pronoun must also be singular. If the antecedent is plural, the pronoun must also be plural. Few people make mistakes when matching a pronoun with a noun antecedent. However, sometimes a pronoun is the antecedent for another pronoun. Indefinite pronoun antecedents frequently result in a number mismatch between pronoun and antecedent. In Lesson 12, you learned about singular pronouns. Here is the list again.

each	anyone	nobody
either	everybody	one
neither	everyone	somebody
anybody	no one	someone

- A pronoun with one of the words from this list as its antecedent must be singular.

  <u>Each</u> of the men brought *his* favorite snack to the picnic.

  <u>Everyone</u> who wants to be in the "Toughman" contest should pay up *his* life insurance.

  <u>Somebody</u> left *her* purse underneath the desk.

  <u>Neither</u> of the occupants could locate *his* or *her* key to the apartment.

- If two or more singular nouns or pronouns are joined by *and*, use a plural pronoun.

  <u>Buddha and Muhammad</u> built religions around *their* philosophies.

  If <u>he and she</u> want to know where I was, *they* should ask me.

- If two or more singular nouns or pronouns are joined by *or*, use a singular pronoun.

  <u>Matthew or Jacob</u> will loan you *his* calculator.

  The <u>elephant or the moose</u> will furiously protect *its* young.

- If a singular and a plural noun or pronoun are joined by *nor*, the pronoun agrees with the closest noun or pronoun it represents.

  Neither the soldiers nor the <u>sergeant</u> was sure of *his* location.

Neither the sergeant nor the <u>soldiers</u> were sure of *their* location.

Practice

Circle the correct pronoun in each of the following sentences. The answers to each set of questions can be found at the end of the lesson.

1. No one in (his, their) right mind would turn down that amazing job offer.

2. Anyone who wants to become a member should pay (her, their) dues by the last day of the month.

3. Nathan or Andrew will volunteer (his, their) time this Sunday afternoon at the hospital.

4. Tell someone in the human resources department about your situation, and (she, they) will speak to your supervisor.

5. If you order peanut butter and jelly instead, (it, they) will cost less.

6. Neither Lily nor Emily will volunteer (herself, themselves) to work late this evening.

7. Everyone can decide whether (he or she, they) will attend the seminar or not.

8. I know someone who calls (her, their) great-grandmother Mama.

9. When you want to impress a client, remember to send (him, them) a personalized thank-you note.

Pronoun Case

Most people know when to use *I*, when to use *me*, or when to use *my*. These three pronouns illustrate the three cases of the first-person singular pronoun: nominative (*I*), objective (*me*), and possessive (*my*). The following table shows the cases of all the personal pronouns, both singular and plural.

PERSONAL PRONOUN CASE		
NOMINATIVE	OBJECTIVE	POSSESSIVE
I	me	my
we	us	our(s)
you	you	your(s)
he	him	his
she	her	her(s)
they	them	their(s)
it	it	its

Nominative case pronouns (those in the first column) are used as subjects or as complements following linking verbs (*am, is, are, was, were*—any form of *be*). Nominative case pronouns following a linking verb may sound strange to you because so few people use them correctly.

> **They** left a few minutes early to mail the package. [subject]
>
> **I** looked all over town for the type of paper you wanted. [subject]
>
> The doctor who removed my appendix was **he**. [follows a linking verb]
>
> "This is **she**," said Barbara into the phone. [follows a linking verb]
>
> "It was **I** who ate the cookies," said John. [follows a linking verb]

Objective case pronouns (those in the middle column in the table) are used as objects following an action verb or as objects of a preposition.

> The help-line representative gave **him** an answer over the phone. [follows an action verb]

Of all these samples, I prefer **them**. [follows an action verb]

We went to lunch with Sammy and **him**. [object of the preposition *with*]

We couldn't tell whether the package was for **them** or **us**. [object(s) of the preposition *for*]

Possessive case pronouns (those in the third column in the table), sometimes used as adjectives, show ownership. Few English speakers misuse the possessive case pronouns. Most pronoun problems occur with the nominative and objective cases.

Problems with Pronoun Case

A single pronoun in a sentence is easy to use correctly. In fact, most English speakers would readily identify the mistakes in the following sentences.

> **Me** worked on the project with **he**.
>
> My neighbor gave **she** a ride to work.

Most people know that **Me** in the first sentence should be **I** and that **he** should be **him**. They would also know that **she** in the second sentence should be **her**. Such errors are easy to spot when the pronouns are used alone in a sentence. The problem occurs when a pronoun is used with a noun or another pronoun. See if you can spot the errors in the following sentences.

Wrong:
    The grand marshall rode with Shane and I.
    Donna and me are going to the Civic Center.
    The stage manager spoke to my brother and I.

The errors in these sentences are harder to see than those in the sentences with a single pronoun. If you turn the sentence with two pronouns into two separate sentences, the error becomes very obvious.

Correct:
    The grand marshall rode with Shane.
    The grand marshall rode with **me**. (not *I*)
    Donna is going to the Civic Center. [Use the singular verb *is* in place of *are*.]
    I (not *me*) am going to the Civic Center. [Use the verb *am* in place of *are*.]
    The stage manager spoke to my brother.
    The stage manager spoke to **me**. (not *I*)

Splitting a sentence in two does not work as well with the preposition *between*. If you substitute *with* for *between*, then the error is easier to spot.

    The problem is between (she, her) and (I, me).
    The problem is with **her**. (not *she*)
    The problem is with **me**. (not *I*)

Practice

Circle the correct pronouns in the following sentences. Answers are at the end of the lesson.

10. (Them, They) and (I, me) made an effort to try to agree on the terms.

11. Benny and (he, him) went to the movies with Bonnie and (I, me).

12. Neither my cousins nor my uncle knows what (he, they) will do tomorrow.

13. Why must it always be (I, me) who cleans up the lounge?

14. The pilot let (he, him) and (I, me) look at the instrument panel.

15. Lauren and (her, she) went to our friend Kim's house to visit with (them, they).

16. My friend and (I, me) both want to move to another location.

Noun-Pronoun Pairs

Sometimes, a noun is immediately followed by a pronoun in a sentence. To make certain you use the correct pronoun, delete the noun from the pair. Look at the following examples to see how this is done.

PRONOUNS IN NOUN-PRONOUN PAIRS	
WHICH PRONOUN?	**REMOVE THE NOUN**
(We, Us) support personnel wish to lodge a complaint.	**We** wish to lodge a complaint.
They gave the job to (we, us) inventory staffers.	They gave the job to **us**.
The committee threw (we, us) retirees a huge end-of-the-year party.	The committee threw **us** a huge end-of-the-year party.

Incomplete Constructions

Sometimes, a pronoun comes at the end of a sentence following a comparative word such as *than* or *as*.

> Harold spent as much time on this project as (they, them).
> Duane can build cabinets better than (I, me).
> The long day exhausted us more than (they, them).
> My youngest child is now taller than (I, me).

In each of these sentences, part of the meaning is implied. To figure out which pronoun is correct, complete the sentence in your head and use the pronoun that makes more sense.

> Harold spent as much time on this project as *they did.*
> Harold spent as much time on this project as *he spent on them.*

The first sentence makes more sense, so *they* would be the correct choice.

> Duane can build cabinets better than *I can.*
> Duane can build cabinets better than *he can build me.*

The first sentence makes more sense, so *I* is the correct pronoun.

> The long day exhausted us more than *they did.*
> The long day exhausted us more than *it did them.*

The second sentence makes more sense, so *them* is the correct choice.

> My youngest child is now taller than *I am.*

There is no way to complete the sentence using the pronoun *me*, so *I* is the correct choice.

Pronoun choice is especially important if the sentence makes sense either way. The following sentence can be completed using both pronouns, either of which makes good sense. The pronoun choice controls the meaning. The writer must be careful to choose the correct pronoun if the meaning is to be accurately portrayed.

> I work with Assad more than (she, her).
> I work with Assad more than *she does.*
> I work with Assad more than *I work with her.*

Use the pronoun that portrays the intended meaning.

Ambiguous Pronoun References

Sometimes, a sentence is written in such a way that a pronoun can refer to more than one antecedent. When this happens, the meaning is *ambiguous.* In the following examples, the ambiguous pronouns are italicized, and the possible antecedents are underlined.

> When <u>Eric</u> spoke to his girlfriend's <u>father</u>, *he* was very polite.
> Remove the <u>door</u> from the <u>frame</u> and paint *it.*
> <u>Jamie</u> told <u>Linda</u> *she* should be ready to go within an hour.
> <u>Pat</u> told <u>Craig</u> *he* had been granted an interview.

See how the sentences are rewritten below to clarify the ambiguous references.

> Eric was very polite when he spoke to his girlfriend's father.
> Paint the door after removing it from the frame.
> Jamie told Linda to be ready to go within an hour.
> Pat told Craig that Craig had been granted an interview.

Improper Reflexive Pronouns

A *reflexive pronoun* is one that includes the word *self* or *selves*: *myself, yourself, himself, herself, ourselves, themselves*. The following section explains ways in which reflexive pronouns are sometimes misused.

- The possessive pronouns *his* and *their* cannot be made reflexive.

  Wrong:

  They decided to do the remodeling theirselves.
  Mark wanted to arrange the meeting hisself.

  Correct:

  They decided to do the remodeling *themselves*.
  Mark wanted to arrange the meeting *himself*.

- Avoid using a reflexive pronoun when a personal pronoun works in the sentence.

  Wrong:

  Three associates and myself chose the architect for the building.
  The preliminary results of the poll were revealed only to ourselves.

  Correct:

  Three associates and *I* chose the architect for the building.
  The preliminary results of the poll were revealed only to *us*.

Answers

1. his
2. her
3. his
4. she
5. it
6. herself
7. he or she
8. her
9. him
10. They, I
11. he, me
12. he
13. I
14. him, me
15. she, them
16. I

TIP

Identify the pronoun mistake or two that you make most often. In your conversation, make a conscious effort to use the pronouns correctly at least three times.

 ▶ PROBLEM VERBS AND PRONOUNS

I never made a mistake in grammar but one in my life and as soon as I done it I seen it.

—CARL SANDBURG, American poet (1878–1967)

LESSON SUMMARY

Sit or *set*? *Your* or *you're*? *There* or *their*? Or is it *they're*? Knowing how to use such problem pairs is the mark of the educated writer. This lesson shows you how.

This lesson covers problem verbs such as *lie/lay, sit/set, rise/raise,* and their various forms. It also covers problem pronouns such as *its/it's, your/you're, whose/who's, who/that/which,* and *there/they're/their.* You can distinguish yourself as an educated writer if you can use these verbs and pronouns correctly in formal writing situations. In the **Problem** column on the next page, underline where these problem verbs are misused, and check your answers with the **Solution** column.

Problem

When I couldn't find my keys, I decided to retrace my steps from this afternoon. I'd had the keys in my hand when I got home from the grocery store. I sit the keys down, put away the groceries, than went to lay down on the couch for a nap. Marie woke me up a little while later, and asked me to raise so I could go help make dinner in the kitchen. I'd forgotten some groceries in the car, so I went out to get those—and I hoped that the warm whether wouldn't effect the cheese too much, but it was already melted. I accidentally left my keys on the seat of the car, which was were they where when I finally retracted my steps later in the evening. Mystery solved!

Solution

When I couldn't find my keys, I decided to retrace my steps from this afternoon. I'd had the keys in my hand when I got home from the grocery store. I <u>set</u> the keys down, put away the groceries, <u>then</u> went to <u>lie</u> down on the couch for a nap. Marie woke me up a little while later, and asked me to <u>rise</u> so I could go help make dinner in the kitchen. I'd forgotten some groceries in the car, so I went out to get those—and I hoped that the warm <u>weather</u> wouldn't <u>affect</u> the cheese too much, but it was already melted. I accidentally left my keys on the seat of the car, which was <u>where</u> they <u>were</u> when I finally <u>retraced</u> my steps later in the evening. Mystery solved!

Problem Verbs

Lie/Lay

Few people use *lie* and *lay* and their principal parts correctly, perhaps because few people know the difference in meaning between the two. The verb *lie* means *to rest or recline*. The verb *lay* means *to put or place*. The following table shows the principal parts of each of these verbs. Their meanings, written in the correct form, appear in parentheses.

FORMS OF *LIE* AND *LAY*			
PRESENT	**PROGRESSIVE**	**PAST**	**PAST PARTICIPLE***
lie, lies	lying	lay	lain
(rest, rests)	(resting)	(rested)	(rested)
lay, lays	laying	laid	laid
(place, places)	(placing)	(placed)	(placed)

The past participle is the form used with have, has, *or* had.

To choose the correct form of *lie* or *lay*, simply look at the meanings in parentheses. Choose the word in parentheses that makes the most sense and use the corresponding form of *lie* or *lay*. Sometimes, none of the words seem especially appropriate. Nevertheless, choose the option that makes more sense than any of the others. If a sentence contains the word *down*, mentally delete the word from the sentence to make the appropriate verb more obvious. Examine the sample sentences to see how this is done.

> The garbage cans are _____ in the middle of the street. [Requires progressive]
> *Resting* makes better sense than *placing*.
> Choose *lying*.

> Keith told Nan to _____ the mail on the dining room table. [Requires present]
> *Place* makes better sense than *rest*.
> Choose *lay*.

> The sandwiches _____ in the sun for over an hour before we ate them. [Requires past]
> *Rested* makes better sense than *placed*.
> Choose *lay*.

> Yesterday afternoon, I _____ down for an hour. [Requires past]
> Remove the word *down*.
> *Rested* makes better sense than *placed*.
> Choose *lay*.

> Barry thought he had _____ the papers near the copy machine. [Requires past participle]
> *Placed* makes better sense than *rested*.
> Choose *laid*.

Practice

Write the correct form of *lie* or *lay* in each of the blanks that follow. Answers are at the end of the lesson.

1. Sara _____ her hat and gloves on the table when she came in.

2. _____ the packages on the mailroom floor.

3. Gary _____ on the sofa until three o'clock in the morning.

4. Gramps has _____ in bed with a headache most of the day.

5. No one had any idea how long the sandwiches had _____ in the sun, or who had _____ them there in the first place.

Sit/Set

These two verbs are very similar to *lie* and *lay*. *Sit* means *to rest*. *Set* means *to put or place*. The following table shows the principal parts of each of these verbs. Their meanings, written in the correct form, appear in parentheses.

FORMS OF *SIT* AND *SET*			
PRESENT	PROGRESSIVE	PAST	PAST PARTICIPLE*
sit, sits (rest, rests)	sitting (resting)	sat (rested)	sat (rested)
set, sets (put, place; puts, places)	setting (putting, placing)	set (put, placed)	set (put, placed)

The past participle is the form used with have, has, *or* had.

Choose the correct form of *sit* or *set* by using the meanings (the words in parentheses) in the sentence first. Decide which meaning makes the most sense, and then choose the corresponding verb. See how this is done in the following examples.

> The speaker _____ the chair next to the podium.
> *Put* or *placed* makes more sense than *rested*. Choose *set*.

> The speaker _____ in the chair next to the podium.
> *Rested* makes more sense than *put* or *placed*. Choose *sat*.

Practice

Write the correct form of *sit* or *set* in each of the blanks that follow. Answers are at the end of the lesson.

6. The board of directors _____ aside additional money for research and development.

7. Heather _____ the glass on the table next to the picture of Daniella _____ with Jack, the family's pet cat.

8. I can't remember where I _____ the mail down.

9. Logan _____ by Pauline in class every day; they _____ their books on the rack under their chairs.

10. We had _____ in the waiting room for almost an hour before the doctor saw us.

Rise/Raise

The verb *rise* means *to go up*. The verb *raise* means *to move something up*. *Raise* requires an object. In other words, something must receive the action of the verb raise (*raise your hand, raise the flag, raise the objection, raise children*). This table shows the principal parts of both verbs.

FORMS OF *RISE* AND *RAISE*			
PRESENT	PROGRESSIVE	PAST	PAST PARTICIPLE*
rises, rise	rising	rose	risen
(goes up, go up)	(going up)	(went up)	(gone up)
(comes up, come up)	(coming up)	(came up)	(come up)
raises, raise	raising	raised	raised
(moves up, move up)	(moving up)	(moved up)	(moved up)

The past participle is the form used with have, has, or had.

Choose the correct form of *rise* or *raise* by using the meanings (the words in parentheses) in the sentence first. Decide which meaning makes the most sense, and choose the corresponding verb. See how this is done in the following examples. Sometimes, none of the words seem especially appropriate. Nevertheless, choose the option that makes more sense than any of the others.

The sun _____ a little bit earlier each day of the spring.
Comes up makes the most sense.
Choose *rises*.

Without realizing it, we began to _____ our voices.
Move up makes more sense than any of the other options.
Choose *raise*.

The river _____ over two feet in the last hour.

Went up makes the most sense.
Choose *rose*.

Practice

Write the correct form of *rise* or *raise* in each of the blanks that follow. Answers are at the end of the lesson.

11. The guard _____ the flag every morning before the sun _____.

12. The McDermotts _____ six children; two were twins.

13. By late morning, the fog had _____ enough for us to see the neighboring farm.

14. The reporters _____ their hands and _____ from their seats when they were called upon by the president.

Problem Pronouns

Its/It's

Its is a possessive pronoun that means *belonging to it*. *It's* is a contraction for *it is* or *it has*. You will use only *it's* when you can also substitute the words *it is*. Take time to make this substitution, and you will never confuse these two words.

> A doe will hide **its** [belonging to it (the doe)] fawn carefully before going out to graze.
> **It's** [it is] time we packed up and moved to a new location.
> The new computer system has proven **its** [belonging to it] value.
> We'll leave the game as soon as **it's** [it is] over.

Your/You're

Your is a possessive pronoun that means *belonging to you*. *You're* is a contraction for the words *you are*. You will only use *you're* when you can also substitute the words *you are*. Take time to make this substitution, and you will never confuse these two words.

> Is this **your** [belonging to you] idea of a joke?
> As soon as **you're** [you are] finished, you may leave.
> **Your** [belonging to you] friends are the people you most enjoy.
> **You're** [you are] friends whom we value.

Whose/Who's

Whose is a possessive pronoun that means *belonging to whom*. *Who's* is a contraction for the words *who is* or *who has*. Take time to make this substitution, and you will never confuse these two words.

> **Who's** [Who is] in charge of the lighting for the show?
> **Whose** [belonging to whom] car was that?

> This is the nurse **who's** [who is] on duty until morning.
> Here is the man **whose** [belonging to whom] car I ran into this morning.

Who/That/Which

Who refers to people. *That* refers to things. *Which* is generally used to introduce nonrestrictive clauses that describe things. (See Lesson 4 for nonrestrictive clauses.) Look at the following sentences to see how each of these words is used.

> There is the woman **who** helped me fix my flat tire.
> The man **who** invented the polio vaccine died in 1995.
> This is the house **that** Jack built.
> The book **that** I wanted is no longer in print.
> Abigail, **who** rescued my cat from the neighbor's tree, lives across the street.
> Yasser Arafat, **who** headed the PLO, met with Israeli leaders.
> The teacher asked us to read *Lord of the Flies*, **which** is my favorite novel.
> Mount Massive, **which** is the tallest peak in the Rocky Mountains, looms above Leadville, Colorado.

There/Their/They're

There is an adverb telling where an action or item is located. *Their* is a possessive pronoun that shows ownership. *They're* is a contraction for the words *they are*. Of all the confusing word groups, this one is misused most often. Here is an easy way to distinguish among these words.

- Take a close look at this version of the word: t**HERE**. You can see that *there* contains the word *here*. Wherever you use the word *there*, you should be able to substitute the word *here*, and the sentence should still make sense.

■ *Their* means *belonging to them*. Of the three words, *their* can be most easily transformed into the word *them*. Try it. You'll discover that two short markings—connecting the *i* to the *r* and then drawing a line to make the *ir* into an *m*—will turn *their* into *them*. This clue will help you avoid misusing *their*.

■ Finally, imagine that the apostrophe in *they're* is actually a very small letter *a*. If you change *they're* to *they are* in a sentence, you'll never misuse the word. Look over the following example sentences.

> **There** [here] is my paycheck.
>
> The new chairs are in **there** [here].
>
> **Their** [belonging to them] time has almost run out.
>
> This is **their** [belonging to them] problem, not mine.
>
> **They're** [they are] planning to finish early in the morning.
>
> I wonder how **they're** [they are] going to work this out.

Practice

Circle the correct word in each set of parentheses. Answers are at the end of the lesson.

15. Call her when (its, it's) time to go to lunch.

16. The company was known for (its, it's) excellent healthcare benefits.

17. (Its, It's) ball field becomes a muddy mess when (it's, its) raining.

18. Don't forget (your, you're) umbrella when you leave the house this morning.

19. (Your, You're) scheduled to meet with the new client tomorrow morning.

20. (Your, You're) schedule for tomorrow is finalized.

21. (It's, Its) (your, you're) number (their, they're, there) going to call, not mine.

22. This is the scarf (who, which, that) I borrowed from Jessica.

23. My friend Evan is the one (who, which, that) lives in Seattle.

24. The new grocery store, (who, which, that) is located in the center of town, is scheduled to open next week.

25. Georgia O'Keeffe, (who, which, that) is my favorite artist, lived in New Mexico for many years.

26. He was on the team (who, which, that) won last year's title.

27. (There, Their, They're) scheduled to arrive in London next week.

28. (Your, You're) never going to find the books in (there, their, they're).

29. The teller (who, which, that) gave me the deposit slip is over (there, their, they're).

30. (Its, It's) been five years since (there, their, they're) apartment was painted.

31. (Whose, Who's) calculator needs batteries?

32. (Who's Whose) been handling the supply orders for our department?

33. (Who's, Whose) birthday is it?

34. Jacob met with the person (who's, whose) organizing the conference.

Answers

1. laid
2. Lay
3. lay
4. lain
5. lain, laid
6. set
7. set, sitting
8. set
9. sits, set
10. sat
11. raised, rose *or* raises, rises
12. raised
13. risen
14. raised, rose
15. it's
16. its

17. Its, it's
18. your
19. You're
20. Your
21. It's, your, they're
22. that
23. who
24. which
25. who
26. that
27. They're
28. You're, there
29. who, there
30. It's, their
31. Whose
32. Who's
33. Whose
34. who's

TIP

Identify the special verb or pronoun problem that gives you the most trouble. Explain the correct way to use it to a friend or family member. Make a conscious effort to use it correctly at least three times today.

MODIFIERS

Language exerts hidden power, like the moon on the tides.
—RITA MAE BROWN, American writer (1944–)

LESSON SUMMARY

Modifiers brighten and enliven our writing, but can wreak havoc on structure if used improperly. This lesson shows you how to avoid common problems with adjectives and adverbs.

Words and phrases that describe other words are called *modifiers*. Words that describe nouns and pronouns are called *adjectives*. Words that describe verbs, adjectives, or adverbs are called *adverbs*. Entire phrases or groups of words can also function as modifiers. The English language is structured in such a way that modifiers play a vital part in communication. Using them correctly is an important skill. Identify and underline the modifiers in the **Problem** passage on the next page, and check your answers against the **Solution** column.

Problem

Last night's dinner was an enjoyable experience. We met at the trendy new restaurant at 8:00, just in time for our reservation. The restaurant was decorated very luxuriously, with deep colors, nice table cloths, and impressive artwork on the walls. The waiter was very courteous, and pleasantly answered our questions about the menu. When the food came out, it was steaming hot, and smelled delicious. My steak was cooked perfectly; however, my friend said her overcooked fish was underwhelming. Dessert made up for the bad fish, though: my friend's towering piece of chocolate cake looked more like delicious architecture than cake! I thoroughly enjoyed my own ice cream, which was covered in fresh fruit. I will definitely be going back to this wonderful restaurant in the future.

Solution

Last night's dinner was an <u>enjoyable</u> experience. We met at the <u>trendy</u> <u>new</u> restaurant at 8:00, just in time for our reservation. The restaurant was decorated <u>very</u> <u>luxuriously</u>, with <u>deep</u> colors, <u>nice</u> table cloths, and <u>impressive</u> artwork on the walls. The waiter was <u>very</u> <u>courteous</u>, and <u>pleasantly</u> answered our questions about the menu. When the food came out, it was <u>steaming</u> <u>hot</u>, and smelled <u>delicious</u>. My steak was cooked <u>perfectly</u>; however, my friend said her <u>overcooked</u> fish was <u>underwhelming</u>. Dessert made up for the bad fish, though: my friend's <u>towering</u> piece of <u>chocolate</u> cake looked more like delicious architecture than cake! I <u>thoroughly</u> enjoyed my own ice cream, which was covered in <u>fresh</u> fruit. I will <u>definitely</u> be going <u>back</u> to this <u>wonderful</u> restaurant in the future.

Adjectives

Adjectives describe a noun or pronoun in a sentence. Here is an easy way to tell if a word is an adjective. Adjectives answer one of three questions about another word in the sentence: *Which one? What kind?* and *How many?* The following table illustrates this. The adjectives are highlighted to make them easy to identify.

ADJECTIVES		
WHICH ONE?	**WHAT KIND?**	**HOW MANY?**
that cubicle	**sports** car	**many** examples
the **other** arrangement	**red** stickers	**three** containers
our **first** project	**wise** mentor	**several** desks

Pay special attention to adjectives that follow linking verbs. Here, the adjective follows the verb, but it describes the noun or pronoun that comes before the verb. The following sentences illustrate this. The italicized adjectives describe the underlined nouns.

This <u>cheesecake</u> tastes *delicious.* [delicious cheesecake]

Chris's <u>change</u> of heart seemed *appropriate.* [appropriate change]

The <u>room</u> smelled *strange.* [strange room]

Fewer/Less, Number/Amount

Use the adjective *fewer* to modify plural nouns that can be counted. Use *less* for singular nouns that represent a quantity or a degree. Most nouns to which an *-s* can be added require the adjective *fewer*.

> The promotional staff had **fewer** innovative ideas [plural noun] than the marketing staff.
>
> The marketing staff had **less** time [singular noun] to brainstorm than the promotional staff.

The same principle applies to the nouns *number* and *amount*. Use the noun *number* when referring to things that can be made plural or that can be counted. Use the noun *amount* when referring to singular nouns.

> The **number** of hours [plural noun] we have for this telethon has been reduced.
>
> The **amount** of time [singular noun] we have for this telethon has been reduced.

Adverbs

Use adverbs to describe verbs, adjectives, and other adverbs. Here is an easy way to tell if a word is an adverb. Adverbs answer one of these questions about another word in the sentence: *Where? When? How?* and *To what extent?* The following table illustrates this. The adverbs are highlighted.

ADVERBS			
WHERE?	WHEN?	HOW?	TO WHAT EXTENT?
The line moved **forward**.	I saw him **yesterday**.	They spoke **softly**.	I could **hardly** understand.
Store your gear **below**.	Come around **later**.	Cindy types **quickly**.	You **narrowly** missed that car.
Stand **here**.	We'll talk **tonight**.	He sang **happily**.	We **still** won't give in.

This next table shows examples of adverbs modifying verbs, adjectives, and other adverbs. The adverbs are highlighted; the words they modify are underlined.

ADVERBS THAT MODIFY		
VERBS	ADJECTIVES	OTHER ADVERBS
Mail arrives **regularly**.	an **extremely** exciting time	**most** cleverly presented
Doves sing **mournfully**.	a **hopelessly** difficult problem	**very** calmly answered
I responded **immediately**.	an **unusually** sound approach	declined **quite** dramatically

Adjective or Adverb?

Sometimes, writers mistakenly use adjectives in the place of adverbs. This error is illustrated in the following sentences. The italicized words are adjectives incorrectly used in place of adverbs. The adverb form follows the sentence.

Megan can think of answers very *quick*. [**quickly**]
Store these antiques very *careful*. [**carefully**]
Ernie whispered the news as *quiet* as he could. [**quietly**]

Take special care to choose the correct word when using verbs that deal with the senses: *feel, taste, look, smell, sound*. If the word following the verb describes a noun or pronoun that comes before the verb, use an adjective. On the other hand, if the word following the verb describes the verb, use an adverb. In the following table, the adjectives and adverbs are highlighted and the nouns or verbs they modify are underlined.

MODIFIERS WITH "SENSE" VERBS	
ADJECTIVES	**ADVERBS**
The entire group felt **sick** after lunch.	The massage therapist felt **gently** along the patient's spine.
The new keyboard looked **strange** to me.	The detective looked **carefully** at the evidence gathered by the pathologist.
The explanation sounded **plausible** to us.	The biologist smelled the container **gingerly**.

Good *and* Well

Good is an adjective. *Well* is an adverb. Sometimes, *good* is mistakenly used to describe a verb. Use *well* to describe an action. The words modified by *good* and *well* are underlined in these examples.

Brenton did **well** on the test.
Raul felt **good** after the marathon.
The new marketing strategy was **well** planned.
The lasagna smelled **good** when I walked through the door.

Comparisons

Adjectives and adverbs change form when they are used in comparisons. When you compare two items, use the *comparative* form of the modifier. If you are comparing more than two items, use the *superlative* form of the modifier.

The comparative and superlative forms are created in one of two ways:

1. Add-*er* (comparative) or -*est* (superlative) to the modifier if it is a short word of one or two syllables.
2. Place the word *more* or the word *less* before the modifier if it is a multisyllable word.

In addition, some modifiers change form completely. Examine the samples in the following table. The first six lines of the table illustrate these special modifiers that change form. The rest use the two rules previously mentioned.

MODIFIERS IN COMPARISONS		
MODIFIER	COMPARATIVE (FOR TWO ITEMS)	SUPERLATIVE (MORE THAN TWO)
good	better	best
well	better	best
many	more	most
much	more	most
bad	worse	worst
little	less or lesser	least
neat	neater	neatest
lovely	lovelier	loveliest
funny	funnier	funniest
extreme	more [or less] extreme	most [or least] extreme
intelligent	more [or less] intelligent	most [or least] intelligent
precisely	more [or less] precisely	most [or least] precisely

When comparing items in a prepositional phrase, use *between* for two items and *among* for three or more. Look at how the comparative and superlative forms are used in the following sentences.

Up is the **better** direction for the stock market to be going. [comparing two directions]
Blue looks **better** than any other color we've seen. [comparing one color to other colors considered as a group]
The classic coupe is the **best** luxury car available. [comparing more than two cars]
The Mississippi is the **best** river for walleye fishing. [comparing more than two rivers]
The first run model was **more thoroughly** tested than the prototype. [comparing two models]

Avoid Illogical or Unclear Comparisons

"Ellie is more disorganized than any woman" is an illogical statement. It implies that Ellie, who is a woman, is more disorganized than herself. Always include the words *other* or *else* to keep your comparisons from being illogical.

> Ellie is more disorganized than any **other** woman.
> Ted can concentrate better than anyone **else** in our division.

Avoid Double Comparisons

A double comparison occurs when a writer uses both *-er* or *-est* and *more* or *most*. The following table provides examples of common mistakes and how to correct them.

DOUBLE COMPARISONS	
WRONG	**CORRECT**
Diane is the most friendliest person I know.	Diane is the friendliest person I know.
Judi is less sleepier than I am.	Judi is less sleepy than I am.
The writing in this sample seems more plainer than the writing in the other sample.	The writing in this sample seems plainer than the writing in the other sample.

Avoid Double Negatives

When a negative word is added to a statement that is already negative, a double negative results. Avoid double negatives in your writing. The words *hardly* and *barely* can cause problems; they function as negative words. In the following example sentences, the negative words are highlighted. Pay close attention to how the incorrect sentences are rewritten to avoid the double negative.

DOUBLE NEGATIVES	
WRONG	**CORRECT**
The warehouse **doesn't** have **no** surplus stock at this time.	The warehouse has **no** surplus stock at this time. The warehouse **doesn't** have **any** surplus stock at this time.
I **can't hardly** understand this financial report.	I **can hardly** understand this financial report. I **can't** understand this financial report.
The cash on hand **won't barely** cover this expense.	The cash on hand **will barely** cover this expense. The cash on hand **won't** cover this expense.

Misplaced and Dangling Modifiers

Misplaced Modifiers

Place words, phrases, or clauses that describe nouns and pronouns as closely as possible to the words they describe. Failure to do this often results in a misplaced modifier—and a sentence that means something other than what was intended.

Words

For example, the words *only, almost,* and *just* should be placed as closely as possible to the word described. The best place is right before the words they describe. The placement of the word affects the meaning of the sentence.

The customers **only** looked at two samples.
The customers looked at **only** two samples.

In the first sentence, the customers "only looked" at the samples; they didn't touch them. In the second sentence, the customers looked at "only two," not three or four, samples. The placement of *only* changes the meaning.

Here's an example with *almost:*

Chad **almost** scored three touchdowns.
Chad scored **almost** three touchdowns.

In the first version, Chad "almost scored" three times—he must have come close to the goal line three times without actually crossing. In the second version, Chad scored "almost three" touchdowns—maybe 2.2 touchdowns. How many points are awarded for that?

Here's how placing *just* can affect the meaning of a sentence:

The Hill family **just** leases a car.
The Hill family leases **just** a car.

In the first version, the Hill family "just leases" a car, so they don't own or buy a car. In the second, they lease "just a car," not a truck or a van or any other vehicle.

Phrases and Clauses

Phrases and clauses that describe nouns or pronouns must also be placed as closely as possible to the words they describe. The sentences in the following table contain misplaced modifiers. Pay close attention to how they are rewritten to clarify the meaning.

MISPLACED MODIFIERS	
WRONG	**CORRECT**
The veterinarian explained how to vaccinate hogs in the community center basement. [Why would you want hogs in the community center?]	In the community center basement, the veterinarian explained how to vaccinate hogs. The veterinarian in the community center basement explained how to vaccinate hogs.
A big dog followed the old man that was barking loudly. [Why was the man barking?]	A big dog that was barking loudly followed the old man. Barking loudly, a big dog followed the old man.

Dangling Modifiers

Words, phrases, or clauses that begin a sentence and are set off by commas sometimes mistakenly modify the wrong noun or pronoun. These are called *dangling modifiers*. The following sentences contain dangling modifiers. Pay close attention to how the sentences are rewritten to avoid the problem.

DANGLING MODIFIERS	
WRONG	**CORRECT**
Flat and useless, Jason removed the bicycle tire. [Why was Jason flat?]	Jason removed the flat and useless bicycle tire. Flat and useless, the bicycle tire was removed by Jason.
Attached to an old stump, Janette saw a "No Fishing" sign. [Why was Janette attached to an old stump?]	Janette saw a "No Fishing" sign attached to an old stump. The "No Fishing" sign attached to an old stump caught Janette's attention.
While cleaning up after dinner, the phone rang. [Don't you wish you had a phone that cleaned up after dinner?]	While I was cleaning up after dinner, the phone rang. While cleaning up after dinner, I heard the phone ring. The phone rang while I was cleaning up after dinner.

Practice

Circle the correct word in each of the following sentences. The answers to this set of questions can be found at the end of the lesson.

1. Marta dashed as (quick, quickly) as she could to the store for some sugar.

2. Charlotte seemed (bored, boredly) during the long meeting.

3. The old door doesn't open as (easy, easily) as it used to.

4. The line moved too (slow, slowly), frustrating Justin.

5. If you ask (polite, politely), she is more likely to grant your request.

6. The customer at the end of the line looked (angry, angrily).

7. When the phone rang (loud, loudly), it woke up the baby.

8. The new mattress was more (comfortable, comfortably) than our old one.

9. Lauren played especially (well, good) at the recital.

10. Lisa looked (careful, carefully) for any errors in the report.

11. They searched (thorough, thoroughly) in the attic and the basement.

12. Franklin had (fewer, less) difficulty with the decision because he had (fewer, less) choices.

13. Josie is the (younger, youngest) of the twins and the (shorter, shortest) one in the whole family.

14. Macaroni and cheese tastes especially (good, well) if the ingredients are mixed (good, well).

15. The staff hasn't heard (anything, nothing) about the new vacation policy.

16. Divide these cookies (between, among) the two girls, but split the cake (between, among) all the guests at the party.

Choose the correctly written sentence from each of the following sets.

17. a. I like olives and pimentoes boiled in oil.
    b. Boiled in oil, I like olives and pimentos.

18. a. While speeding along a country road, two deer dashed across the road in front of our car.
    b. Two deer dashed across the road in front of our car as we were speeding along a country road.

19. a. Even Rachel sang with the choir with a broken leg.
    b. Even with a broken leg, Rachel sang with the choir.

20. a. We heard about the bank robbers who were arrested on the evening news.
    b. We heard on the evening news about the bank robbers who were arrested.

Answers

1. quickly
2. bored
3. easily
4. slowly
5. politely
6. angry
7. loudly
8. comfortable
9. well
10. carefully
11. thoroughly
12. less, fewer
13. younger, shortest
14. good, well
15. anything
16. between, among
17. a.
18. b.
19. b.
20. b.

TIP

Practice what you have learned in this lesson by listening to others speak. Many people make mistakes with modifiers as they speak. When you hear such a mistake, think about how you might rephrase what the person said to make it correct. Once again, don't feel compelled to correct the mistakes; just use them as opportunities for mental practice so that no one will have the opportunity to correct *you*.

16 ▶ EASILY CONFUSED WORD PAIRS

I have been a believer in the magic of language since, at a very early age, I discovered that some words got me into trouble and others got me out.

—KATHERINE DUNN, American novelist (1945–)

LESSON SUMMARY
Threw or *through*? *To, two,* or *too*? *Brake* or *break*? This lesson and the next review a host of words that are often confused with other words, and show you when to use them.

This lesson covers some of the most commonly confused word pairs you are likely to use in your writing. If you learn to distinguish these words, you can avoid errors in your writing. These words are divided into three separate sections with practice exercises at the end of each section. The italicized words following some of the entries are *synonyms*, words that can be substituted in a sentence for the easily confused words.

Problem

In last night's soccer match against the Hoovertown High Sharks, team captain Melanie Schwartz lead the Plattsville High Piranhas to they're forth straight win. The final score was 3-0.

Despite playing with a wrist injury, Schwartz seemed not to be effected by it, staying in the game until well into the second have. Goalkeeper Joanie Mitchell shone as well, preventing the Sharks from scoring any goals in the game.

Piranhas coach Bella Sweeney had nothing but complements for her team. "They get out their and play every game like its the championship," she said.

The Sharks, who had hoped to brake the Piranhas' winning streak, had trouble excepting their difficult loss. "This is a game we could of won," lamented team captain Shirley Henderson. "Its just not our night."

Solution

In last night's soccer match against the Hoovertown High Sharks, team captain Melanie Schwartz <u>led</u> the Plattsville High Piranhas to <u>their</u> <u>fourth</u> straight win. The final score was 3-0.

Despite playing with a wrist injury, Schwartz seemed not to be <u>affected</u> by it, staying in the game until well into the second <u>half</u>. Goalkeeper Joanie Mitchell shone as well, preventing the Sharks from scoring any goals in the game.

Piranhas coach Bella Sweeney had nothing but <u>compliments</u> for her team. "They get out <u>there</u> and play every game like <u>it's</u> the championship," she said.

The Sharks, who had hoped to <u>break</u> the Piranhas' winning streak, had trouble <u>accepting</u> their difficult loss. "This is a game we could <u>have</u> won," lamented team captain Shirley Jefferson. "<u>It's</u> just not our night."

Three-Way Confusion

Lead/Led/Lead

- **Lead** as a verb means *guide, direct*. As a noun, it means *front position*. It rhymes with *seed*.
- **Led** is a verb, the past tense of **lead**, meaning *guided, directed*. It rhymes with *red*.
- **Lead** is a noun that is *the name of a metal*. It rhymes with *red*.

  Examples:

  Geronimo **led** (*guided*) the small band to safety.

  We hope the next elected officials will **lead** (*guide*) us to economic recovery.

  A pound of styrofoam weighs as much as a pound of **lead** (*the metal*).

  Jake took the **lead** (*front position*) as the group headed out of town.

Quite/Quit/Quiet

- **Quite** is an adverb meaning *completely, very, entirely*. It rhymes with *fight*.
- **Quit** is a verb meaning *stop, cease* or *stopped, ceased*. It rhymes with *sit*.
- **Quiet** as an adjective means *calm, silent, noiseless*. As a verb, it means *soothe, calm*. As a noun, it means *tranquility, peacefulness*. It almost rhymes with *riot*.

  Example:

  The firm was **quite** (*very*) surprised when its most productive investment specialist **quit** (*stopped*) work and opted for the **quiet** (*calm*) life of a monk.

Right/Write/Rite

- **Right** is an adjective meaning *correct, proper, opposite of left*.
- **Write** is a verb meaning *record, inscribe*.
- **Rite** is a noun meaning *ceremony, ritual*.
  Example:
  > I will **write** (*record*) the exact procedures so you will be able to perform the **rite** (*ceremony*) in the **right** (*proper*) way.

Sent/Cent/Scent

- **Sent** is a verb, the past tense of *send*. It means *dispatched, transmitted*.
- **Cent** is a noun meaning *one penny*, a coin worth .01 of a dollar.
- **Scent** is a noun meaning *odor, smell*.
  Example:
  > For a mere **cent** (*penny*), I bought an envelope perfumed with the **scent** (*odor*) of jasmine, which I **sent** (*dispatched*) to my grandmother.

Sight/Site/Cite

- **Sight** as a noun means *ability to see*. As a verb, it means *see, spot*.
- **Site** is a noun meaning *location, position*.
- **Cite** is a verb meaning *quote, make reference to*.
  Examples:
  > At 95, my grandmother's **sight** (*ability to see*) was acute enough to **sight** (*spot*) even the smallest error in a crocheted doily.
  >
  > This is the proposed **site** (*location*) for the new building.
  >
  > You must **cite** (*make reference to*) the source of your information.

To/Too/Two

- **To** is a preposition or part of an infinitive. Use it only to introduce a prepositional phrase, which usually answers the question *where*, or before a verb. Use **to** for introducing a prepositional phrase: *to the store, to the top, to my home, to our garden, to his laboratory, to his castle, to our advantage, to an open door, to a song, to the science room*, etc. Use **to** as an infinitive (*to* followed by a verb, sometimes separated by adverbs): *to run, to jump, to want badly, to seek, to propose, to write, to explode, to sorely need, to badly botch, to carefully examine*, etc.
- **Too** is an adverb meaning *also, very*.
- **Two** is an adjective, *the name of a number*, as in *one, two, three*.
  Example:
  > The couple went **to** (*preposition*) the deli **to** (*infinitive*) pick up **two** (*the number*) dinners because both of them were **too** (*very*) tired **to** (*infinitive*) cook.

Where/Wear/Were

- **Where** is an adverb referring to *place, location*.
- **Wear** as a verb means *put on, tire*. As a noun, it means *deterioration*.
- **Were** is a verb, the plural past tense of *be*.
  Examples:
  > The slacks **were** (*form of* be) too tight.
  > The tires showed excessive **wear** (*deterioration*).
  > They will **wear** (*tire*) out these shoes if they **wear** (*put on*) them too much.
  > **Where** (*location*) are the clothes you **were** (*form of be*) planning to **wear** (*put on*) tomorrow?

Practice

Circle the correct word in the parentheses. Answers can be found at the end of the lesson.

1. The (sent, cent, scent) of freshly baked bread filled the house.

2. I (cent, sent, scent) for the police dog, which quickly picked up the (cent, sent, scent), helping us solve the case. He was worth every (cent, sent, scent) we invested in him.

3. When you (right, write, rite) the final report, please be sure you use the (right, write, rite) statistics.

4. The (right, write, rite) of baptism will be performed at Sunday's service.

5. If you (quite, quit, quiet) talking for a minute and give us some (quite, quit, quiet), I will be (quite, quit, quiet) happy to ask the others to maintain this (quite, quit, quiet) atmosphere for the duration of the meeting.

6. While in the (lead, led) at the competition, Morris's pencil (lead, led) broke, which (lead, led) us to believe he would lose.

7. The health inspector will (lead, led) the effort to educate citizens about the dangers of paint chips that might contain (lead, led).

8. The researcher asked permission to (sight, site, cite) my study in his report.

9. From the top floor, we were able to (sight, site, cite) the (sight, site, cite) that was chosen for the new office building.

10. (Where, wear, were) did you vacation last summer?

11. I planned to (where, wear, were) my new sneakers, but I forgot (where, wear, were) I put them.

Easy Misses

Brake/Break

- **Brake** as a verb means *slow, stop*. As a noun, it means *hindrance, drag*.
- **Break** as a verb means *separate, shatter, adjourn*. As a noun, it means *separation, crack, pause, opportunity*.

Examples:

During our **break** (*pause*), we spotted a **break** (*crack*) in the pipeline.

Brake (*slow*) gently when driving on glare ice by applying slight pressure to the **brake** (*drag*).

Passed/Past

- **Passed** is a verb, the past tense of *pass*, meaning *transferred, went ahead or by, elapsed, finished*.
- **Past** as a noun means *history*. As an adjective, it means *former*. As an adverb, it means *by* or *beyond*.

Examples:

The first runner **passed** (*transferred*) the baton to the second just as she **passed** (*went by*) the stands. Three seconds **passed** (*elapsed*) before the next runner came by.

Harriet **passed** (*finished*) her bar exam on the first try.

I must have been a dolphin in a **past** (*former*) life.

Avoid digging up the **past** (*history*) if you can.

Nathan walks **past** (*by*) the library every day.

Peace/Piece

- **Peace** is a noun meaning *tranquility*.
- **Piece** as a noun means *division, creation*. As a verb, it means *patch, repair*.

Example:

If you can **piece** (*patch*) together the **pieces** (*bits*) of this story, perhaps we can have some **peace** (*tranquility*) around here.

Plain/Plane

- **Plain** as an adjective means *ordinary, clear, simple.* As a noun, it refers to *flat country,* also sometimes written as **plains.**
- **Plane** is a noun meaning *airship* or *flat surface.* It is occasionally used as a verb or adjective meaning *level.*

Examples:

They wore **plain** (*ordinary*) clothes.

It was **plain** (*clear*) to see.

The meal we ate on the **plains** (*flat country*) was quite **plain** (*simple*).

It was **plain** (*clear*) to us that the enemy did not see our **plane** (*airship*) sitting on the open **plain** (*flat country*).

Scene/Seen

- **Scene** is a noun meaning *view, site, commotion.*
- **Seen** is a verb, the past participle of *see,* meaning *observed, noticed.*

Example:

We caused quite a **scene** (*commotion*) at the **scene** (*site*) of the accident. It was the worst we had ever **seen** (*observed*).

Threw/Through

- **Threw** is a verb, the past tense of *throw,* meaning *tossed.*
- **Through** is an adverb or a preposition meaning *in one side and out the other.* Use **through** to introduce a prepositional phrase: *through the door, through the lobby, through the mist.*

Example:

Fred **threw** (*tossed*) the ball **through** (*in one side and out the other*) the hoop.

Weak/Week

- **Weak** is an adjective meaning *flimsy, frail,* and *powerless.*
- **Week** is a noun meaning *a period of seven days.*

Example:

The patient's heartbeat was so **weak** (*frail*) that the doctor was certain he would be dead within a **week** (*seven days*).

Which/Witch

- **Which** is a pronoun dealing with *choice.* As an adverb, it introduces a subordinate clause.
- **Witch** is a noun meaning *sorceress, enchantress.*

Examples:

Which (*choice*) one do you want?

This car, **which** (*introduces subordinate clause*) I have never driven, is the one I'm thinking about buying.

I don't know **which** (*choice*) **witch** (*enchantress*) I should dress up as for Halloween.

Practice

Circle the correct word in the parentheses. Answers can be found at the end of the lesson.

12. (Which, Witch) (which, witch) costume did you decide to wear to the party?

13. When we were (threw, through) with exams, we (threw, through) a big party to celebrate.

14. When she saw the biker ahead (brake, break), Sally slammed on her (brake, break) to avoid the (brake, break) in the concrete path.

15. Have you (scene, seen) the love (scene, seen) in the movie?

16. The confused (which, witch) didn't know (which, witch) ingredients to use in her potion.

17. The (scene, seen) at the Grand Canyon was breathtaking. Have you (scene, seen) it before?

18. Even a (week, weak) after returning from the hospital, Virginia still felt (week, weak) and needed rest.

19. It took only one (peace, piece) of good news to restore her (peace, piece) of mind.

20. The private (plain, plane) had a (plain, plane) tan interior.

To Split or Not to Split

Already/All Ready
- **Already** is an adverb meaning *as early as this, previously, by this time.*
- **All ready** means *completely ready, totally ready.*
  Examples:
    At age four, Brigitta is reading **already** (*as early as this*).
    We had **already** (*previously, by this time*) finished.
    Are we **all ready** (*completely ready*) to go?

Altogether/All Together
- **Altogether** is an adverb meaning *entirely, completely.*
- **All together** means *simultaneously.*
  Examples:
    These claims are **altogether** (*entirely*) false.
    The audience responded **all together** (*simultaneously*).

Everyday/Every Day
- **Everyday** is an adjective meaning *ordinary, usual.*
- **Every day** means *each day.*
  Examples:
    These are our **everyday** (*usual*) low prices.
    The associates sort the merchandise **every day** (*each day*).

Maybe/May Be
- **Maybe** is an adverb meaning *perhaps.*
- **May be** is a verb phrase meaning *might be.*
  Example:
    Maybe (*perhaps*) the next batch will be better than this one. On the other hand, it **may be** (*might be*) worse.

Always Split
- **A lot.** There's no such word as *alot.* There's a word *allot,* which means *to portion out* something.
  Example:
    I thought it was all right that we **allotted** tickets to **a lot** of our best customers.

Practice
Circle the correct word in the parentheses.

21. I (where, wear, were) my (everyday, every day) clothes almost (everyday, every day).

22. There (maybe, may be) more storms tomorrow, so (maybe, may be) you should plan something else to do.

23. If you had been (already, all ready), we could have (already, all ready) begun.

24. He always makes (some time, sometime) in the afternoon to exercise. You should try it (some time, sometime).

25. There were (a lot, alot) of spectators at the game Friday night.

Answers

1. scent
2. sent, scent, cent
3. write, right
4. rite
5. quit, quiet, quite, quiet
6. lead, lead, led
7. lead, lead
8. cite
9. sight, site
10. Where
11. wear, where
12. Which, witch
13. through, threw
14. brake, brake, break
15. seen, scene
16. witch, which
17. scene, seen
18. week, weak
19. piece, peace
20. plane, plain
21. wear, everyday, every day
22. may be, maybe
23. all ready, already
24. some time, sometime
25. a lot

TIP

How many easily confused words can you spot in your reading? Try substituting the synonyms you learned.

17 ▶ MORE EASILY CONFUSED WORDS

Words have a longer life than deeds.

—PINDAR, Greek poet (522 B.C.E.–443 B.C.E.)

LESSON SUMMARY

Some of the most commonly used words in the English language are easily confused with other equally common words. To avoid confusing readers, you need to know which ones are which.

This lesson covers more of the most commonly confused word pairs, those you are likely to use in your writing. If you learn to distinguish these words, you can avoid errors. The words are divided into three separate sections with practice exercises at the end of each section. The words in italics following some of the entries are *synonyms*, words that can be substituted in a sentence for the easily confused words. In the **Problem** column on the next page, underline the incorrect words from these word pairs. Compare your answers with the **Solution** column.

Problem

Seasonal Affective Disorder (also known as SAD) is a health issue that effects alot of people every year. Sometimes called "the winter blues" because it seems to occur during times of seasonal change, the principle symptoms of the mood disorder include lethargy (lack of energy), trouble sleeping, difficulty concentrating, and depression. Anyone who suffers from these symptoms should seek farther advise from a doctor. If a person is found to be suffering from true SAD, treatment may include melatonin, lightbox therapy, cognitive behavioral therapy, or other types of therapy.

The disorder is also controversial. Some medical experts rise concerns that the symptoms maybe triggered by other underlying medical or mental health issues; others site studies going back to the 1970s and 1980s that show this phenomenon as a long-standing medical issue. The first diagnosis of SAD was made in 1984 by Dr. Norman Rosenthal, who's associates at the National Institute of Mental Health where researching the possible disorder.

Solution

Seasonal Affective Disorder (also known as SAD) is a health issue that <u>affects</u> <u>a lot</u> of people every year. Sometimes called "the winter blues" because it seems to occur during times of seasonal change, the <u>principal</u> symptoms of the mood disorder include lethargy (lack of energy), trouble sleeping, difficulty concentrating, and depression. Anyone who suffers from these symptoms should seek <u>further</u> <u>advice</u> from a doctor. If a person is found to be suffering from true SAD, treatment may include melatonin, lightbox therapy, cognitive behavioral therapy, or other types of therapy.

The disorder is also controversial. Some medical experts <u>raise</u> concerns that the symptoms <u>may be</u> triggered by other underlying medical or mental health issues; others <u>cite</u> studies going back to the 1970s and 1980s that show this phenomenon as a longstanding medical issue. The first diagnosis of SAD was made in 1984 by Dr. Norman Rosenthal, <u>whose</u> associates at the National Institute of Mental Health <u>were</u> researching the possible disorder.

Small but Tricky

By/Buy

- **By** is a preposition used to introduce a phrase (*by the book*, *by the time*, *by the way*).
- **Buy** as a verb means *purchase*. As a noun, it means *bargain, deal*.
   Examples:
   We stopped **by** *(preposition)* the store to **buy** *(purchase)* some groceries.
   That car was a great **buy** (deal).

Dear/Deer

- **Dear** is an adjective meaning *valued, loved.*
- **Deer** is a noun referring to an *animal,* a four-legged one that lives in the woods and looks like Bambi.

    Example:

    My **dear** *(loved)* daughter's favorite movie is *Bambi,* about a **deer** *(animal).*

Die/Dye

- **Die** is a verb meaning *pass away, fade.*
- **Dye** as a verb means to *color, tint.* As a noun, it refers to *coloring, pigment.*

    Example:

    We waited for the wind to **die** *(fade)* before we decided to **dye** *(color)* the sheets.

Hear/Here

- **Hear** is a verb meaning *listen to.*
- **Here** is an adverb meaning *in this place, to this place.*

    Example:

    Please come **here** *(to this place)* so you can **hear** *(listen to)* what I have to say.

Hole/Whole

- **Hole** is a noun meaning *opening, gap.*
- **Whole** as an adjective means *entire, intact.* As a noun, it means *entire part or amount.*

    Examples:

    The **whole** *(entire)* group heard the message. They patched the **hole** *(opening)* in the wall.

Knew/New

- **Knew** is a verb, the past tense of *know.* It means *understood, recognized.*
- **New** is an adjective meaning *fresh, different, current.*

    Example:

    I **knew** *(understood)* they were planning to buy a **new** *(different)* car.

Know/No

- **Know** is a verb meaning *understand, recognize.*
- **No** as an adverb means *not so, not at all.* As an adjective, it means *none, not one.*

    Example:

    As far as I **know** *(understand),* we have **no** *(not one)* more of these shoes in stock.

Meat/Meet

- **Meat** is a noun meaning *food, flesh, main part.*
- **Meet** as a verb means *assemble, greet, fulfill.* As a noun, it means *assembly.*

    Examples:

    Before a track **meet** *(assembly),* it is better to eat foods high in carbohydrates rather than **meat** *(flesh).*

    The **meat** *(main part)* of his message was that our efforts did not **meet** *(fulfill)* his standards.

One/Won

- **One** can be an adjective meaning *single.* It can also be a noun used to mean a single person or thing.
- **Won** is a verb, the past tense of *win.* It means *prevailed, achieved, acquired.*

    Example:

    Jacquez is the **one** *(noun referring to* Jacquez*)* who **won** *(achieved)* the most improved bowler trophy this year.

Seam/Seem

- **Seam** is a noun meaning *joint, joining point.*
- **Seem** is a verb meaning *appear.*

    Example:

    Does it **seem** *(appear)* to you as if this **seam** *(joint)* is weakening?

Practice

Circle the correct word in the parentheses. Answers can be found at the end of the lesson.

1. Would you run (by, buy) the store on your way home to (by, buy) a gallon of milk?

2. The best (by, buy) in the store is that new book written (by, buy) the famous talk show host. You should (by, buy) it.

3. My (deer, dear) friend and I saw five (deer, dear) in my backyard.

4. If you want to change the color of that shirt, you can (die, dye) it.

5. The rosebush started to (die, dye) soon after we planted it.

6. I can (hear, here) the speaker much better now that I am sitting (hear, here).

7. The (hole, whole) flood began by water leaking through a (hole, whole) in the pipe.

8. I just (knew, new) the (knew, new) toaster would be a good as my old one.

9. I didn't (know, no) that that you had (know, no) idea how to get to the restaurant.

10. We asked to (meat, meet) the chef so we could tell her how much we enjoyed the (meat, meet) dish we ordered.

11. The undefeated varsity baseball team (one, won) the game by only (one, won) point.

12. I (seam, seem) to remember that the tailor did a flawless job repairing the (seam, seem) on my coat.

Often Used and Misused

Choose/Chose
- **Choose** is a verb meaning *select*. It rhymes with *bruise*.
- **Chose** is past tense of *choose*; it means *selected*. It rhymes with *hose*.

  Example:
  Henry **chose** (*selected*) flex hours on Friday afternoons. I will **choose** (*select*) the same option.

Loose/Lose/Loss
- **Loose** is an adjective meaning *free, unrestrained, not tight*. It rhymes with *goose*.
- **Lose** is a verb meaning *misplace, to be defeated, fail to keep*. It rhymes with *shoes*.
- **Loss** is a noun meaning *defeat, downturn, the opposite of victory or gain*. It rhymes with *toss*.

  Examples:
  The chickens ran **loose** (*free*) in the yard.
  The knot holding the boat to the dock was **loose** (*not tight*).
  Where did you **lose** (*misplace*) your gloves?
  The investors will **lose** (*fail to keep*) considerable capital if the market suffers a **loss** (*downturn*).

Suppose/Supposed
- **Suppose** is a verb meaning *assume, imagine*.
- **Supposed** as a verb is the past tense of *suppose* and means *assumed, imagined*. As an adjective, it means *expected, obligated*.

  Examples:
  I **suppose** (*assume*) you'll be late, as usual.
  We all **supposed** (*assumed*) you would be late.
  You were **supposed** (*expected*) to have picked up the copies of the report before you came to the meeting.

Than/Then

- **Than** is a conjunctive word used to make a comparison.
- **Then** is an adverb telling *when* or meaning *next*.
  Example:
  > **Then** *(next)*, the group discussed the ways in which the new procedures worked better **than** *(conjunction making a comparison)* the old.

Use/Used

- **Use** as a verb means *utilize, deplete*. It rhymes with *lose*. As a noun, it rhymes with *goose* and means *purpose*.
- **Used** as a verb is the past tense of *use* and means *utilized, depleted*. As an adjective, it means *secondhand*.
- **Used to** can be used as an adjective, meaning *accustomed to*, or as an adverb meaning *formerly*. (Note that you never write *use to* when you mean *accustomed to* or *formerly*.)
  Examples:
  > Just **use** *(utilize)* the same password we **used** *(utilized)* yesterday.
  > What's the **use** *(purpose)* in trying yet another time?
  > We should consider buying **used** *(secondhand)* equipment.
  > We **used to** *(formerly)* require a second opinion.
  > Residents of Buffalo, New York, are **used to** *(accustomed to)* cold temperatures.

Weather/Whether

- **Weather** is a noun referring to the *condition outside*.
- **Whether** is an adverb used when referring to *a possibility*.
  Examples:
  > The **weather** *(condition outside)* took a turn for the worse.
  > Let me know **whether** *(a possibility)* you are interested in this new system.

Practice

Circle the correct word in the parentheses. The answers can be found at the end of the lesson.

13. Ms. Wallace interviewed each candidate twice to (choose, chose) the best person for the job.

14. Although it was hard to (choose, chose), Tabitha (choose, chose) the chocolate cake with the raspberry filling over the white cake with strawberry filling.

15. After the (loose, lose, loss) of her job, she began to (loose, lose, loss) confidence.

16. The shoes she ordered from the catalogue were too (loose, lose, loss).

17. I can tell when I (loose, lose, loss) weight because my pants get (loose, lose, loss).

18. It's 7:30; aren't you (suppose, supposed) to be at the airport by 8:00?

19. I waited until I'd collected more (then, than) enough donations, and (then, than) I contacted the director of the homeless shelter.

20. We (use, used) to buy (use, used) records whenever we went to thrift stores, but now we have no (use, used) for them.

21. You are (suppose, supposed) to enjoy your vacation (weather, whether) or not the (weather, whether) is beautiful.

Killer *a*'s and *al*'s

Accept/Except/Expect
- **Accept** is a verb meaning *receive, bear.*
- **Except** is a preposition meaning *but, excluding.*
- **Expect** is a verb meaning *anticipate, demand, assume.*

  Examples:

  This client **expects** (*demands*) nothing **except** (*but*) the most sophisticated options available.

  Will you **accept** (*bear*) the responsibility for this decision?

  We **expect** (*anticipate*) everyone to come **except** (*excluding*) John.

Advice/Advise
- **Advice** is a noun meaning *suggestion, suggestions.* It rhymes with *ice.* (Hint: Think *adv*ICE.)
- **Advise** is a verb meaning *suggest to, warn.* It rhymes with *wise.*

  Examples:

  We **advise** (*suggest to*) you to proceed carefully.

  That was the best **advice** (*suggestion*) I've received so far.

Affect/Effect
- **Affect** is a verb meaning *alter, inspire* or *move emotionally, imitate.* **Affected**, besides being the past tense of *affect*, can also be used as an adjective meaning *imitated, pretentious.* **Affect** is also a noun referring to *feeling* or *emotion.*
- **Effect** as a noun means *consequence.* As a verb, it means *cause.*

  Examples:

  How will this plan **affect** (*alter*) our jobs? What **effect** (*consequence*) will this restructuring have on profits? Will it **effect** (*cause*) an increase?

  The movie **affected** (*moved emotionally*) Marian.

  He **affected** (*imitated*) an English accent.

  The **affected** (*pretentious*) speech fooled no one.

Capital/Capitol
- **Capital** as a noun means either *assets* or *the city that is the seat of government.* As an adjective, it means *main, very important,* or *deserving of death.*
- **Capitol** is a noun referring to *the building that houses the government.*

  Examples:

  How much **capital** (*assets*) are you willing to invest?

  I think that's a **capital** (*main*) objective.

  First-degree murder is a **capital** (*deserving of death*) crime.

  Albany is the **capital** (*city*) of New York.

  No legislators were injured in the explosion in the **capitol** (*building*).

Personal/Personnel
- **Personal** is an adjective meaning *private.*
- **Personnel** as a noun means *staff, employees* or as an adjective means *dealing with staff or employees.*

  Example:

  The director of **personnel** (*staff*) keeps all the **personnel** (*employee*) files in order and guards any **personal** (*private*) information they contain.

Principal/Principle
- **Principal** as a noun refers to the *head of a school* or an *investment.* As an adjective, it means *primary, major.*
- **Principle** is a noun meaning *rule, law, belief.*

  Examples:

  The **principal** (*head*) of Calbert High School used the **principal** (*investment*) of an endowment fund to cover this month's salaries.

  The **principal** (*primary*) objective is to make decisions that are in keeping with our **principles** (*beliefs*).

Practice

Circle the correct word in the parentheses. The answers can be found at the end of the lesson.

22. Surely you didn't (accept, except, expect) Weldon to (accept, except, expect) responsibility for this decision when everyone (accept, except, expect) him was consulted.

23. (Accept, Except, Expect) for Mr. Nelson, Mrs. Lawrence didn't (accept, except, expect) anyone else to (accept, except, expect) the committee's costly construction proposal.

24. The soothsayer will (advice, advise) you to seek her (advice, advise) often.

25. The new work schedule (affected, effected) production in a positive way.

26. How will this new work schedule (affect, effect) production?

27. What (affect, effect) will this new work schedule have on production?

28. We plan to tour the (capital, capitol) building whenever we visit a state's (capital, capitol) city.

29. The (personnel, personal) information you submit to (personnel, personal) will be kept strictly confidential.

30. The employees' (principal, principle) concern is workload.

31. The (principle, principal) of the school is a man of great (principle, prinicpal).

Answers

1. by, buy
2. buy, by, buy
3. dear, deer
4. dye
5. die
6. hear, here
7. whole, hole
8. knew, new
9. know, no
10. meet, meat
11. won, one
12. seem, seam
13. choose
14. choose, chose
15. loss, lose
16. loose
17. lose, loose
18. supposed
19. than, then
20. used, used, use
21. supposed, whether, weather
22. expect, accept, except
23. except, expect, accept
24. advise, advice
25. affected
26. affect
27. effect
28. capitol, capital
29. personal, personnel
30. principal
31. principal, principle

TIP

Make a conscious effort to use the correct forms of these easily confused words in your writing. You may find it helpful to copy the words and their synonyms onto a separate sheet of paper. This will provide a good review and serve as a handy reference you can keep with you as you write.

18 ▶ DICTION

A special kind of beauty exists which is born in language, of language, and for language.

—GASTON BACHELARD, French philosopher (1884–1962)

LESSON SUMMARY

What does writing have to do with diction? Diction often refers to speaking components, such as intonation, inflection, and enunciation, but it also encompasses word choice and style. Effective language means concise, precise writing. Lessons 18 and 19 will focus on helping you learn to choose the words that will best communicate your ideas.

 word is a terrible thing to waste. Or is it better to say, "It is a terrible thing to waste a word"? The difference between these two versions is a matter of *diction*, using appropriate words and combining them in the right way to communicate your message accurately. This lesson discusses ways to avoid some of the most common diction traps: wordiness, lack of precison, clichés, and jargon. Learning to recognize and avoid such writing weaknesses will turn a mediocre writer into a good one—this means expressing ideas in the *best* and *clearest* possible way. Underline the instances of wordiness and cliché in the **Problem** column on the following page, and check your answers with the **Solution** column.

Problem

When it comes to fixing our nation's energy crisis, we need to think outside the box. We will need to roll up our sleeves and dig in, finding ways to reduce our current energy footprints while developing alternative forms of energy. Children are our future, and if we deplete this planet and leave them with no resources, we leave them up the creek without a paddle. Sustainability studies and research can tell us the writing on the wall, and show us areas where we can be more "green" as a society. Information is our friend as we look to conserve, create, and maintain resources for a brighter tomorrow.

Solution

When it comes to fixing our nation's energy crisis, we need to <u>think outside the box</u>. We will need to <u>roll up our sleeves and</u> <u>dig in,</u> finding ways to reduce our current energy footprints while developing alternative forms of energy. <u>Children are our future</u>, and if we deplete this planet and leave them with no resources, we leave them <u>up the creek without a paddle</u>. Sustainability studies and research can tell us <u>the writing on the wall</u>, and show us areas where we can be more "green" as a society. Information <u>is our friend</u> as we look to conserve, create, and maintain resources <u>for a brighter tomorrow</u>.

Wordiness

Excess words in communication waste space and time. Not only that, but they may also distort the message or make it difficult for the reader to understand. Get in the habit of streamlining your writing, making the sentences as concise as possible. If you use five words where three would do, delete the extra words or structure your sentences to avoid them. See if you can rewrite the sentences in the first column to make them less wordy. Check yourself against the version in the second column.

The additional words in the first column add no information. All they do is take up space.

WORDY	REVISED
It was a three-hour period after the accident when the rescue squad that we knew was going to help us arrived. [21 words]	The rescue squad arrived three hours after the accident. [9 words]
It was decided that the church would organize a committee for the purpose of conducting a search for a new pastor. [21 words]	The church organized a committee to search for a new pastor. [11 words]

Buzzwords and Fluffy Modifiers

Buzzwords—such as *aspect, element, factor, scope, situation, type, kind, forms,* and so on—sound important, but add no meaning to a sentence. They often signal a writer who has little or nothing to say, yet wishes to sound important. Likewise, modifiers such as *absolutely, definitely, really, very, important, significant, current, major,* and *quite* may add length to a sentence, but they seldom add meaning.

Wordy:

> The *nature of the* scheduling system is a *very important matter* that can *definitely* have a *really significant* impact on the morale *aspect* of an employee's attitude. *Aspects of* our current scheduling policy make it *absolutely necessary* that we undergo a *significant* change.

Revised:

> The scheduling system can affect employee morale. Our policy needs to be changed.

The following table lists a host of phrases that can be reduced to one or two words.

WORDY	CONCISE	WORDY	CONCISE
puzzling in nature	puzzling	at this point in time	now; today
of a peculiar kind	peculiar	at that point in time	then
regardless of the fact that	although	in order to	to
due to the fact that	because	by means of	by
of an indefinite nature	indefinite	exhibits a tendency to	tends to
concerning the matter of	about	in connection with	with
in the event that	if	in relation to	with

Passive Voice

Some wordiness is caused by using passive voice verbs when you could use the active voice. (See Lesson 11 if you don't remember passive voice.)

PASSIVE	ACTIVE
It has been decided that your application for grant money is not in accordance with the constraints outlined by the committee in the application guidelines.	The committee denied your grant because it did not follow the application guidelines.
The letter of resignation was accepted by the Board of Directors.	The Board of Directors accepted the resignation.

Intellectual-ese

Those passive sentences suffer not only from passive voice wordiness, but also from the writer's attempt to make the writing sound intellectual, to make the message more difficult than necessary. Writers make this error in many ways. One way is to turn adjectives and verbs into nouns. This transformation usually means extra words are added to the sentence.

WORDY	REVISED
Water *pollution* [noun] is not as serious in the northern parts of Canada.	Water is not as *polluted* [adjective] in northern Canada.
Customer *demand* [noun] is reducing in the area of sales services.	Customers *demand* [verb] fewer sales services.

Another way writers add words without adding meaning is to use a pretentious tone. What follows is an actual memo issued by a bureaucrat during World War II. When it was sent to President Franklin Roosevelt for his approval, he edited the memo before sending it on.

Original pretentious memo:

In the unlikely event of an attack by an invader of a foreign nature, such preparations shall be made as will completely obscure all Federal buildings and non-Federal buildings occupied by the Federal government during an air raid for any period of time from visibility by reason of internal or external illumination.

Roosevelt's revised memo:

If there is an air raid, put something across the windows and turn off the lights outside in buildings where we have to keep the work going.

Here's another example of pretentious writing, along with a clearer, revised version.

Pompous memo:

As per the most recent directive issued from this office, it is incumbent upon all employees and they are henceforth instructed to reduce in amount the paper used in the accomplishment of their daily tasks due to the marked increase in the cost of such supplies.

Revised:

Since paper costs have increased, employees must use less paper.

WORD ECONOMY	
STRETCHED SENTENCE	**CONCISE SENTENCE**
Cassandra seems to be content.	Cassandra seems content.
We must know what it is that we are doing.	We must know what we're doing.
This is the book of which I have been speaking.	I spoke about this book.
It is with pleasure that I announce the winner.	I am pleased to announce the winner.
The reason we were late was because of traffic.	We were late because of traffic.
These plans will be considered on an individual basis.	These plans will be considered individually.
The caterer, who was distressed, left the party.	The distressed caterer left the party.
There are new shipments arriving daily.	New shipments arrive daily.
Due to the fact that we were late, we missed the door prizes.	We came late and missed the door prizes.
The consideration given in the latest promotion is an example of how I was treated unfairly.	I was not fairly considered for the latest promotion.

Writers sometimes stretch their sentences with unnecessary words, all to sound intelligent. The previous table illustrates stretched sentences that have been rewritten more concisely.

Redundancy

Another writing trap that takes up space is *redundancy*, repeating words that express the same idea or in which the meanings overlap. If you stop to think about phrases like the following—and many others—you'll see that the extra words are not only unnecessary but often just plain silly.

> enclosed *with this letter*
> remit *payment*
> *absolutely* necessary
> weather *outside*
> postpone *until later*
> refer *back*
> *past* history

> ask *the question*
> continue *on*, proceed *ahead*
> repeated *over again*
> gather *together*
> *compulsory* requirement
> *temporarily* suspended
> *necessary* requirements
> plain *and simple*

Enclosed means it's in this letter, doesn't it? *Remit* means *pay*. And how can something be more *necessary* than *necessary*? The weather *outside* as opposed to the weather *inside*? *Past* history as opposed to . . . ? You see the point. Keep it simple. (Not *plain and simple.*)

Practice

Try rewriting the following sentences to remove the fluffy wording. Suggested revisions are at the end of this lesson, but your versions may be different; there's more than one way to rewrite these sentences.

1. It gives us great pleasure to take this opportunity to announce the opening of the newly built playground at the Municipal Park in Succasunna.

2. Some educators hold with the opinion that corporal punishment should in fact be reinstated in our schools to act as a deterrent to those students who are considering engaging in inappropriate behavior.

3. It is certainly a true statement that bears repeating over and over again that technological advancements such as computers can assist employees in performing in a very efficient manner, and that these self-same computers may in fact result in considerable savings over a period of time.

4. I arrived at a decision to allow the supervisor of my department to achieve a higher golf score in order to enhance my opportunities for advancement in the event that such opportunities became available.

Precise Language

Make your writing as precise as possible. In doing so, you communicate more meaning using fewer words. In other words, you make your writing more concise. Choose exact verbs, modifiers, and nouns to help you transmit an exact meaning, such as the examples in the following table.

IMPRECISE VS. PRECISE	
VERBS	
Emilia participated in the protest.	Emilia organized the march on the capital.
Hannah won't deal with sales meetings.	Hannah won't attend sales meetings.
Dick can relate to Jane.	Dick understands Jane's feelings.
MODIFIERS	
These bad instructions confused me.	These disorganized, vague instructions left me with no idea how to repair the leak.
Toy Story is a good movie with fun for all.	*Toy Story* is a clever animated film with humor, adventure, and romance.
We had a nice time with you.	We enjoyed eating your food, drinking your cola, and swimming in your pool.
NOUNS	
I always have trouble with this computer.	I can never get this computer to save or print.
I like to have fun when I take a vacation.	I like to swim, fish, and eat out when I'm on vacation.
Let me grab some things from my locker.	Let me grab my purse and books from my locker.

Abstract vs. Concrete

Abstract language refers to intangible ideas or to classes of people and objects rather than the people or things themselves. Abstractions are built on concrete ideas. Without a grasp of the concrete meanings, a reader can't be expected to understand an abstract idea. Journalists and law enforcement professionals are especially aware of the distinction between abstract and concrete as they write. They strive to present the facts clearly, so the reader can draw conclusions. They avoid making the assumptions for the reader, hoping the facts will speak for themselves. Concrete language requires more time and thought to write, but it communicates a message more effectively. Additional words are an advantage if they add meaning or increase precision.

ABSTRACT ASSUMPTION	CONCRETE DETAILS
Strader was amazing.	Strader scored 28 points, grabbed 12 rebounds, and blocked five shots.
The couple was in love.	The couple held hands, hugged, and ignored everything around them.
Billie is reliable and responsible.	Billie always arrives on time, completes her assignments, and helps others if she has time.

Clichés

A *cliché* is a tired, overworked phrase that sucks the life out of writing. These are cliché phrases: *a needle in a haystack, quiet as a mouse, crack of dawn, tough as nails, naked truth, hear a pin drop,* and so on. Authors use clichés when they don't have the time or ability to come up with more precise or more meaningful language. Although clichés are a sort of "communication shorthand," they rely on stereotypical thinking for their meaning. A writer who uses clichés is relying on unoriginal, worn-out thinking patterns to carry a message. If the message is important, fresh language will make a stronger impression than old, overused phrases. Original language stimulates thought and heightens the reader's concentration. Moreover, a fresh image rewards an attentive reader.

Imagine that a writer wanted to explain how difficult it was to find the source of a problem. Look at the following two versions. One relies on a cliché to communicate the message, while the other uses a fresher, more original approach. Which version is likely to make the stronger impression, to communicate the message more effectively?

Finding the source of this problem was harder than finding a needle in a haystack.
Finding the source of this problem was harder than finding a fact in a political advertisement.

Here are more examples contrasting clichés with fresher, more original language. When you check your writing, look for ways to replace frequently used words and phrases with something fresh and original.

We rose at the crack of dawn.
We rose with the roosters.

Having Sam at our negotiations meetings was like having a loose cannon on deck.
Having Sam at our negotiations meetings was like having a German shepherd's tail in your crystal closet.

Jargon

Jargon is the technical, wordy language used by those associated with a trade or profession. Often, it is full of passive voice, acronyms, technical terms, and abstract words. Writers use jargon to sound educated, sophisticated, or knowledgeable. Actually, jargon muddies and even distorts the message. Compare the following two paragraphs.

> Alex demonstrates a tendency to engage inappropriately in verbal social interaction during class time. His grades are deficient because he suffers from an unwillingness to complete supplementary assignments between class periods.

> Alex talks in class when he isn't supposed to. He has low grades because he doesn't do his homework.

The first paragraph leaves the impression that Alex is a sociopath with a serious problem. The second portrays him as a student who needs to talk less and work more. When you write, strive for clear, plain language that communicates your message accurately. Clear communication leaves a better impression by far than pretentious, abstract, jargon-filled words.

Practice

Choose the option that expresses the idea most clearly and concisely. Answers are at the end of the lesson.

5. a. Doubtless, the best choice we could make would reflect our association's founding principles.
   b. It is without a doubt that the most advantageous selection we could choose would be one that best reflects our association's principles that it has had since its origin.

6. a. The least expensive option in a situation such as this is inevitably also the most advantageous option.
   b. The cheapest way is the best way.

7. a. Too many youngsters prefer using their spare time with popular modern pastimes to improving their minds with more analytical options.
   b. Too many youngsters prefer using their spare time to play video games, instant message, and text message friends than to improve their minds with reading.

8. a. The marketing department found that customers prefer the vanilla scent.
   b. Consumer attitude studies conducted by our marketing department seem to indicate that a large majority of our customers had good things to say about the vanilla scent.

Answers

1. We are pleased to announce the opening of Succasunna's new Municipal Park playground.
2. Some educators believe that unruly students should be spanked.
3. Using computers can save time and money.
4. I let my supervisor beat me at golf so she would promote me.

5. a.
6. b.
7. b.
8. a.

TIP

Listen to public officials as they deliver prepared speeches. Do they speak clearly and plainly, or are they trying to sound "official"? A truly competent, intelligent speaker or writer doesn't need a mask of pretentious, abstract, sophisticated-sounding language.

19 ▶ MORE DICTION

The English language is nobody's special property. It is the property of the imagination: It is the property of the language itself.

—DEREK WALCOTT, poet and playwright (1930–)

LESSON SUMMARY

We continue learning about diction and writing clearly and accurately. Here we look at colloquialisms, loaded language, consistent points of view, parallelisms, and gender-neutral language.

Good writers know that communicating requires choosing words carefully. Writing styles that are too formal or informal, inappropriate, or just plain emotional turn readers off. You may have the best ideas in the world, but if you can't get them across in writing, no one will ever act on your great ideas. On the other hand, well-expressed, commonplace ideas are more likely to get attention. How you choose your words has everything to do with whether your writing gets the attention it deserves. In the **Practice** column on the next page, underline the instances of colloquialism and improper tone. Check your answers against the **Solution** column.

Problem

Hey boss,

The presentation for tomorrow's meeting is ready. Fred and I were hanging out late last night, pulling together our research and our ideas so we could whip them into shape. After we were done, I e-mailed the dude over in the graphics department to finish the formatting. This morning, I eyeballed the information to make sure everything was included, and I think we're good to go. Lemme know if there's anything else you'd like me to do before tomorrow's meeting.

Solution

Hey boss,

The presentation for tomorrow's meeting is ready. Fred and I were hanging out late last night, pulling together our research and our ideas so we could whip them into shape. After we were done, I e-mailed the dude over in the graphics department to finish the formatting. This morning, I eyeballed the information to make sure everything was included, and I think we're good to go. Lemme know if there's anything else you'd like me to do before tomorrow's meeting.

Colloquialism

Colloquialisms are informal words and phrases such as *a lot, in a bind, pulled it off,* and so on. These words and phrases are widely used in conversations between friends, but in written communication, they portray an attitude of chumminess or close friendship that may cause your message to be taken less seriously than you intended. You may even insult your reader without meaning to. A friendly, colloquial tone is fine in a personal letter; however, a more formal tone is better for business communications, which are meant to be taken seriously. Compare the following paragraphs. If you received these two memos from an employee, which would you take more seriously?

I think the way we promote people around here stinks. People who aren't that good at their jobs get promoted just because they pal around with the right people. That puts across the idea that it doesn't matter how much time I put in at work or how good of a job I do; I won't get promoted unless I kiss up to the boss. I'm not that kind of guy.

I think our promotion system is unfair. Average and below-average employees receive promotions simply because they befriend their superiors. This practice leaves the impression that commitment and quality of work are not considered. I choose not to socialize with my supervisors, and I feel as though I am not being promoted for that reason alone.

The writer of the first paragraph sounds as if he doesn't take his job all that seriously. And yet he probably does; he just hasn't managed to communicate his seriousness in writing because he has used language that is more appropriate in a conversation with his friends than a memo to his supervisor. The writer of the second paragraph, on the other hand, conveys his seriousness by using more formal language. He has done so without falling into the opposite trap, discussed in the last lesson, of trying to sound *too* intelligent. He has used plain, but not colloquial, language.

The sentences in the following table illustrate the difference between colloquial and formal diction. By substituting the highlighted words, the sentence becomes more formal rather than colloquial.

Tone

Tone describes a writer's emotional attitude toward the subject or the audience. The more reasonable and objective a message seems, the more likely it is to be considered seriously. Raging emotions seldom convince anyone to change an opinion, and they seldom convince anyone who is undecided. Persuasion requires clearly presented facts and logically presented arguments. A reader or listener will give the most credibility to an argument that seems fair and objective. Emotion can reduce credibility. Use it carefully.

Avoid Anger

Avoid accusatory, angry words that make demands. Consider the two paragraphs that follow. Which one is most likely to persuade the reader to take action?

COLLOQUIAL	MORE FORMAL WORDS
I have **around** three hours to finish this task.	I have **about** three hours to finish this task.
The pasta was **real** good.	The pasta was **very** good.
We **got sick** from the food.	We **became ill** from the food.
It looks **like** we could win.	It looks **as if** we could win.
I'm **awful** tired.	I'm **very** (or **quite** or **extremely**) tired.

I just got this stupid credit card bill in the mail. None of these outrageous charges are mine. I can't believe some big corporation like yours can't find a way to keep its records straight or keep its customers from being cheated. If you can't do any better than that, why don't you just give it up? I reported my stolen credit card five days before any of these charges were made, and yet you idiots have charged me for these purchases. The fine print you guys are so fond of putting in all of your contracts says I am not (I'll say it again just to help you understand) **not** responsible for these charges. I want them removed immediately.

The credit card bill I received on April 25 contains several charges that need to be removed. I reported my stolen credit card on April 20. When I called to make the report, the representative referred me to the original contract that states, "No charges in excess of $50.00 nor any made more than 24 hours after the card has been reported stolen shall be charged to the customer's account." Naturally, I was quite relieved. All of the charges on this account were made more than 24 hours after I reported the stolen card. Please remove the charges from my account. Thank you very much.

No matter how angry you might be, giving your reader the benefit of the doubt is not only polite but also more likely to get results. (This principle is even more important when you're writing a supervisor, employee, or client than when you're writing a big credit card company.) The first letter is the one you might write in the heat of the moment when you first get your credit card bill. In fact, writing that letter might help you get the anger out of your system. Tearing it up will make you feel even better. *Then* you can sit down and write the letter you're actually going to send—the second version.

Use *sarcasm* (bitter, derisive language) and *irony* (saying the opposite of what you actually mean) carefully in your writing. Like anger, sarcasm brings your credibility into question. Overusing sarcasm can make you seem childish or petty rather than reasonable and logical. Furthermore, for irony to be successful, the reader must immediately recognize it. Unless the reader fully understands, you risk confusing or distorting your message. A little well-placed irony or sarcasm may invigorate your writing, but it requires careful, skillful use.

Avoid Cuteness

Avoid words that make your writing sound flippant, glib, or cute. Although the writing may be entertaining to the reader, it might not be taken seriously. The following paragraph protests a decision, but fails to offer a single reason why the decision was wrong. It may get the attention of the reader, but it won't produce any results, except perhaps the dismissal of its author.

> I'm just a li'l ol' girl, but it's clear to me that this decision is dead wrong. I'm afraid that the people who made it have a serious intelligence problem. If they took their two IQ points and rubbed them together, they probably couldn't start gasoline on fire. If you were one of those people . . . Oh well, it's been nice working for you.

The conclusion implied in this writer's last sentence—that she doesn't expect to work here much longer—is probably accurate.

Avoid Pompousness

Avoid words that make your writing sound pompous or preachy. Few people respond positively to a condescending, patronizing tone. Compare the following two paragraphs, both written by employees seeking a promotion. Which employee would you promote if they were both vying for the same position and had nearly identical work records and qualifications?

> If you examine my service and work record for the past two years, I believe you will find a dedicated, hardworking employee who is ideal for the floor manager position. I believe all employees should be on time for their jobs. You will see that my attendance record is impeccable, no absences and no tardies. You can see from my monthly evaluations that I was a high-quality employee when I was hired and that I have consistently maintained my high standards. I strive to be the kind of employee all managers wish to hire, and I believe my record shows this. I am also extremely responsible. Again, my record will reflect that my supervisors have confidence in me and assign additional responsibility readily to me because I am someone who can handle it. I am a man of my word, and I believe that responsibility is something to be treasured, not shirked. As you compare me with other employees, I feel confident that you will find I am the most competent person available.

> Thank you for considering me for the position of floor manager. As you make your decision, I would like to highlight three items from my service and work record. First, in two years, I have not missed work and have been tardy only once, as the result of an accident. Second, my supervisors have given me the highest ratings on each of the monthly evaluations. Finally, I was pleased to have been given additional responsibilities during my supervisors' vacation times, and I learned a great deal about managing sales and accounts as a result. I welcome the challenge that would come with a promotion. Thank you again for your consideration.

Both writers highlight the same aspects of their employment records. Yet the first writer seems so full of himself that his superiors might wonder whether he has the people skills to be an effective supervisor. No one wants to work for a supervisor who is prone to such pronouncements as "responsibility is something to be treasured, not shirked." The other writer's just-the-facts approach is bound to make a better impression on the decision makers.

Avoid Cheap Emotion

Avoid language that is full of sentimentality or cheap emotion. You risk making your reader gag. The following paragraph illustrates this error.

We were so deeply hurt by your cruel thoughtlessness in failing to introduce us to Jack Nicholson. He is the most wonderful, talented actor to have ever walked the face of the earth. My friend Charlotte and I so admire him and have ever since we can remember. Our admiration is a deep-channeled river that will never stop flowing. I'm sure you can imagine just how sorely disappointed and deeply wounded we were when we were not given the opportunity and honor to shake the hand and hear the voice of this great man. Neither I nor my dearest friend can seem to forget this slight, and I'm sure we will remain scarred for many years to come.

Are you gagging yet? Instead of regretting not having introduced the writer to the great Jack Nicholson, the reader probably congratulates himself on not having let this nut case get near him.

Consistent Point of View

Authors can write using the first-person point of view (*I, me, we, us, my, our*), second-person point of view (*you, your*), or third-person point of view (*she, he, one, they, her, him, them, hers, his, one's, theirs*). Avoid switching points of view within or between sentences. Keep the point of view consistent throughout.

INCONSISTENT	CONSISTENT
Citizens pay taxes, which entitles them [third person] to have some say in how their [third person] government is run. We [first person] have a right to insist on efficient use of our tax dollars.	We citizens pay taxes, which entitles us to have some say in how our government is run. We have a right to insist on efficient use of our tax dollars.
I [first person] enjoyed my trip to the park. You [second person] could see trees budding, flowers blooming, and baby animals running all over.	I enjoyed my trip to the park. I saw trees budding, flowers blooming, and baby animals running all over.

Parallelism

Two or more equivalent ideas in a sentence that have the same purpose should be presented in the same form. This is called *parallel structure*. Using parallel sentence structures not only helps your writing flow smoothly, but also helps readers quickly recognize similar ideas. Look at the following examples of parallel words, phrases, and clauses.

NOT PARALLEL	PARALLEL
My roommate is miserly, sloppy, and a bore.	My roommate is miserly, sloppy, and boring. My roommate is a miser, a slob, and a bore.
My vacuum cleaner squealed loudly, shook violently, and dust filled the air.	My vacuum cleaner squealed loudly, shook violently, and filled the air with dust.
We soon discovered that our plane tickets were invalid, that our cruise reservations had never been made, and our travel agent left town.	We soon discovered that our plane tickets were invalid, that our cruise reservations had never been made, and that our travel agent had left town.

Pairs of ideas should always be presented in parallel constructions. The following sentences present two or more equivalent ideas using similar forms.

> The committee finds no original and inspiring ideas in your proposal. What is original is not inspiring, and what is inspiring is not original.
> We came, we saw, we conquered.
> Belle was a timid, talented, and creative person.
> Ask not what your country can do for you; ask what you can do for your country.

Using Gender-Neutral Language

It may seem that language is neutral, simply a tool for expressing ideas. Although this is partly true, our language reflects our values and communicates to others our social biases about gender and other issues. If an entire culture is gender-biased, the language automatically becomes a vehicle for expressing and perpetuating those biases. One of the first steps toward overcoming such a prejudice is to examine the language and change it so that it no longer perpetuates false stereotypes about gender.

Some people resist changing the language, thinking that the words are harmless and that those who are offended are simply too sensitive. The fact remains that many readers are sensitive to, and offended by, the traditional use of masculine pronouns to refer to both sexes or by diminutive suffixes indicating gender. Saying, "Man must fulfill his destiny" or "Emily Dickinson was a great poetess" strikes them as archaic at best and insulting at worst.

Whenever emotionally charged words distract a reader, the message suffers. A reader who is offended by the words won't get the meaning.

Gender Traps

The following are samples of the type of language to avoid because the emotional charge may sidetrack the ideas.

Masculine Nouns or Pronouns

The most serious difficulty comes when using pronouns. If the pronoun *he* is used to refer to an indefinite person—a teacher, a student, a postal carrier—the underlying assumption seems to be that all teachers or students or postal carriers are male. The same problem comes up with words such as *someone, somebody, everyone, no one,* or *nobody*. Here are some examples of gender traps in sentences and possible ways to revise them.

POOR	BETTER
A presidential candidate must realize that his life is no longer his own.	Presidential candidates must realize that their lives are not their own.
If a student wishes to change his schedule, he must see his advisor, who will tell him how to proceed.	a) If a student wishes to change his or her schedule, he or she must see his or her advisor, who will tell him or her how to proceed. [This sentence solves the mismatching number problem by using both a masculine and a feminine singular pronoun. However, the writing seems awkward and unwieldy.]
	b) If students wish to change their schedule, they must see their advisor, who will tell them how to proceed. [In this sentence, making the noun *student* into plural *students* solves the pronoun mismatch problem.]
	c) If you wish to change your schedule, see your advisor, who will tell you how to proceed. [This sentence uses the second-person pronouns "you" and "your."]
If anyone wants to improve his test scores, he should take good notes and study.	a) Anyone who wants improved test scores should take good notes and study. [Restructure the sentence to avoid the pronoun reference.]
	b) Students who want to improve their test scores should take good notes and study. [Turn *anyone* into the plural *students*.]
	c) Anyone who wants to improve his or her test scores should take good notes and study. [Use both the masculine and feminine singular pronouns.]

Note that you cannot simply change the words *he* and *his* to *they* and *theirs*. "If anyone wants to improve their test scores, they should good take notes and study" is grammatically incorrect. The pronouns *they* and *their* don't match their antecedent, anyone, in number, because *anyone* is singular and *they* is plural.

Women as Subordinate to Men

Writers can make it seem as if men are always leaders and women are always subordinate in many subtle ways.

POOR	BETTER
A principal and his staff need to establish good communication.	The principal and staff need to establish good communication.
If you ask the nurse, she will summon the doctor if he is available.	If you ask, a nurse will summon an available doctor.
Bob took his wife and children to a movie.	Bob and Mary took their children to a movie.
Emil asked his secretary to check the mail.	Emil asked the secretary to check the mail.

Writers also fall into a similar kind of trap when they refer to men according to their abilities, while referring to women according to their appearance.

POOR	BETTER
Dr. Routmeir and his attractive, blond wife arrived at the party at 9:00 P.M.	a) Dr. and Ms. Routmeir arrived at the party at 9:00 P.M. b) Herman and Betty Routmeir arrived at the party at 9:00 P.M.
The talented violinist and his beautiful accompanist took the stage.	The violinist and the accompanist took the stage.

Note that in both sentences in the first column, the man is referred to by his profession, while the woman is referred to by her appearance. To avoid the appearance of assigning value to men because of their accomplishments and to women because of their appearance, refer to both in the same context, either physical or professional. Furthermore, in the first example, the man is addressed by a formal title, and the woman is not identified except as the wife belonging to the man. To avoid the appearance of referring to the woman strictly as the possession of the man, refer to both by name.

"Men's" Jobs and "Women's" Jobs

Avoid making special note of gender when discussing a job traditionally done by men or women—those traditions don't hold anymore! The first sentence makes traditional assumptions, while the second does not.

> When a man on board collapsed, a lady pilot emerged from the cockpit, and a male nurse offered assistance.
>
> When a passenger collapsed, a pilot emerged from the cockpit, and a nurse offered assistance.

The references *lady pilot* and *male nurse* call attention to themselves because they assume that the reader will automatically assign a gender to the job. Readers who do not think in terms of the traditional stereotypes will be offended by the writer's assumption that they do engage in stereotypical thinking.

Avoiding Gender Traps

As a writer, you must understand the effect of gender references on readers. You can avoid offending readers unintentionally with gender-specific language in three ways: using gender-neutral terms, using the plural, or restructuring sentences altogether to avoid a gender reference. All these tactics have already been illustrated in the previous revised sentences. More examples appear next.

Use Gender-Neutral Terms

There are a lot of words in English that traditionally have taken different forms for male and female persons. These distinctions are becoming obsolete. Today, most people prefer one term to refer to both men and women in their particular roles. And this change doesn't have to be awkward, as you can see in the following table.

In the past, it was common to use the word *man* to refer to all humanity, both men and women. Today, that usage will offend many readers. The following sentence demonstrates this kind of usage while the second one offers a more appropriate alternative.

> If man wishes to improve his environment, he must improve himself.
> If humanity wishes to improve its environment, each individual must improve.

Convert to the Plural

One of the stickiest gender-reference problems is how to deal with a sentence such as "A student must do *his* homework if *he* wants to succeed in *his* classes." The easiest way to avoid those troublesome *he* words is to turn the singular pronouns *he, she, him, hers,* or *his* into the plural pronouns *they* and *their.* Of course, then you must also revise the antecedents of those pronouns so they are also plural (see Lesson 13): "*Students* must do *their* homework if *they* want to succeed in *their* classes." The table on the next page offers some other examples.

GENDER-SPECIFIC	GENDER-NEUTRAL
waiter, waitress	server
stewardess, steward	flight attendant
policeman, policewoman	police officer
chairwoman, chairman	chairperson, chair
man-made	synthetic, artificial
foreman	supervisor
manpower	employees, personnel
man, mankind	humanity, people

GENDER-SPECIFIC	GENDER-NEUTRAL
The doctor uses his best judgment.	Doctors use their best judgment.
Every student must do his homework.	Students must do their homework.
A company executive is wise to choose his words carefully.	Company executives are wise to choose their words carefully.
If a manager wants respect, he should behave respectably.	Managers who want respect should behave respectably.

Restructure Sentences to Avoid Gender Reference

Finally, you can avoid gender references altogether by restructuring your sentences. See how this is done in the following examples.

GENDER-SPECIFIC	GENDER-NEUTRAL
Man has always turned to his intellect to solve problems.	People have always turned to their intellect to solve problems.
A company executive is wise to drive himself relentlessly.	Anyone who desires success must work relentlessly.
A nurse must take her job seriously.	A nurse must take the job seriously.
Someone left his umbrella in the cloakroom. He should call Lost and Found.	The person who left an umbrella in the cloakroom should call Lost and Found.
The ladies enjoyed the shopping trip.	The shoppers enjoyed their trip.

TIP

Pay close attention to the tone and style of everything you write or read. Is the degree of formality appropriate for the message and the audience? Do you sense emotional overload? Is the point of view consistent? Are equivalent ideas presented equally? Does the writing contain gender references? If so, are they likely to offend the reader?

  COMMUNICATING YOUR IDEAS

Often when I write I am trying to make words do the work of line and color. I have the painter's sensitivity to light. Much (and perhaps the best) of my writing is verbal painting.

—ELIZABETH BOWEN, Irish novelist (1899–1973)

LESSON SUMMARY

The previous lessons have dealt with words and sentences. This final lesson is about the bigger issues involved in a piece of writing as a whole. By focusing on the purpose of your writing, you can develop your ideas in a logical, effective way to have the biggest possible impact on your readers.

Mastering writing detail is important, but the main purpose of writing is to communicate a message with a specific purpose to an audience. Most writing does one of three things: inform, explain, or present an argument. Writing effectively involves discovering what you want to say, organizing your ideas, and presenting them in the most logical, effective way. This lesson discusses all of these issues.

Writing to Inform

Good, informational writing is clear, simple, and orderly. In business writing, it's important to get right to the point. No one has time to spend reading your warm-ups, the words you write while you're trying to get to the point. The best communications state the point directly and present the information clearly.

However, sometimes getting started is difficult. Ask yourself a few key questions to help clarify your thoughts and get to the point.

1. Summarize the main idea of your communication in a single sentence. If you can do this, the rest of the writing will come more easily. State it as simply and clearly as possible. If your communication presents a list of information, facts, or statistics, try summarizing the purpose of the information. The sentence should answer the question: Why am I writing this?

2. Next, think about your audience. Who will be reading your writing? What is your relationship with the audience: superior, colleague, customer? Thinking about the audience helps you use an appropriate tone or attitude.

3. Brainstorm all the information that must be included in the communication. This can be in the form of a list or a piece of paper with words and pictures connected by lines; use whatever works best for you. Get all the information down on paper where you can look at it.

4. Once the information is assembled, think about the most efficient way to organize it. Think about your message as a train of thought, one in which all the parts are connected. How can you organize the information in such a way that connections seem easy and natural? Consider these organizational patterns:

   - Spatial order: the order in which items are arranged in relationship to each other
   - Chronological order: time order
   - Logical order: begin with the most basic premise, follow with what can be derived from the premise
   - General to specific: begin with a general statement, arrive at a specific fact
   - Specific to general: arrive at a generalization from a series of specific facts

5. Now it's time to start writing. Begin with a sentence or short paragraph that states the purpose of the communication, revising what you came up with in Step 1 now that you know what your main points are.

6. Develop each of the ideas you identified in Steps 3 and 4 in a single paragraph. If the supporting ideas can be presented as effectively in list form as they can in sentence form, use a bulleted or numbered list similar to this one, which outlines organizational patterns. Stick to one idea in each paragraph, and keep the paragraphs as short and concise as possible.

If you're writing for business, use numbered and bulleted lists like the previous ones. Strive for a clear, logical presentation, one that is well organized and free of excess words that say nothing. Here's a map of one writer's organizational process in responding to a request: the planning, the organization, the main idea, the audience, and the completed memo.

The Planning

Main idea: Ms. Rhinehart has asked for information about our accounting staff (how many, job titles, and levels) and justification for the personnel requests we made.

Purpose: Provide the information so the department can hire additional staff.

Audience: Ms. Rhinehart, vice-president and chief financial officer

I. Data
   A. Current senior staff
      1. One accounting manager
      2. Two senior accountants
      3. Three senior accounts receivable managers
      4. Three senior payroll managers
   B. Current entry-level staff
      1. One assistant to the accounting manager
      2. One assistant to the senior accountants
      3. One assistant to the accounts receivable managers
      4. One assistant to the payroll managers

II. Requests
  A. Additional entry-level staff
    1. Three assistants to provide support to senior accountants, accounts receivable managers, and payroll managers
    2. One assistant to rotate throughout the department as needed
    3. Reason: The acquisition of the new company has doubled the department's workload. At the moment, senior staff members, with high salaries, are spending too much time on entry-level work. Hiring new assistants will allow senior staff to delegate much of this work and return their focus to more complicated projects.
  B. Promoting current staff
    1. Promote assistant to the accounting manager to executive assistant
    2. Reason: In addition to assistant to the accounting manager, the executive assistant can also oversee all department assistants, again relieving the senior staff workload.

The Memo

To: Ms. Rhinehart
From: Allie Leonard
Re: Staff assessment and needs of accounting department as requested
Date: July 7, 2009

I am providing the information you requested about the accounting staff. I am also outlining our requests for hiring additional staff and the reasons for these requests.

This is the staff, both senior and entry-level, that we have at this time.

- One accounting manager and one assistant to the accounting manager
- Two senior accountants and one assistant to the two senior accountants
- Three senior accounts receivable managers and one assistant to the three accounts receivable managers
- Three senior payroll managers and one assistant to the three senior payroll managers

Due to the acquisition of the new company, the accounting department's workload has doubled, and senior staff members are spending too much time performing tasks that can be handled by assistants. We are requesting four more assistants for our department as well as the promotion of one of the existing assistants. One assistant would work with the senior accountant, another would work with the accounts receivable managers, one would assist the payroll managers, and the fourth assistant would rotate as necessary throughout the department. Additionally, we request the promotion of the existing assistant to the accounting manager to executive assistant to the entire department. In this capacity, she will assist the accounting manager as well as oversee all department assistants. These changes will allow the senior staff to focus their time and energy on crucial high-level projects that are currently being ignored.

Thank you for considering our request.

Writing to Explain

Another form of writing you're likely to use often is explanation. You may need to provide reasons for an action or policy, or you may need to explain how a product is used.

For this type of writing, follow the same planning process as you would for a written communication designed to present information.

1. Summarize the main idea and purpose.
2. Determine the audience.
3. Brainstorm ideas.
4. Organize the ideas.
5. Begin by stating the purpose.
6. Develop the ideas in paragraphs.

Keep these tips in mind as you write.

- Present the steps in a logical order. Chronological order is usually best for a process.
- Be certain you've explained each step clearly, accurately, and thoroughly enough so readers can understand.
- Use the facts and examples to support each of your points.
- Pay special attention to the introduction and conclusion. These two paragraphs lay the foundation for understanding and give the reader a quick review of the information you've just presented. Make the beginning and ending paragraphs work for you.

Here's a real-world example: It outlines the planning a writer did before drafting a letter to a customer explaining how to operate a new copy machine.

Main idea: Explain how to use a new copy machine to new customers

Audience: Members of promotional staff at KCBD-TV, all of whom use the copier

Purposes: (1) Clearly explain use, (2) clearly outline maintenance procedures, (3) provide basic troubleshooting suggestions, (4) assure them that the copier is reliable and that service is quick, should they need it.

I. Daily use
   A. Copying
   B. Enlarging/reducing
   C. Handling multiple-page documents
II. Maintenance
   A. Routine
      1. Loading paper
      2. Adding toner
      3. Clearing paper jams
   B. Troubleshooting
      1. Electrical problems
      2. Paper jams
      3. Failure to copy
   C. Calling the technician
      1. Business day number
      2. Emergency service
III. Reliability
   A. Warranties
   B. Weekly maintenance checks
   C. Service
   D. Two-hour replacement guarantee

First paragraph: Everyone in the promotional department at KCBD-TV will find this new Sharp copy machine a huge improvement over the older model. You'll appreciate how easy it is to use this new copier for daily tasks, and anyone can perform the routine maintenance on the machine. This, our most reliable copier, is backed by a long-term warranty and a quick, efficient service plan.

Writing to Persuade

The other most common type of writing involves presenting a clear, convincing argument. Your written communication may be a single message, or it may be the first in a series of exchanges that will eventually result in a compromise. Each type of argument requires a different approach; however, both kinds of persuasive communications must have three common characteristics: logical order, solid support, and credibility.

Logical Order

Even the brightest and best ideas make no impact if a reader cannot recognize or follow them. Arguments must be carefully organized to create the desired effect on the reader.

The strongest positions are the beginning and the ending of a communication. Place your strongest argument in one position or the other and arrange the rest in such a way that they can be clearly stated and easily linked together.

Solid Support

Good persuasion not only makes a clear, strong claim but also proves the claim with solid support. Here are some ways to support your assertions:

- **Examples**, either personal or researched.
- **Objective evidence**, such as facts and statistics.
- **Citing an authority**. Use a qualified, timely authority whose opinions are applicable to your special situations. If the reader is not familiar with the authority, explain why the person is qualified.
- **Analogy**. If you can think of a clear comparison with which the reader is automatically familiar, present the comparison clearly. Carefully point out all the similarities and explain why the comparison is useful and applicable.

If you are supporting a moral or emotional claim, use logic or emotional appeals made with vivid description and concrete language.

Credibility

A written communication is *credible* if the reader believes the writer or finds the writer trustworthy. Regardless of the history between the writer and reader, each communication provides a fresh opportunity to establish credibility.

In any communication, you can establish credibility in one of three ways:

1. **Demonstrate your knowledge of the subject.** Show that you have personal experience that makes your perspective on the subject reliable. If you have no personal experience from which to draw, show that you have consulted a variety of reliable, neutral sources and that your views are based on your research.
2. **Demonstrate fairness and objectivity.** Show that you have taken into account all of the significant viewpoints. Convince your reader that you understand and value other perspectives on the subject and that you see their merit. Show that you have carefully considered all of the evidence, even that which does not support your point of view.
3. **Seek areas of agreement.** This is especially valuable if your communication is the beginning of a process that will result in a compromise. Find out what the viewpoints have in common and begin building trust and credibility on common ground.

Use the same six steps outlined on page 182 to plan a persuasive communication. Examine the following writer's plan for a written communication that argues in favor of a new scheduling policy.

Claim: Store needs a better system for scheduling employees.
Audience: Store's general manager
Purposes: (1) Point out problems inherent in the current policy, (2) outline the qualities a new scheduling policy should have, (3) point out the advantages

of a scheduling policy with those qualities, (4) show that customers will receive better service, (5) show that employees understand and are willing to share the burden of developing and implementing a new policy.

I. Problems with current policy
   A. Based solely upon seniority
   B. Arbitrary within seniority brackets
   C. Equal number for all shifts
      1. Doesn't allow for employees willing to be flexible
      2. Not enough employees during peak sales times
      3. Too many employees during off-peak sales times
      4. Leads to minimal employee commitment
   D. No incentive for good attendance
II. Qualities of an effective scheduling policy
   A. Continues to take seniority into account
   B. Allows for individual preferences
   C. Allows for flex time
   D. Allows for increased numbers during peak times, reduced numbers during off times
   E. Provides an incentive for reliable attendance
   F. Provides an incentive to work least desirable hours

III. Advantages of a policy with these characteristics
   A. Improved customer service
      1. Better service during peak times
      2. Quality service during off-peak times
   B. Less absenteeism
   C. Improved employee morale
   D. Sense of ownership among employees
IV. Development and implementation
   A. Management responsibilities
   B. Employee responsibilities
      1. Committee willing to develop plan during unpaid time
      2. Willing to assume some responsibility for implementation

First paragraph: Since we value customer service, our store needs to develop a scheduling system that will provide better customer service, while at the same time fostering an increased sense of commitment among employees.

Whenever you write, keep in mind that you want to present your message as clearly and simply as possible. Write to *express*, not to *impress*. The words should deliver the message, not get in the way of it.

TIP

Write a memo asking for a raise. If you can do that, you know the time you've spent with this book has been worth your while. Go ahead, do it. Worst case scenario: Whoever reads the memo will speak or write back and deny the request. Even if this happens, your writing will have made an impression. If you presented a few good arguments, they'll stick in your supervisor's mind even if you don't get the raise. The next one will come sooner than it would have if you hadn't written the memo. Best case scenario: You get a raise. How can you lose? Even if you don't send the memo, write it. It will build your confidence, and maybe you'll send it at a more opportune time. You can think about it, revise it, add to it, and then send it.

Whenever you have an idea you want to be taken seriously, write a memo. It won't be long before people begin to notice that you have the power of the pen. A word of caution: Some people are intimidated by others who can write, and they may even try to discourage you. Don't let them. Just use softer words when you write, and write to them often. In time, they will come to appreciate your ideas and your ability.

Review

Now that you've gone through the lessons and are just about ready to take your posttest, how about a warm-up quiz first? Review the following essay, and see how many grammatical mistakes you can identify and fix. Good luck!

Problem

During our weekend trip to Connecticut, we drove down to the coastline to visit a little town called mystic. It was a great place to see the bright colors of autumn leaves, we found plenty to do on an October saturday.

We visited the Mystic Seaport an outdoor museum that recreates a 19th century fishing village. Full of historic buildings and activities. We went onboard the *star eagle* a replica of an 18th-century cutter ship used by the U.S. coast guard. While at the seaport, we also watched a woman make johnnycakes a staple of colonial New England cuisine and learned how to make proper sailors knots.

After we left the seaport, we drove threw town and visited another famous landmark mystic pizza, the restaurant from the Julia Roberts Movie Mystic Pizza. No colonial cooking here And no Julia Roberts, either, but there where pictures of the films cast and crew adorning the walls. The pizza was tasty and we followed it with desert from the nearby Mystic drawbridge ice cream shop. All in all, it was a very fun day.

Solution

During our weekend trip to Connecticut, we drove down to the coastline to visit a little town called <u>Mystic</u>. It was a great place to see the bright colors of autumn leaves<u>, and</u> we found plenty to do on an October <u>Saturday</u>.

We visited the Mystic Seaport, an outdoor museum that recreates a <u>19th-century</u> fishing <u>village full</u> of historic buildings and activities. We went onboard the <u>*Star Eagle*</u>, a replica of an 18th-century cutter ship used by the U.S. <u>Coast Guard</u>. While at the seaport, we also watched a woman make johnnycakes <u>(a staple of colonial New England cuisine)</u> and learned how to make proper <u>sailor's</u> knots.

After we left the seaport, we drove <u>through</u> town and visited another famous <u>landmark: Mystic Pizza</u>, the restaurant from the Julia Roberts <u>movie *Mystic Pizza*</u>. No colonial cooking <u>here!</u> And no Julia Roberts, either, but there <u>were</u> pictures of the cast and crew adorning the walls. The pizza was <u>tasty</u>, and we followed it with dessert from the nearby Mystic <u>Drawbridge</u> ice cream shop. All in all, it was a very fun <u>day!</u>

Posttest ▶

Now that you've spent a good deal of time improving your grammar and writing skills, take this posttest to see how much you've learned. If you took the pretest at the beginning of this book, you have a good way to compare what you knew when you started the book with what you know now.

When you complete this test, grade yourself, and then compare your score with your score on the pretest. If your score now is much greater, congratulations—you've profited noticeably from your hard work. If your score shows little improvement, perhaps you should review certain chapters. Do you notice a pattern to the types of questions you got wrong? Whatever you score on this posttest, keep this book around for review and refer to it when you are unsure of a grammatical rule.

There's an answer sheet you can use for filling in the correct answers on page 191. Or, if you prefer, simply circle the answer numbers in this book. If the book doesn't belong to you, write the numbers 1–50 on a piece of paper, and record your answers there. Take as much time as you need to do this short test. When you finish, check your answers against the answer key that follows. Each answer tells you which lesson of this book teaches you about the grammatical rule in that question.

1.	ⓐ	ⓑ	ⓒ	ⓓ
2.	ⓐ	ⓑ	ⓒ	ⓓ
3.	ⓐ	ⓑ	ⓒ	ⓓ
4.	ⓐ	ⓑ	ⓒ	ⓓ
5.	ⓐ	ⓑ	ⓒ	ⓓ
6.	ⓐ	ⓑ	ⓒ	ⓓ
7.	ⓐ	ⓑ	ⓒ	ⓓ
8.	ⓐ	ⓑ	ⓒ	ⓓ
9.	ⓐ	ⓑ	ⓒ	ⓓ
10.	ⓐ	ⓑ	ⓒ	ⓓ
11.	ⓐ	ⓑ	ⓒ	ⓓ
12.	ⓐ	ⓑ	ⓒ	ⓓ
13.	ⓐ	ⓑ	ⓒ	ⓓ
14.	ⓐ	ⓑ	ⓒ	ⓓ
15.	ⓐ	ⓑ	ⓒ	ⓓ
16.	ⓐ	ⓑ	ⓒ	ⓓ
17.	ⓐ	ⓑ	ⓒ	ⓓ

18.	ⓐ	ⓑ	ⓒ	ⓓ
19.	ⓐ	ⓑ	ⓒ	ⓓ
20.	ⓐ	ⓑ	ⓒ	ⓓ
21.	ⓐ	ⓑ	ⓒ	ⓓ
22.	ⓐ	ⓑ	ⓒ	ⓓ
23.	ⓐ	ⓑ	ⓒ	ⓓ
24.	ⓐ	ⓑ	ⓒ	ⓓ
25.	ⓐ	ⓑ	ⓒ	ⓓ
26.	ⓐ	ⓑ	ⓒ	ⓓ
27.	ⓐ	ⓑ	ⓒ	ⓓ
28.	ⓐ	ⓑ	ⓒ	ⓓ
29.	ⓐ	ⓑ	ⓒ	ⓓ
30.	ⓐ	ⓑ	ⓒ	ⓓ
31.	ⓐ	ⓑ	ⓒ	ⓓ
32.	ⓐ	ⓑ	ⓒ	ⓓ
33.	ⓐ	ⓑ	ⓒ	ⓓ
34.	ⓐ	ⓑ	ⓒ	ⓓ

35.	ⓐ	ⓑ	ⓒ	ⓓ
36.	ⓐ	ⓑ	ⓒ	ⓓ
37.	ⓐ	ⓑ	ⓒ	ⓓ
38.	ⓐ	ⓑ	ⓒ	ⓓ
39.	ⓐ	ⓑ	ⓒ	ⓓ
40.	ⓐ	ⓑ	ⓒ	ⓓ
41.	ⓐ	ⓑ	ⓒ	ⓓ
42.	ⓐ	ⓑ	ⓒ	ⓓ
43.	ⓐ	ⓑ	ⓒ	ⓓ
44.	ⓐ	ⓑ	ⓒ	ⓓ
45.	ⓐ	ⓑ	ⓒ	ⓓ
46.	ⓐ	ⓑ	ⓒ	ⓓ
47.	ⓐ	ⓑ	ⓒ	ⓓ
48.	ⓐ	ⓑ	ⓒ	ⓓ
49.	ⓐ	ⓑ	ⓒ	ⓓ
50.	ⓐ	ⓑ	ⓒ	ⓓ

Posttest

1. Which of the following is a sentence fragment (not a complete sentence)?
   a. The memo was distributed on Friday.
   b. Although the managers and the support staff had been called.
   c. The company was being acquired by a large corporation.
   d. Be sure to attend the meeting.

2. Which version is correctly capitalized?
   a. After we headed west on interstate 70, my uncle Paul informed us that his Ford Taurus was almost out of gas.
   b. After we headed west on Interstate 70, my Uncle Paul informed us that his Ford Taurus was almost out of gas.
   c. After we headed West on Interstate 70, my Uncle Paul informed us that his Ford Taurus was almost out of gas.
   d. After we headed West on interstate 70, my Uncle Paul informed us that his Ford taurus was almost out of gas.

3. Which version is punctuated correctly?
   a. That building, with the copper dome is our state capitol.
   b. That building with the copper dome, is our state capitol.
   c. That building, with the copper dome, is our state capitol.
   d. That building with the copper dome is our state capitol.

4. Which version is punctuated correctly?
   a. The temperature was 80 degrees at noon; by 6:00 P.M. it had dropped to below 40.
   b. The temperature was 80 degrees at noon, by 6:00 P.M. it had dropped to below 40.
   c. The temperature was 80 degrees at noon by 6:00 P.M., it had dropped to below 40.
   d. The temperature was 80 degrees at noon by 6:00 P.M. it had dropped to below 40.

5. Which version is punctuated correctly?
   a. It was one managers' idea to give us a month's vacation.
   b. It was one manager's idea to give us a months vacation.
   c. It was one manager's idea to give us a month's vacation.
   d. It was one managers idea to give us a month's vacation.

6. Which version is punctuated correctly?
   a. "Watch out! yelled the police officer. There's an accident ahead."
   b. "Watch out!" yelled the police officer. "There's an accident ahead."
   c. "Watch out"! yelled the police officer. "There's an accident ahead."
   d. "Watch out! yelled the police officer." "There's an accident ahead."

7. Which version used parentheses correctly?
   a. We celebrated one wedding anniversary (we'd been married five years at the time), by spending a week in Italy.
   b. We celebrated (one wedding anniversary) we'd been married five years at the time, by spending a week in Italy.
   c. We celebrated one wedding anniversary we'd been married five years at the time, (by spending a week in Italy).
   d. We celebrated one wedding anniversary we'd been married (five years at the time), by spending a week in Italy.

8. Choose the subject that agrees with the verb in the following sentence.

_____ of the musicians have arrived at the concert.

a. Each
b. Neither
c. One
d. Two

9. Which of the following sentences is most clearly and correctly written?
a. Bart told us all about the fish he caught while waiting in line at the movie theater.
b. At the movie theater, Bart told us about the fish he caught while we waited in line.
c. As we waited in line at the movie theater, Bart told us about the fish he caught.
d. As we waited in line, Bart told us about the fish he caught at the movie theater.

10. Which version is in the active voice?
a. The president of the P.T.A. requested donations for the new auditorium.
b. For the new auditorium, donations had been requested by the P.T.A. president.
c. Donations for the new auditorium were requested by the president of the P.T.A.
d. Donations were requested by the P.T.A. president for the new auditorium.

11. Which version has a consistent point of view?
a. Last Sunday, we went canoeing on the Platte River. You could see bald eagles high in the trees above us.
b. While we were canoeing last Sunday on the Platte River, high in the trees above us, you could see bald eagles.
c. We went canoeing last Sunday on the Platte River, and high in the trees above us, we could see bald eagles.
d. High in the trees above, the bald eagles were looking down at you, as we canoed on the Platte River last Sunday.

12. Which version uses punctuation correctly?
a. Help! Do you know where I can find a babysitter on such short notice.
b. Help! Do you know where I can find a babysitter on such short notice?
c. Help? Do you know where I can find a babysitter on such short notice!
d. Help: Do you know where I can find a babysitter on such short notice?

13. Which of the underlined words in the following sentence should be capitalized?

My <u>brother</u> has been teaching <u>history</u> at the <u>university</u> of California since last <u>fall</u>.

a. Brother
b. History
c. University
d. Fall

For questions 14 and 15, choose the correct verb form.

14. When she was asked which employee should be promoted, Ms. Garcia _____ Caroline Martin.
  a. has chosen
  b. choosed
  c. choose
  d. chose

15. The snow _____ to fall late yesterday afternoon.
  a. began
  b. begun
  c. had began
  d. begins

16. Which version is most clearly and correctly written?
  a. Jeff told Nathan that his car battery was dead.
  b. When Jeff spoke to Nathan, he said his car battery was dead.
  c. Jeff told Nathan about his dead car battery.
  d. Jeff told Nathan that the battery in Nathan's car was dead.

For questions 17–19, choose the option that correctly completes the sentence.

17. The cat _____ in a patch of sun on the front porch.
  a. is laying
  b. is lying
  c. lays
  d. laid

18. When I heard the unusual sound, I _____ walked through the house and searched each room very _____.
  a. calmly, carefully
  b. calmly, careful
  c. calm, careful
  d. calm, carefully

19. I have _____ idea how these _____ got in my sweater.
  a. know, wholes
  b. know, holes
  c. no, holes
  d. no, wholes

20. Which of the following sentences contains a redundancy? (It repeats words that express the same idea.)
  a. Del shouted as loudly as he could, but no one heard him.
  b. Twenty minutes had passed before the fire trucks arrived.
  c. Yesterday, the senator made the same speech at three different locations.
  d. For a wide variety of different reasons, more people are using computers.

21. Which version has a parallel structure?
  a. He is a man of many talents. He repairs small machines, he cooks gourmet meals, and you should see his lilies and orchids.
  b. He is a man of many talents. There's a talent for repairing small machines, he cooks gourmet meals, and then there are the lilies and orchids.
  c. He is a man of many talents. He repairs small machines, he cooks gourmet meals, and he grows lilies and orchids.
  d. He is a man of many talents: repairing small machines, cooking gourmet meals, and he grows lilies and orchids.

22. Which of the following sentences contains a cliché?
  a. Looking for Harriet's ring was like searching for a needle in a haystack.
  b. The reason I can't have lunch with you is because I have a dentist appointment.
  c. The crooked fence looked like a row of teeth in need of braces.
  d. As costs go up, so do prices.

23. Which version uses periods correctly?
   a. T.J. McCloud and Dr Sheila Brown will represent the U.S. at the 3 PM ceremony.
   b. T.J. McCloud and Dr. Sheila Brown will represent the U.S. at the 3 P.M. ceremony.
   c. T.J. McCloud and Dr. Sheila Brown will represent the US at the 3 P.M. ceremony.
   d. TJ McCloud and Dr Sheila Brown will represent the U.S. at the 3 PM ceremony.

24. Which version is correctly capitalized?
   a. Many Meteorologists are predicting that the West will have the wettest winter on record.
   b. Many meteorologists are predicting that the west will have the wettest winter on record.
   c. Many Meteorologists are predicting that the West will have the wettest Winter on record.
   d. Many meteorologists are predicting that the West will have the wettest winter on record.

25. Three of the following sentences are either run-ons or comma splices. Which one is NOT?
   a. A group of lions is called a pride a group of elephants is called a herd.
   b. Josh told me he would meet us at the zoo at noon, he never showed up.
   c. We waited three hours, finally, Karen decided to give him a call.
   d. A young sheep is known as a lamb, but a young goat is known as a kid.

26. Which version is punctuated correctly?
   a. There are many reasons—aside from the obvious ones—why she is not the right person for this job.
   b. There are many reasons: aside from the obvious ones—why she is not the right person for this job.
   c. There are many reasons—aside from the obvious ones, why she is not the right person for this job.
   d. There are many reasons aside from the obvious ones—why she is not the right person for this job.

27. Which is the correct punctuation for the underlined portion?

   The explosion broke several windows in the <u>factory however</u> no one was injured.

   a. factory, however
   b. factory however;
   c. factory; however,
   d. factory, however;

28. Which version uses hyphens correctly?
   a. My soft-spoken brother-in-law did not raise his voice when he saw that his car had been damaged in the parking-lot.
   b. My soft spoken brother-in-law did not raise his voice when he saw that his car had been damaged in the parking-lot.
   c. My soft-spoken brother-in-law did not raise his voice when he saw that his car had been damaged in the parking lot.
   d. My soft-spoken brother in-law did not raise his voice when he saw that his car had been damaged in the parking lot.

29. Which version is punctuated correctly?
 a. Ms. Jeffers who is my physics teacher, coaches the girls' basketball team.
 b. Ms. Jeffers, who is my physics teacher, coaches the girls' basketball team.
 c. Ms. Jeffers who is my physics teacher coaches the girls' basketball team.
 d. Ms. Jeffers who, is my physics teacher, coaches the girls' basketball team.

For questions 30–34, choose the option that correctly completes the sentence.

30. Several manuals, each with detailed instructions, _____ with your new computer.
 a. were sent
 b. was sent
 c. has been sent
 d. sent

31. Jessica and _____ are looking in the grass for one of her earrings; _____ will be hard to find.
 a. me, it
 b. me, they
 c. I, they
 d. I, it

32. Yesterday, I _____ my watch on this table, but now _____ gone.
 a. set, it's
 b. set, its
 c. sat, its
 d. sat, it's

33. I didn't want Lisa's _____ because I knew she would tell me not to _____ the job.
 a. advice, except
 b. advice, accept
 c. advise, accept
 d. advise, except

34. Carlos _____ the basketball team because he had _____ many sports-related injuries.
 a. quite, too
 b. quite, to
 c. quit, to
 d. quit, too

35. Which version is punctuated correctly?
 a. The recreation center will show the following movies: *Charlotte's Web, Jungle Book,* and *Annie,* the cost will be $2.50 per ticket.
 b. The recreation center will show the following movies; *Charlotte's Web, Jungle Book,* and *Annie;* the cost will be $2.50 per ticket.
 c. The recreation center will show the following movies: *Charlotte's Web, Jungle Book,* and *Annie.* The cost will be $2.50 per ticket.
 d. The recreation center will show the following movies—*Charlotte's Web, Jungle Book,* and *Annie.* The cost will be $2.50 per ticket.

36. Which version is punctuated correctly?
 a. Excited about her European vacation Eva spent hours in the bookstore looking at travel guides.
 b. Excited about her European vacation, Eva, spent hours in the bookstore looking at travel guides.
 c. Excited about her European vacation, Eva spent hours in the bookstore looking at travel guides.
 d. Excited about her European vacation Eva spent, hours in the bookstore looking at travel guides.

37. Which version is punctuated correctly?
  a. The woman who lives across the street was born on July 4, 1922, in Washington, D.C.
  b. The woman, who lives across the street, was born on July 4, 1922, in Washington, D.C.
  c. The woman who lives across the street, was born on July 4, 1922 in Washington, D.C.
  d. The woman who lives across the street was born on July 4, 1922 in Washington D.C.

For question 38, choose the correct verb tense.

38. By next fall, I _____ to all fifty of the United States.
  a. would be
  b. should have been
  c. will have been
  d. had been

39. Three of the following sentences are punctuated correctly. Which one is punctuated incorrectly?
  a. My son's baseball game was postponed; it was raining too hard.
  b. Because it was raining too hard; my son's baseball game was postponed.
  c. My son's baseball game was postponed because it was raining too hard.
  d. It was raining too hard, and my son's baseball game was postponed.

40. Which of the following should NOT be hyphenated?
  a. one-fifteen in the morning
  b. the sixteenth-president of the United States
  c. a thirty-second commercial
  d. a thousand-dollar profit

41. In which of the following sentences is the underlined verb NOT in agreement with the subject of the sentence?
  a. There <u>is</u> only one store that sells that brand.
  b. Why <u>are</u> the girls on the team so excited?
  c. Here <u>are</u> the shoes I wanted to show you.
  d. What <u>is</u> the causes of her constant complaints?

42. In which of the following sentences is the underlined pronoun incorrectl?
  a. The teacher who won the award was <u>her</u>.
  b. <u>He and I</u> plan to visit you tomorrow.
  c. When can <u>she</u> come over for dinner?
  d. Both Michael and Steven will finish <u>their</u> homework early.

43. Which version is punctuated correctly?
  a. Dianes' completed forms aren't in our files.
  b. Diane's completed forms are'nt in our files.
  c. Diane's completed forms' aren't in our files.
  d. Diane's completed forms aren't in our files.

44. Which version is written correctly?
  a. <u>Friends'</u> was one of the most popular shows ever on television.
  b. *Friends* was one of the most popular shows ever on television.
  c. "Friends" was one of the most popular shows ever on television.
  d. FRIENDS was one of the most popular shows ever on television.

45. Which of the following sentences is in the passive voice?
  a. Every morning this week, Zeke brought bagels to work.
  b. Each day, he selected several different kinds.
  c. Generally, more than half of the bagels were eaten before 9:00.
  d. We've asked him to stop because we've all gained a few pounds.

46. We noticed the _____ of his cologne when he _____ in front of us.
   a. scent, past
   b. scent, passed
   c. sent, passed
   d. sent, past

47. Ian is the _____ of the triplets, but _____ all the members of his family, he is the only one with a talent for music.
   a. smallest, among
   b. smallest, between
   c. smaller, between
   d. smaller, among

48. _____ the person _____ found my wallet.
   a. Your, who
   b. Your, which
   c. You're, that
   d. You're, who

49. I _____ you thought he would be much older _____ I am.
   a. supposed, then
   b. suppose, then
   c. suppose, than
   d. supposed, than

50. Evan doesn't like chocolate; he _____ away his _____ of cake.
   a. through, piece
   b. through, peace
   c. threw, peace
   d. threw, piece

Answers

If you miss any of the answers, you can find help for that kind of question in the lesson shown to the right of the answer.

1. b. Lesson 3	**26. a.** Lesson 7
2. b. Lesson 1	**27. c.** Lesson 6
3. d. Lesson 4	**28. c.** Lesson 9
4. a. Lesson 5	**29. b.** Lesson 4
5. c. Lesson 7	**30. a.** Lesson 12
6. b. Lesson 8	**31. d.** Lesson 13
7. a. Lesson 9	**32. a.** Lesson 14
8. d. Lesson 12	**33. b.** Lesson 17
9. c. Lesson 15	**34. d.** Lesson 16
10. a. Lesson 11	**35. c.** Lesson 6
11. c. Lesson 19	**36. c.** Lesson 4
12. b. Lesson 2	**37. a.** Lesson 5
13. c. Lesson 1	**38. c.** Lesson 10
14. d. Lesson 10	**39. b.** Lesson 6
15. a. Lesson 10	**40. b.** Lesson 9
16. d. Lesson 13	**41. d.** Lesson 12
17. b. Lesson 14	**42. a.** Lesson 13
18. a. Lesson 15	**43. d.** Lesson 7
19. c. Lesson 17	**44. b.** Lesson 8
20. d. Lesson 18	**45. c.** Lesson 11
21. c. Lesson 19	**46. b.** Lesson 16
22. a. Lesson 18	**47. a.** Lesson 15
23. b. Lesson 2	**48. d.** Lesson 14
24. d. Lesson 1	**49. c.** Lesson 17
25. d. Lesson 3	**50. d.** Lesson 16

Answer Explanations

1. Choice **B** is correct. This sentence does have a subject (*the managers and the support staff*) and a verb phrase (*had been called*). However, one word changes everything: *Although* is a conjunction, which tells you that this is a dependent clause. This dependent clause cannot stand alone as a sentence, so it is a sentence fragment.

   Choice **A** is incorrect. This sentence has a subject (*The memo*) and a verb phrase (*was distributed*), so it is complete.

   Choice **C** is incorrect. The sentence has a subject (*the company*) and a verb phrase (*was being acquired*), with no elements left hanging. This is a complete sentence.

   Choice **D** is incorrect. This one is a bit trickier, as there seems to be a missing subject. However, in a case like this where the speaker is clearly addressing someone, *you* (or the listener) are the unspoken subject of the sentence. So if you look at the sentence as *You, be sure to attend the meeting*, it is complete.

2. Choice **B** is correct. *West* should be lowercase because it refers to a compass direction, not a particular region. *Uncle* should be capitalized because it is being used as part of his name. Finally, *Ford Taurus* is a brand name, which is always capitalized.

   Choice **A** is incorrect. *Interstate* should be capitalized, as it's the name of the highway. *Uncle* should be capitalized because it's being used as part of the uncle's name.

   Choice **C** is incorrect. *West* should not be capitalized because it refers to a compass direction here, not a specific place or geographic region.

   Choice **D** is incorrect. *West* should not be capitalized because it refers to a compass direction here, not a specific place or geographic region. *Taurus* is part of a brand name (it's the name of the car), so it should be capitalized.

3. Choice **D** is correct. Restrictive clauses (which contain information essential to the sentence) do not require commas, so the sentence is correct as written here.

   Choice **A** is incorrect. The comma is placed in a spot that creates two phrases that cannot stand on their own: *That building* and *with the copper dome is our state capitol* (which makes no sense on its own).

   Choice **B** is incorrect. The comma is placed in a spot that creates two phrases that cannot stand on their own: *That building with the copper dome* and *is our state capitol*. They make no sense when separated into two different thoughts by the comma.

   Choice **C** is incorrect. The comma placement suggests that the phrase *with the copper dome* is a nonrestrictive clause and could be removed from the sentence without changing its meaning. But without that phrase, how do you know which building *that* is?

4. Choice **A** is correct. Both *The temperature was 80 degrees at noon* and *by 6:00 P.M. it had dropped to below 40* are independent clauses. If there is no coordinating conjunction, a semicolon is needed to separate the two clauses.

   Choice **B** is incorrect. Using a comma instead of a semicolon to separate two independent clauses creates a comma splice, which is incorrect.

   Choice **C** is incorrect. With no punctuation at all to indicate a pause in the thought, this choice becomes a run-on sentence. The comma after *6 P.M.* is unnecessary and confusing.

   Choice **D** is incorrect. With no punctuation at all to indicate a pause in the thought, this choice becomes a run-on sentence.

5. Choice **C** is correct. Both *manager* and *month* are correctly treated as singular possessives (with the apostrophe before the *s*).

   Choice **A** is incorrect. The sentence tells you that it was one person's idea, but *managers'* (with the apostrophe following the *s*) is plural.

   Choice **B** is incorrect. *Manager's* is correct, but *months* is incorrectly plural when it should be possessive. (The sentence explicitly tells you that the time period in question is *a* month.)

   Choice **D** is incorrect. *Managers* is a plural noun, but the adjective *one* indicates that it should be singular.

6. Choice **B** is correct. The tag is separated from the quotation, and the punctuation marks are correctly placed within the quotation marks.

   Choice **A** is incorrect. This choice is missing quotation marks within the sentence to let the reader know where the police officer's direct quote begins and ends. *Yelled the police officer* is a tag, or a speaker identifier, which is separate from the actual quotation.

   Choice **C** is incorrect. End marks like exclamation points should always be placed within a quotation mark if they are part of the statement.

   Choice **D** is incorrect. The second quotation mark is placed incorrectly after *officer*. When you read the sentence, think about what makes sense for the quotation: is it likely that the speaker actually said, "yelled the police officer"? That can help you figure out where the quotation marks should be.

7. Choice **A** is correct. In this case, the parentheses surround a side comment that can be removed from the sentence without affecting its meaning. It offers extra information that isn't directly related to their trip to Italy.

   Choice **B** is incorrect. Parentheses are used to surround a side comment that is nonessential to the sentence's meaning. If you remove the parenthetical information in this sentence, you're left with an incomplete thought, so this choice is incorrect.

   Choice **C** is incorrect. Parentheses are used to surround a side comment that is nonessential to the sentence's meaning. If you remove the parenthetical information in this sentence, you're left with an incomplete thought, so this choice is incorrect.

   Choice **D** is incorrect. These parentheses are partly correct (they separate extra information about how long the couple had been married at the time), but they leave out part of the clause. *We'd been married* should be moved inside the parentheses to join the other additional information (*five years at the time*).

8. Choice **D** is correct. *Two* is a plural subject, so it agrees with the plural verb *have arrived*.

   Choice **A** is incorrect. *Each* is a singular pronoun, and the verb *have arrived* is plural, so the subject should be plural.

   Choice **B** is incorrect. N*either* is a singular pronoun, so is requires a singular verb. However, the verb *have arrived* is plural.

   Choice **C** is incorrect. *One* is a singular pronoun, and the verb *have arrived* is plural, so the subject should be plural.

9. Choice **C** is correct. This sentence is divided into two proper clauses: a dependent clause setting the scene (*As we waited in line at the movie theater*), and an independent clause describing the action (*Bart told us about the fish he caught*). It clearly expresses the actual meaning of the sentence.

   Choice **A** is incorrect. In this sentence, it's unclear whether Bart caught the fish while he was waiting in line at the theater, or if he was telling the story while waiting in line at the theater. The sentence should be rewritten for clarity.

Choice **B** is incorrect. In this sentence, it's unclear whether Bart caught the fish while he was waiting in line, or if he was telling the story while waiting in line at the theater. The sentence should be rewritten for clarity.

Choice **D** is incorrect. This sentence makes it sound like Bart caught the fish at the movie theater, which is not the correct meaning. The sentence should be rewritten for clarity.

10. Choice **A** is correct. The action verb *requested* makes it clear that this sentence is written in active voice.

    Choice **B** is incorrect. *Donations had been requested* contains a passive verb phrase because there are additional verbs separating the subject (*Donations*) and the active verb (*requested*).

    Choice **C** is incorrect. *Donations . . . were requested* contains a passive verb phrase because there is an additional verb separating the subject (*Donations*) and the active verb (*requested*).

    Choice **D** is incorrect. *Donations were requested* contains a passive verb phrase because there is an additional verb separating the subject (*Donations*) and the active verb (*requested*).

11. Choice **C** is correct. The perspective stays in the first person throughout the entire sentence (*we/us/we*).

    Choice **A** is incorrect. This choice starts with the first person (*We went canoeing . . .*), but then switches over to the second person (*You could see . . .*).

    Choice **B** is incorrect. This choice starts with the first person (*While we were canoeing . . .*), but then switches over to the second person (*you could see . . .*).

    Choice **D** is incorrect. This choice starts with the second person (*down at you . . .*), but then switches over to the first person (*we canoed . . .*).

12. Choice **B** is correct. Both the exclamation and the question have the appropriate punctuation.

    Choice **A** is incorrect. The sentence, *Do you know where I can find a babysitter on such short notice* is a question and should end with a question mark.

    Choice **C** is incorrect. *Help* is an interjection, not a question, and should end with an exclamation point. *Do you know where I can find a babysitter on such short notice* is a question for the reader, not an exclamatory statement.

    Choice **D** is incorrect. The question is punctuated correctly, but short interjections like *help* should end with an exclamation point.

13. Choice **C** is correct. If the sentence talked about *a* university or *the* university, the word would not be capitalized. But the sentence mentions a specific university, so *University* is part of the full name and should be capitalized.

    Choice **A** is incorrect. *Brother* is not used as a name here, so it should not be capitalized.

    Choice **B** is incorrect. *History* is a general subject in this case, not a specific class, so it should not be capitalized.

    Choice **D** is incorrect. *Fall* is used generically here to describe the season, so it should not be capitalized.

14. Choice **D** is correct. *Chose* is the correct past tense of the verb *choose* and agrees with the rest of the sentence.

    Choice **A** is incorrect. *Has chosen* is the present perfect tense, which expresses a past event in the present. However, the rest of the sentence is in the past tense, so the verb should be past tense as well.

    Choice **B** is incorrect. *Choosed* is not a word, so it does not correctly complete this sentence.

    Choice **C** is incorrect. *Choose* is a present tense verb, but the verb *was asked* is past tense. The two verbs must agree and both be in the past tense.

15. Choice **A** is correct. *Yesterday afternoon* tells you that the action takes place in the past, so a past tense verb is needed. *Began* is the correct past tense of the verb *begin*.

    Choice **B** is incorrect. *Begun* is the past participle of *begin*, not the past tense. The past participle is generally preceded by *has/have/had*, which is not part of this sentence.

    Choice **C** is incorrect. This is a past participial phrase, but it has the wrong past participle, so it does not correctly complete this sentence.

    Choice **D** is incorrect. *Yesterday afternoon* tells you that the action takes place in the past, so a past tense verb is needed. *Begins* is a present, not a past, tense verb.

16. Choice **D** is correct. It may seem like overkill to use Nathan's name twice in one sentence, but when both Nathan and Jeff could be the antecedent of the pronoun *he*, you need to be as specific as possible about who is doing what.

    Choice **A** is incorrect. The antecedent of the pronoun *his* is unclear in this sentence: Does *his* refer to the subject (*Jeff*) or the object (*Nathan*)? It's unclear whose car battery is dead.

    Choice **B** is incorrect. The antecedents of the pronouns *he* and *his* are unclear, so you don't know which person corresponds to what pronoun.

    Choice **C** is incorrect. The antecedent of the pronoun *his* is unclear: did Jeff tell Nathan about Jeff's dead car battery, or Nathan's dead car battery? There is no way to tell from the way this sentence is written.

17. Choice **B** is correct. *Lying* is the correct present participle of *lie*, which has the correct meaning to complete this sentence.

    Choice **A** is incorrect. While similar, *lay* actually means *to put* or *to set*, while *lie* means *to recline*. It's much more likely that the cat is *reclining* on the porch rather than being *set* on the porch, so *laying* is incorrect.

Choice **C** is incorrect. The present tense verb *lays* does not have the correct meaning in the context of this sentence.

Choice **D** is incorrect. *Laid* is the past participle of *lay*, which does not have the correct meaning in the context of this sentence.

18. Choice **A** is correct. Both of the blanks must be filled with adverbs because they modify two verbs (*walked* and *searched*). Both *calmly* and *carefully* are adverbs that correctly complete the sentence.

    Choice **B** is incorrect. Both of the blanks must be filled with adverbs because they modify two verbs (*walked* and *searched*). *Calmly* is an adverb, but *careful* is an adjective (it modifies a noun, not a verb), so it does not fit in the second blank.

    Choice **C** is incorrect. Both of the blanks must be filled with adverbs because they modify two verbs (*walked* and *searched*). *Calm* and *careful* are both adjectives, not adverbs.

    Choice **D** is incorrect. Both of the blanks must be filled with adverbs because they modify two verbs (*walked* and *searched*). *Carefully* is an adverb, but *calm* is an adjective, so it does not fit in the sentence.

19. Choice **C** is correct. *No* is used as an adjective to modify *idea*, and *holes* is the correct noun in the context of the sentence.

    Choice **A** is incorrect. The first blank must be filled with an adjective that describes *idea*. *Know* is a verb, so this choice can be eliminated. Also, *wholes* is not a real word.

    Choice **B** is incorrect. The first blank must be filled with an adjective that describes *idea*. *Know* is a verb, so this choice can be eliminated.

    Choice **D** is incorrect. While the adjective *no* is correct, *wholes* is not a real word, so it cannot correctly complete this sentence.

20. Choice **D** is correct. The quickest indicator of redundancy is when synonyms appear multiple times in a sentence, as with *variety* and *different* in this sentence. Both words are expressing the same thing. A less redundant sentence would read, *For a wide variety of reasons . . .* or *For different reasons. . . .*

    Choice **A** is incorrect. This sentence has two distinct ideas (that Del shouted as loudly as he could and that no one heard him), with no overlap.

    Choice **B** is incorrect. This sentence has no conflict or redundancy among any of its elements.

    Choice **C** is incorrect. This sentence has no conflict or redundancy among any of its elements.

21. Choice **C** is correct. The pronoun *he* is applied to each part of the sentence; also, the tenses are used consistently (*he is . . . he repairs . . . he cooks*).

    Choice **A** is incorrect. This sentence is not parallel; it uses the pronoun *he* to list his accomplishments, then switches to *you*, which changes the point of view from third person to second person.

    Choice **B** is incorrect. In a parallel sentence, the phrasing is similar for each clause. This sentence switches from the direct pronoun *he* to a passive voice that removes him from the action.

    Choice **D** is incorrect. This sentence is not parallel; the tense shifts from the present perfect (*repairing, cooking*) to the simple present (*grows*).

22. Choice **A** is correct. The *needle in a haystack* is a phrase we've all heard countless times to describe a task that is difficult, even though needles and haystacks have little to do with Harriet or her ring.

    Choice **B** is incorrect. A dentist's appointment may be an excuse, but it's not a common, overused expression.

    Choice **C** is incorrect. The fence and crooked teeth are simply a simile, or a comparison

based on the writer's observation. This is not a cliché.

    Choice **D** is incorrect. This is a statement that is more of a principle or a concept than a common phrase used to characterize an idea. It is not an example of a cliché.

23. Choice **B** is correct. T.J.'s name, the abbreviation *Dr.*, the abbreviation *U.S.*, and the abbreviation *P.M.* should all use periods.

    Choice **A** is incorrect. *Dr.* is an abbreviation and should always be followed by a period, as should abbreviations like *P.M.*

    Choice **C** is incorrect. The abbreviation *U.S.* must be contain periods.

    Choice **D** is incorrect. Initials in names (like *T.J.*) should always contain periods, as should *Dr.* (and other abbreviated titles) and the abbreviation *P.M.*

24. Choice **D** is correct. The only proper noun in the sentence is *West*, as it refers to a specific region and not just a compass direction.

    Choice **A** is incorrect. In this sentence, *meteorologists* refers to a generic group of meteorologists, not a specific title. Therefore, it is not a proper noun and should not be capitalized.

    Choice **B** is incorrect. Because *west* is referring to a specific region in this sentence (suggested by the use of *the*), it should be capitalized.

    Choice **C** is incorrect. *Meteorologists* is not a proper noun when the word is not part of a specific title, so it should not be capitalized. *Winter* should also not be capitalized when it describes the season in general.

25. Choice **D** is correct. There are two independent clauses joined by a comma and a conjunction (*but*), so the sentence is correct.

    Choice **A** is incorrect. This sentence is a run-on because it contains two independent clauses that are not separated with punctuation.

Choice **B** is incorrect. This sentence is a comma splice because it separates the two independent clauses with a comma, but no conjunction.

Choice **C** is incorrect. This sentence is a comma splice because it separates the two independent clauses with a comma, but no conjunction. *Finally* is not a coordinating conjunction.

26. Choice **A** is correct. The em-dashes are used to set off the speaker's own side comment and separate it from the rest of the sentence.

    Choice **B** is incorrect. The punctuation is uneven, and the colon is not correct. A leading em-dash should be inserted with a second em-dash when setting off a comment within a sentence.

    Choice **C** is incorrect. The punctuation is uneven and inconsistent. A leading em-dash should be followed by a second em-dash when setting off a comment within a sentence.

    Choice **D** is incorrect. While an em-dash can be used to create a dramatic pause in a sentence, there's no reason to pause in this spot. It separates the same idea into two unnecessarily different parts.

27. Choice **C** is correct. *However* is a conjunctive adverb, which should be accompanied by a semicolon. In this case, *however* is also an introductory clause, so it is followed by a comma.

    Choice **A** is incorrect. Using a comma here creates a comma splice; joining the two independent clauses should be done with either a period or a semicolon.

    Choice **B** is incorrect. The adverb *however* should come after the semicolon because it belongs to the second independent clause.

    Choice **D** is incorrect. Because *however* is a conjunctive adverb, it should be preceded by a semicolon, not a comma. Also, it is an introductory clause and should be followed by a comma.

28. Choice **C** is correct. *Soft-spoken* and *brother-in-law* should both be hyphenated because they form a single adjective and a single noun, respectively.

    Choice **A** is incorrect. *Soft-spoken* (a compound adjective) and *brother-in-law* (a compound noun) are hyphenated correctly, but *parking lot* should not be hyphenated.

    Choice **B** is incorrect. Because *soft-spoken* is used as a single compound word to modify *brother-in-law*, it should be hyphenated.

    Choice **D** is incorrect. *Brother-in-law* is a compound noun, and all three words must be hyphenated.

29. Choice **B** is correct. The dependent phrase *who is my physics teacher* is correctly set off by commas.

    Choice **A** is incorrect. The phrase *who is my physics teacher* is a nonrestrictive clause (it offers additional information, but is not crucial to the meaning of the sentence), so it should be preceded and followed by commas.

    Choice **C** is incorrect. The phrase *who is my physics teacher* is a nonrestrictive clause (it offers additional information, but is not crucial to the meaning of the sentence), so it should be preceded and followed by commas.

    Choice **D** is incorrect. This choice puts commas around the wrong clause. If you take out the words between the commas, you're left with *Ms. Jeffers who coaches the basketball team.* This is an incomplete thought and a sentence fragment, which indicates that this is not a correctly punctuated sentence.

30. Choice **A** is correct. *Were sent* is the correct past tense verb phrase to modify the plural subject *several manuals.*

    Choice **B** is incorrect. *Was sent* is a singular verb phrase, which does not agree with the plural subject *several manuals.*

Choice **C** is incorrect. *Has been sent* is a singular verb phrase, which does not agree with the plural subject *several manuals*.

Choice **D** is incorrect. *Sent* is the past participle of *send*, and it agrees with the tense of the sentence. However, *sent* is not the correct verb because it is missing the past form of *to be* (*were*).

31. Choice **D** is correct. This uses the nominative case pronoun *I* correctly, and *it* is the pronoun consistent with the phrase it's modifying (*one of her earrings*).

    Choice **A** is incorrect. *Me* is an objective case pronoun, but in this sentence it is acting as the subject, which requires the nominative case pronoun *I*.

    Choice **B** is incorrect. *Me* is an objective case pronoun, but in this sentence it is acting as the subject, which requires a nominative case pronoun. Also, *they* is incorrect because the clause modifies *one of her earrings*. Don't be distracted by the plural *earrings*; *one of* tells you that you're only looking for one earring, so the pronoun form should be singular.

    Choice **C** is incorrect. *I* is the correct pronoun when referring to oneself as a subject; however, *they* should be singular to match *one of her earrings*.

32. Choice **A** is correct. *Set*, meaning *to put* or *to place*, is the correct verb in the context of the sentence. *It's*, a contraction meaning *it is*, is also correct.

    Choice **B** is incorrect. *Set*, meaning *to put* or *to place*, is the correct verb in the context of the sentence. For the second blank, *its* is a possessive pronoun that is being used incorrectly. The contraction *it's* (to replace *it is*) should be used in the second blank.

    Choice **C** is incorrect. *Sat* is the wrong verb choice given the context of the sentence; it is

the past participle of *sit*, which means *to rest*, when you actually want a verb that means *to put*. Additionally, *its* is a possessive pronoun that is being used incorrectly.

    Choice **D** is incorrect. *It's* is punctuated correctly, but *sat* is the wrong verb choice given the context of the sentence. It is the past participle of *sit*, which means *to rest*, when you actually want a verb that means *to put*.

33. Choice **B** is correct. *Advice* is a noun, which fits the structure and meaning of the sentence. *Accept* is the correct verb, and the meaning fits the sentence as well.

    Choice **A** is incorrect. The two blanks must be filled with a noun and a verb, respectively. In the second blank, *except* is incorrect; it is a preposition meaning *excluding*, while the second blank calls for a verb.

    Choice **C** is incorrect. *Advise* is a verb that means *to give advice*, which is incorrect because the first blank requires a noun.

    Choice **D** is incorrect. *Advise* is a verb that means *to give advice*, which is incorrect because the first blank requires a noun, and *except* is a preposition, not the verb needed to fill in the second blank.

34. Choice **D** is correct. The verb *quit* works in the context of the sentence, and the adverb *too* (meaning *excessive*) successfully modifies *many*.

    Choice **A** is incorrect. Based the context of the sentence, the first blank requires a verb (what did Carlos do?). *Quite* is an adverb, which does not fit into the first blank. The adverb *too* is correct.

    Choice **B** is incorrect. Based the context of the sentence, the first blank requires a verb (what did Carlos do?). *Quite* is an adverb, which does not fit into the first blank. *To* is also incorrect, as it is a preposition, while the second blank requires an adverb.

Choice **C** is incorrect. *Quit* is a verb (correctly filling the first blank), but the preposition *to* is not an adverb to modify the phrase *many sports-related injuries*.

35. Choice **C** is correct. The list of movies is punctuated correctly (beginning with a colon and separating list items with commas). This choice also splits the two independent clauses into separate sentences with a period.

    Choice **A** is incorrect. The comma after *Annie* (with no coordinating conjunction) turns the sentence into a comma splice.

    Choice **B** is incorrect. A list should be preceded by a colon, not a semicolon.

    Choice **D** is incorrect. A list should be preceded by a colon, not an em-dash, because the list is an essential component of the sentence.

36. Choice **C** is correct. The only punctuation necessary in this sentence is the comma that separates the introductory phrase from the independent clause that follows it.

    Choice **A** is incorrect. *Excited about her European vacation* is an introductory phrase, which should always be followed by a comma.

    Choice **B** is incorrect. The comma before *Eva* is correct, but the one following her name is incorrect because *Eva* is the subject of the sentence.

    Choice **D** is incorrect. This comma breaks the sentence into two pieces that make little sense: *Excited about her European vacation Eva spent* and *hours in the bookstore looking at travel guides*. These create a choppy, incomplete sentence.

37. Choice **A** is correct. When dates come in the middle of a sentence, they should be followed by commas (as *July 4* and *1922* are here). There should also be a comma between a city name and a state (or U.S. district) abbreviation.

    Choice **B** is incorrect. This sentence sets off *who lives across the street* as a nonrestrictive phrase, when it's really a restrictive phrase that tells you which woman the speaker is talking about. Restrictive phrase should not be set off by commas.

    Choice **C** is incorrect. The comma after *street* creates a false pause in the sentence and separates it into two separate phrases that don't create a logical sentence. Also, dates that appear in the middle of the sentence should always be followed by commas.

    Choice **D** is incorrect. This sentence is missing commas. When dates come in the middle of a sentence, they should always be followed by commas. There should also be a comma between a city name and a state (or U.S. district) abbreviation.

38. Choice **C** is correct. When speculating about future events, you should use the future perfect tense. *Will have been* is the future perfect form of the verb *to be*.

    Choice **A** is incorrect. While the sentence does indicate the future (*By next fall*), the tense you're looking for is the future perfect, which describes an expected event that hasn't yet taken place. *Would be* is the future tense, but it is not the future perfect tense.

    Choice **B** is incorrect. The sentence indicates the future (*By next fall*). However, *should have* is a verb phrase that refers to past events that may have happened, or events that did not happen.

    Choice **D** is incorrect. The sentence indicates the future (*By next fall*). However, *had been* is the past perfect tense, which is used to describe events that have already happened.

39. Choice **B** is correct. An introductory clause like *Because it was raining too hard* should be followed by a comma, not a semicolon.

    Choice **A** is incorrect. This sentence is correctly punctuated because the semicolon separates two distinct (but related) ideas: that the game was postponed and that it was raining.

Choice **C** is incorrect. This sentence is correctly punctuated because the word *because* links the independent and dependent clauses with no additional punctuation necessary.

Choice **D** is incorrect. This sentence is correctly punctuated because the two independent clauses are joined by a comma and the conjunction *and*.

40. Choice **B** is correct. *Sixteenth* is not part of a compound adjective; it is the only word modifying the noun *president*. There does not need to be a hyphen between a noun and its modifier.

    Choice **A** is incorrect. When time is written out in words instead of numbers, the hour and the minute should be hyphenated.

    Choice **C** is incorrect. A compound adjective containing a number (*thirty*) and a word (*second*) should be hyphenated.

    Choice **D** is incorrect. A compound adjective containing a number (*thousand*) and a word (*dollar*) should be hyphenated.

41. Choice **D** is correct. The verb (*is*) is singular, while the subject (*causes*) is plural. The subject and verb are not in agreement.

    Choice **A** is incorrect. *One* is a singular pronoun, so the singular verb *is* is correct.

    Choice **B** is incorrect. *Girls* is a plural noun, so the plural verb *are* is correct.

    Choice **C** is incorrect. *Shoes* is a plural noun, so the plural verb *are* is correct.

42. Choice **A** is correct. The pronoun here is deceptive. It might appear to be an object of *the teacher*, but it is actually a predicate noun renaming the subject of the sentence. The correct nominative pronoun is *she*.

    Choice **B** is incorrect. The pronouns here are used as the subjects of the sentence (who plans to visit you tomorrow?), and *he* and *I* are both nominative case pronouns.

Choice **C** is incorrect. Although it comes in the middle of the sentence, *she* is the subject of the sentence (*she* is the one performing the action of coming over). *She* is the correct nominative case pronoun.

Choice **D** is incorrect. *Michael and Steven* make up the compound subject, and the coordinating word *and* tells you that the subject is plural. *Their* is the correct objective case pronoun to match the plural subject.

43. Choice **D** is correct. *Diane* is correctly punctuated, there are no extraneous apostrophes in the sentence, and *aren't* is contracted properly.

    Choice **A** is incorrect. *Diane* is one person, so the possessive form is created by adding –'s.

    Choice **B** is incorrect. *Diane's* is punctuated correctly, but the contraction *aren't* requires an apostrophe. Contractions with *not* always have the apostrophe between the *n* and the *t*.

    Choice **C** is incorrect. *Forms* is a plural noun and is not possessive, so it should not contain an apostrophe.

44. Choice **B** is correct. The television show title is appropriately italicized.

    Choice **A** is incorrect. Television show titles should be italicized, not underlined. Also, the title *Friends* is not possessive, so it should not contain an apostrophe.

    Choice **C** is incorrect. Television show titles should be italicized, not punctuated with quotation marks.

    Choice **D** is incorrect. There is no reason to put television show titles in all-capital letters.

45. Choice **C** is correct. *Half of the bagels were eaten* contains a passive verb phrase because there is an additional verb separating the subject (*half*) and the active verb (*eaten*). The active sentence would be, *We ate more than half of the bagels before 9:00.*

Choice **A** is incorrect. The subject (*Zeke*) directly performs the action (*brought*), so this is an active sentence.

Choice **B** is incorrect. The subject (*Zeke*) directly performs the action (*selected*), so this is an active sentence.

Choice **D** is incorrect. The subject (*we*) is directly performing the action (*asked*), so this is an active sentence.

46. Choice **B** is correct. *Scent* is the correct noun for this sentence, and *passed* is the correct past tense verb.

Choice **A** is incorrect. Based on the context of the sentence, the two blanks must be filled with a noun and a verb, respectively. *Scent* is the correct noun, but *past* can be either a noun or an adjective—not a verb.

Choice **C** is incorrect. *Sent* is a verb, but a noun is needed to serve as the direct object.

Choice **D** is incorrect. Based on the context of the sentence, the two blanks must be filled with a noun and a verb, respectively. However, *sent* is a verb, and *past* can be either an adjective or a noun.

47. Choice **A** is correct. The adjective *smallest* indicates that Ian is small compared to more than two people, which agrees with the sentence saying he is one of three triplets. Also, *among* indicates that his talent for music is compared with the talents of more than two people, and Ian presumably has more than one other person in his family.

Choice **B** is incorrect. *Between* compares two items. Since Ian has at least three family members (the

reader is tipped off by *triplets*), more than two things are being compared, so the comparative adverb is incorrect.

Choice **C** is incorrect. *Smaller* and *between* compare two items. Since Ian has at least three family members (the reader is tipped off by *triplets*), more than two things are being compared in each instance, so the comparative adverbs are incorrect.

Choice **D** is incorrect. *Smaller* compares two items. Since Ian is one of three triplets, more than two things are being compared, so the comparative adverb is incorrect.

48. Choice **D** is correct. The contraction *you're* is appropriate for the first blank, and *who* correctly modifies *the person.*

Choice **A** is incorrect. The first blank of the sentence is missing the subject and the verb. *You're* (contraction of *you* are) fits that space; the possessive pronoun *your* does not.

Choice **B** is incorrect. The first blank of the sentence is missing the subject and the verb. *You're* (contraction of *you* are) fits that space; the possessive pronoun *your* does not. Also, the second blank of the subject is asking for a pronoun to complete the object. *Which* is a pronoun, but it describes an object or idea, never a person.

Choice **C** is incorrect. The contraction *you're* is correct. However, *that* is incorrect because it is an object pronoun for inanimate things; it never modifies a person.

49. Choice **C** is correct. *Suppose* is the correct verb tense, and the meaning of *than* (showing that one person is older compared to another) fits the sentence as well.

Choice **A** is incorrect. The tense is a bit confusing in this sentence, but the most telling part is *I am*. This tells you that the speaker is comparing him- or herself to someone in the present.

While s/he is talking about a past event (*you thought*), the voice is in the present. Therefore, the past tense verb *supposed* is not correct. *Then* is also not correct because it is an adverb that modifies time. The second blank requires a conjunction that shows a comparison of one thing to another.

Choice **B** is incorrect. The present tense verb *suppose* is correct, but the use of *then* is not because it is an adverb that modifies time. The second blank requires a conjunction that shows a comparison of one thing to another.

Choice **D** is incorrect. The tense is a bit confusing in this sentence, but the most telling part is *I am*. This tells you that the speaker is comparing him- or herself to someone in the present. While s/he is talking about a past event (*you thought*), the voice is in the present. Therefore, the past tense verb *supposed* is not correct.

50. Choice **D** is correct. The verb *threw* fits the meaning of the sentence, and *piece* has the correct meaning as well.

Choice **A** is incorrect. The first blank requires a verb to tell the reader what Evan did. *Through* is a preposition that shows movement from one side to another, which is not the correct part of speech or meaning.

Choice **B** is incorrect. The first blank requires a verb to tell the reader what Evan did. *Through* is a preposition that shows movement from one side to another, which is not the correct part of speech or meaning. *Peace* means *harmony*, which is not the correct meaning for the second blank.

Choice **C** is incorrect. The verb *threw* fits the meaning of the sentence. However, *peace* means *harmony*, which is not the correct meaning for the second blank.

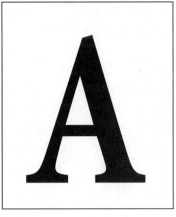

STUDYING FOR SUCCESS

How successful you are at studying has less to do with how much time you put into it than with how you do it. That's because some ways of studying are much more effective than others, and some environments are much more conducive to studying than others. Another reason is that not everyone retains information in the same way. On the following pages, you will discover how to adapt your studying strategies to the ways you learn best. You will probably pick up some new techniques for studying, and will also gain insight on how to prepare for standardized tests.

Learning Styles

Think for a minute about what you know about how you learn. For example, if you need directions to a new restaurant, would you

- ask to see a map showing how to get there.
- ask someone to tell you how to get there.
- copy someone's written directions.

Most people learn in a variety of ways: seeing, touching, hearing, and experiencing the world around them. Many people find, however, that they are more likely to absorb information better from one learning source than from others. The source that works best for you is called your dominant learning method.

There are three basic learning methods: visual, auditory, and kinesthetic (also known as tactile).

- Visual learners understand and retain information best when they can **see** the map, the picture, the text, the word, or the math example.
- Auditory learners learn best when they can **hear** the directions, the poem, the math theorem, or the spelling of a word.
- Kinesthetic learners need to **do**—they must write the directions, draw the diagram, or copy down the phone number.

Visual Learners

If you are a visual learner, you learn best by seeing. Pay special attention to illustrations and graphic material when you study. If you color code your notes with colorful inks or highlighters, you may find that you absorb information better. Visual learners can learn to map or diagram information later in this appendix.

Auditory Learners

If you are an auditory learner, you learn best by listening. Read material aloud to yourself, or talk about what you are learning with a study partner or a study group. Hearing the information will help you to remember it. Some people like to tape-record notes and play them back on the tape player. If you commute to work or school by car or listen to a personal tape player, you can gain extra preparation time by playing the notes to yourself on tape.

Kinesthetic Learners

If you are a kinesthetic learner, you learn best by doing. Interact a lot with your print material by underlining and making margin notes in your textbooks and handouts. Rewrite your notes onto index cards. Recopying material helps you remember it.

How to Study Most Effectively

If studying efficiently is second nature to you, you're very lucky. Most people have to work at it. Try some of these helpful study methods to make studying easier and more effective for you.

Make an Outline

After collecting all the materials you need to review or prepare for the test, the first step for studying any subject is to reduce a large body of information into smaller, more manageable units. One approach to studying this way is to make an outline of text information, handout materials, and class notes.

The important information in print material is often surrounded by lots of extra words and ideas. If you can highlight just the important information, or at least the information you need to know for your test, you can help yourself narrow your focus so that you can study more effectively. There are several ways to make an outline of print material. They include annotating, outlining, and mapping. The point of all three of these strategies is that they allow you to pull out just the important information that you need to prepare for the test.

Annotating

Annotations help you pull out main ideas from the surrounding text to make them more visible and accessible to you. Annotation means that you underline or highlight important information that appears in print material. It also involves responding to the material by engaging yourself with the writer by making margin notes. Margin notes are phrases or sentences in the margins of print material that summarize the content of those passages. Your margin notes leave footprints for you to follow as you review the text.

Here is an example of a passage that has been annotated and underlined.

Loction, Location, Location

<u>Find a quiet spot, use a good reading light, and turn the radio off.</u>

Find Quiet Places

Different quiet places at different times

For many adult test takers, it's difficult to find a quiet spot in their busy lives. Many adults don't even have a bedroom corner that isn't shared with someone else. <u>Your quiet spot may be in a different place at different times of the day.</u>

For example, it could be the kitchen table early in the morning before breakfast, your workplace area when everyone else is at lunch, or a corner of the sofa late at night. If you know you'll have to move around when you study, <u>make sure your study material is portable.</u>

Portable study material

Keep your notes, practice tests, pencils, and other supplies together in a folder or bag. Then you can easily carry your study material with you and study in whatever quiet spot presents itself.

<u>If quiet study areas are nonexistent in your home or work environment, you may need to find a space elsewhere. The public library is the most obvious choice.</u> Some test takers find it helpful to assign themselves study hours at the library in the same way that they schedule dentist appointments, class hours, household tasks, or other necessary uses of daily or weekly time. Studying away from home or work also minimizes the distractions of other people and other demands when you are preparing for a test.

Library!

Lights

Libraries also provide good reading lights. For some people, this may seem like a trivial matter, but the eyestrain that can come from working for long periods in <u>poor light can be very tiring—which you can't afford when you're studying hard.</u>

Need good light

At home, the bedside lamp, the semidarkness of a room dominated by the television, or the bright sunlight of the back porch will be of little help to tired eyes.

Outlining

You are probably familiar with the basic format of the traditional outline:

    I.   Main idea 1
        A.   Major detail
        B.   Major detail
            1. Minor detail
            2. Minor detail
    II.   Main idea 2
        A.   Major detail
        B.   Major detail

You may have used an outline in school to help you organize a writing assignment or take notes. When you outline print material, you're looking for the basic ideas that make up the framework of the text. When you are taking out the important information for a test, then you are looking for the basic ideas that the author wants to convey to you.

Mapping

Mapping is a more visual kind of outline. Instead of making a linear outline of the main ideas of a text, when you map, you make a diagram of the main points in the text that you want to remember. The following diagrams show the same information in a map form.

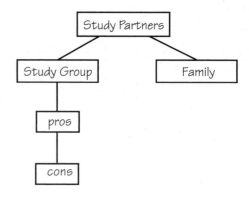

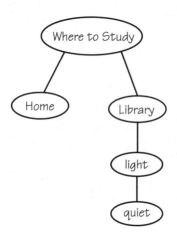

Make Study Notes

The next step after you have pulled out all the key ideas is to make notes from which you will study. You will use these notes for the intensive and ongoing study you'll do over the period of time before the test. They're the specific items that you targeted as important to know for the test. Your notes should help you understand the information you need to know and, in many cases, commit it to memory. You should be sure to include

- the main ideas you underlined or highlighted in the text
- the main ideas and important details you outlined or mapped from the text
- specific terms, words, dates, formulas, names, facts, or procedures that you need to memorize

How Do You Make Study Notes?

Some people like to write study notes in the back pages of their notebooks or on paper folded lengthwise so that it can be tucked between the pages of a text or review book. This format is good to use for notes that can be written as questions and answers, cause and effect, or definition and examples. You can also make notes on index cards.

Using Index Cards

It can be very helpful to write your study notes—especially those that contain material to be memorized—on index cards. Vocabulary words are significantly easier to learn using index cards.

Advantages of making notes on index cards are:

- The information on each card is visually separated from other information. Therefore, it's easier to concentrate on just that one item, separate from the surrounding text. You remember the look of a vocabulary word or a math equation more clearly when it is set off by itself.
- Cards are small and portable. They can be carried in a purse or a pocket and pulled out at any time during the day for review.
- Study cards can help you with the necessary task of memorizing. If you write the key word or topic you are trying to learn on one side, and the information you must know on the other side, you have an easy way to quiz yourself on the material. This method is especially good for kinesthetic learners, who learn by doing.

Making Memorizing Easier

There are many ways to take the drudgery out of memorizing information.

Take Small Bites of Time

Most people memorize information best when they study in small periods over a long period of time.

Memorizing facts from index cards that can be carried with you and pulled out for a few 10-minute sessions each day will yield better results than sitting down with a textbook for an hour straight. Index card notes can be pulled out in odd moments: while you are sitting in the car waiting to pick up your friend, during the 15 minutes you spend on the bus in the morning, while you wait to be picked up from school or work, and so on.

You'll find that these short but regular practices will greatly aid your recall of lots of information. They're a great way to add more study time to your schedule.

Break It Up

When you have a list to memorize, break the list into groups of seven or any other odd number. People seem to remember best when they divide long lists into shorter ones—and, for some reason, shorter ones that have an odd number of items in them. So instead of trying to memorize 10 vocabulary or spelling words, split your list into smaller lists of seven and three, or five and five, to help you remember them.

Create Visual Aids

Give yourself visual assistance in memorizing. If there's a tricky combination of letters in a word you need to spell, for example, circle or underline it in red or highlight it in the text. Your eye will recall what the word looks like. With some information, you can even draw a map or picture to help you remember.

Do It Out Loud

Give yourself auditory assistance in memorizing. Many people learn best if they *hear* the information. Sit by yourself in a quiet room and say aloud what you need to learn. Or give your notes to someone else and let that person ask you or quiz you on the material.

Use Mnemonics

Mnemonics, or memory tricks, are things that help you remember what you need to know.

The most common type of mnemonic is the acronym. One acronym you may already know is **HOMES**, for the names of the Great Lakes (**H**uron, **O**ntario, **M**ichigan, **E**rie, and **S**uperior). **ROY G. BIV** reminds people of the colors in the spectrum (**r**ed, **o**range, **y**ellow, **g**reen, **b**lue, **i**ndigo, and **v**iolet).

You can make a mnemonic out of anything. In a psychology course, for example, you might memorize the stages in death and dying by the nonsense word **DABDA** (**d**enial, **a**nger, **b**argaining, **d**epression, and acceptance.) Another kind of mnemonic is a silly sentence made out of words that each begin with the letter or letters that start each item in a series. You may remember "**P**lease **E**xcuse **M**y **D**ear **A**unt **S**ally" as a device for remembering the order of operations in math (**P**arentheses, **E**xponents, **M**ultiply, **D**ivide, **A**dd, and **S**ubtract).

Sleep on It

When you study right before sleep and don't allow any interference—such as conversation, radio, television, or music—to come between study and sleep, you remember material better. This is especially true if you review first thing after waking as well. A rested and relaxed brain seems to hang on to information better than a tired and stressed-out brain.

On the following pages, try out some of the learning strategies you discovered in this lesson. Then check your answers.

The following is a passage from this text to underline and annotate. Make margin summaries of the key points in each paragraph. Then, make a mnemonic based on your margin notes.

Take Small Bites of Time

Most people memorize information best when they study in small periods over a long period of time
Memorizing facts from index cards that can be carried with you and pulled out for a few 10-minute sessions each day will yield better results than sitting down with a textbook for an hour straight. You'll find that these short but regular practices will greatly aid your recall of lots of information. They're a great way to add more study time to your schedule.

Break It Up

When you have a list to memorize, break the list into groups of seven or any other odd number. People seem to remember best when they divide long lists into shorter ones—and, for some reason, shorter ones that have an odd number of items in them. So instead of trying to memorize ten vocabulary or spelling words, split your list into smaller lists of seven and three, or five and five, to help you remember them.

Create Visual Aids

Give yourself visual assistance in memorizing. If there's a tricky combination of letters in a word you need to spell, for example, circle or underline it in red or highlight it in the text. Your eye will recall what the word looks like.

Do It Out Loud

Give yourself auditory assistance in memorizing. Many people learn best if they hear the information. Sit by yourself in a quiet room and say aloud what you need to learn. Or give your notes to someone else and let that person quiz you on the material.

Use Mnemonics

Mnemonics, or memory tricks, are things that help you remember what you need to know.
The most common type of mnemonic is the acronym. One acronym you may already know is **HOMES**, for the names of the Great Lakes (**H**uron, **O**ntario, **M**ichigan, **E**rie, and **S**uperior). **ROY G. BIV** reminds people of the colors in the spectrum (**r**ed, **o**range, **y**ellow, **g**reen, **b**lue, **i**ndigo, and **v**iolet).

Note Cards

Make note cards with definitions for each kind of learning modality:

- visual
- auditory
- kinesthetic

Mapping

Here is an outline of the learning strategies covered in this chapter. Using the same information, make a map or diagram of the same material.

I. How to study most effectively
    A. Annotating
    B. Outlining
    C. Mapping
II. How to make study notes
    A. Notebook pages
    B. Index cards
        1. Reasons for using index cards
III. Memory methods

Completed Sample Annotation

Take Small Bites of Time

Distributed practice

Most people memorize information best when they study in <u>small periods over a long period of time</u>.

Memorizing facts from portable index cards that can be carried with you and pulled out for a few 10-minute sessions each day will yield better results than sitting down with a textbook for an hour straight. You'll find that these short but regular practices will greatly aid your recall of lots of information. They're a great way to add more study time to your schedule.

Break It Up

Divide lists

When you have a list to memorize, <u>break the list into groups of seven or any other odd number</u>. People seem to remember best when they divide long lists into shorter ones—and, for some reason, shorter ones that have an odd number of items in them. So instead of trying to memorize ten vocabulary or spelling words, split your list into smaller lists of seven and three, or five and five, to help you remember them.

Create Visual Aids

Visual Aids

<u>Give yourself visual assistance in memorizing</u>. If there's a tricky combination of letters in a word you need to spell, for example, circle or underline it in red or highlight it in the text. Your eye will recall what the word looks like.

Do It Out Loud

Auditory

<u>Give yourself auditory assistance in memorizing</u>. Many people learn best if they hear the information. Sit by yourself in a quiet room and say aloud what you need to learn. Or, give your notes to someone else and let that person ask you questions and quiz you on the material.

Use Mnemonics

Acronym

<u>Mnemonics</u>, or memory tricks, are things that help you remember what you need to know.

The most common type of mnemonic is the <u>acronym</u>. One acronym you may already know is **HOMES**, for the names of the Great Lakes (**H**uron, **O**ntario, **M**ichigan, **E**rie, and **S**uperior). **ROY G. BIV** reminds people of the colors in the spectrum (**r**ed, **o**range, **y**ellow, **g**reen, **b**lue, **i**ndigo, and **v**iolet).

Sample Mnemonics
DDVAA

Note Cards
Here are samples of how your note cards might look:

FRONT OF CARD

Visual Modality	Auditory Modality	Kinesthetic Modality

BACK OF CARD

learning by seeing	learning by listening	learning by doing

Mapping
Here is an example of how your map or diagram might look:

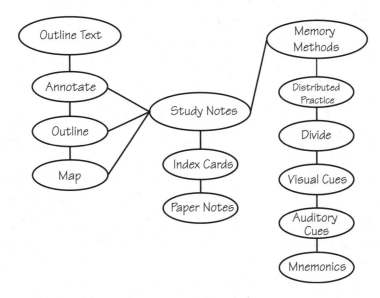

Preparing for a Standarized Test

Most of us get nervous about tests, especially standardized tests, where our scores can have a significant impact on our future. Nervousness is natural—and it can even be an advantage if you know how to channel it into positive energy.

The following pages provide suggestions for overcoming test anxiety, both in the days and weeks before the test and during the test itself.

Two to Three Months before the Test

The number one best way to combat test anxiety is to **be prepared**. That means two things: Know what to expect on the test, and review the material and skills on which you will be tested.

Review the Material and Skills You'll Be Tested On

The fact that you are reading this book means that you've already taken this step. Now, are there other steps you can take? Are there other subject areas you need to review? Can you make more improvement in this or other areas? If you are really nervous or if it has been a long time since you reviewed these subjects and skills, you may want to buy a second study guide, sign up for a class in your neighborhood, or work with a tutor.

The more you know about what to expect on test day and the more comfortable you are with the material and skills to be tested, the less anxious you will be and the better you will do on the test itself.

The Days before the Test

Review, Don't Cram

If you have been preparing and reviewing in the weeks before the exam, there's no need to cram a few days beforehand. Cramming is likely to confuse you and make you nervous. Instead, schedule a relaxed review of all you have learned.

Physical Activity

Get some exercise in the days preceding the test. You'll send some extra oxygen to your brain and allow your thinking performance to peak on the day you take the test. Moderation is the key here. Don't exercise so much that you feel exhausted, but a little physical activity will invigorate your body and brain. Walking is a terrific, low-impact, energy-building form of exercise.

Balanced Diet

Like your body, your brain needs proper nutrients to function well. Eat plenty of fruits and vegetables in the days before the test. Foods high in lecithin, such as fish and beans, are especially good choices. Lecithin is a protein your brain needs for peak performance. You may even consider a visit to your local pharmacy to buy a bottle of lecithin tablets several weeks before your test.

Rest

Get plenty of sleep the nights before the test. Don't overdo it, though, or you'll make yourself as groggy as if you were overtired. Go to bed at a reasonable time, early enough to get the hours of rest you need to function **effectively**. You'll feel relaxed and rested if you've gotten plenty of sleep in the days before you take the test.

Trial Run

At some point before the test, make a trial run to the testing center to see how long it takes to get there. Rushing raises your emotional energy and lowers your intellectual capacity, so you want to allow plenty of time on test day to get to the testing center. Arriving 10 or 15 minutes early gives you time to relax and get situated.

Motivation

Plan some sort of celebration—with family or friends, or just by yourself—for after the test. Make sure it's something you'll really look forward to and enjoy. If you have something planned for after the test, you may find it easier to prepare and keep moving during the test.

Test Day

It's finally here, the day of the big test. Set your alarm early enough to allow plenty of time to get to the testing center. Eat a good breakfast. Avoid anything that's really high in sugar, such as doughnuts. A sugar high turns into a sugar low after an hour or so. Cereal and toast or anything with complex carbohydrates is a good choice. Eat only moderate amounts. You don't want to take a test feeling stuffed! Your body will channel its energy to your digestive system instead of your brain.

Pack a high-energy snack to take with you. You may have a break sometime during the test when you can grab a quick snack. Bananas are great. They have a moderate amount of sugar and plenty of brain nutrients, such as potassium. Most proctors won't allow you to eat a snack while you're testing, but a peppermint shouldn't pose a problem. Peppermints are like smelling salts for your brain. If you lose your concentration or suffer from a momentary mental block, a peppermint can get you back on track. Don't forget the earlier advice about relaxing and taking a few deep breaths.

Leave early enough so you have plenty of time to get to the test center. Allow a few minutes for unexpected traffic. When you arrive, locate the restroom and use it. Few things interfere with concentration as much as a full bladder. Then, find your seat and make sure it's comfortable. If it isn't, tell the proctor and ask to move to something more suitable.

Now relax and think positively! Before you know it, the test will be over, and you'll walk away knowing you've done as well as you can.

Combating Test Anxiety

Okay—you know what the test will be on. You've reviewed the subjects and practiced the skills on which you will be tested. So why do you still have that sinking feeling in your stomach? Why are your palms sweaty and your hands shaking?

Even the brightest, most well-prepared test takers sometimes suffer bouts of test anxiety. But don't worry; you can overcome it. Here are some specific strategies to help you.

Take the Test One Question at a Time

Focus all your attention on the one question you're answering. Avoid thoughts about questions you've already read or concerns about what's coming next. Concentrate your thinking where it will do the most good—on the question you're answering now.

Develop a Positive Attitude

Keep reminding yourself that you're prepared. In fact, if you've read this book, you're probably better prepared than most other test takers. Remember, it's only a test, and you will do your **best**. That's all anyone can ask of you. If that nagging voice inside your head starts sending negative messages, combat them with positive ones of your own. Tell yourself:

- "I'm doing just fine."
- "I've prepared for this test."
- "I know exactly what to do."
- "I know I can get the score I'm shooting for."

You get the idea. Remember to drown out negative messages with positive ones of your own.

If You Lose Your Concentration

Don't worry about it! It's normal. During a long test, it happens to everyone. When your mind is stressed or overexerted, it takes a break whether you want it to or not. It's easy to get your concentration back if you simply acknowledge the fact that you've lost it and take a quick break. You brain needs very little time (seconds, really) to rest.

Put your pencil down and close your eyes. Take a deep breath, hold it for a moment, and let it out slowly. Listen to the sound of your breathing as you repeat this two more times. The few seconds this takes is really all the time your brain needs to relax and refocus. This exercise also helps you control your heart rate, so you can keep anxiety at bay.

Try this technique several times before the test when you feel stressed. The more you practice, the better it will work for you on test day.

If You Freeze

Don't worry about a question that stumps you even though you're sure you know the answer. Mark it and go on to the next question. You can come back to the "stumper" later. Try to put it out of your mind completely until you come back to it. Just let your subconscious mind chew on the question while your conscious mind focuses on the other items (one at a time—of course). Chances are, the memory block will be gone by the time you return to the question.

If you freeze before you ever begin the test, here's what to do:

1. Do some deep breathing to help yourself relax and focus.
2. Remind yourself that you're prepared.
3. Take some time to look over the test.
4. Read a few of the questions.
5. Decide which ones are the easiest, and start there.

Before long, you'll be "in the groove."

Time Strategies

One of the most important—and nerve-wracking—elements of a standardized test is time. You'll be allowed only a certain number of minutes for each section, so it is very important that you use your time wisely.

Pace Yourself

The most important time strategy is **pacing yourself**. Before you begin, take just a few seconds to survey the test, noting the number of questions and the sections that look easier than the rest. Then, make a rough time schedule based on the amount of time available to you. Mark the halfway point on your test and make a note beside that mark of the time when the testing period is half over.

Keep Moving

Once you begin the test, **keep moving**. If you work slowly in an attempt to make fewer mistakes, your mind will become bored and begin to wander. You'll end up making far more mistakes if you're not concentrating. Worse, if you take too long to answer questions that stump you, you may end up running out of time before you finish.

So don't stop for difficult questions. Skip them and move on. You can come back to them later if you have time. A question that takes you five seconds to answer counts as much as one that takes you several minutes, so pick up the easy points first. Besides, answering the easier questions first helps build your confidence and gets you in the testing groove. Who knows? As you go through the test, you may even stumble across some relevant information to help you answer those tough questions.

Don't Rush

Keep moving, but **don't rush**. Think of your mind as a seesaw. On one side is your emotional energy; on the other side, your intellectual energy. When your emotional energy is high, your intellectual capacity is low. Remember how difficult it is to reason with someone when you're angry? On the other hand, when your intellectual energy is high, your emotional energy is low. Rushing raises your emotional energy and reduces your intellectual capacity. Remember the last time you were late for work? All that rushing around probably caused you to forget important things—like your lunch. Move quickly to keep your mind from wandering, but don't rush and get yourself flustered.

Check Yourself

Check yourself at the halfway mark. If you're a little ahead, you know you're on track and may even have a little time left to check your work. If you're a little behind, you have several choices. You can pick up the pace a little, but do this *only* if you can do it comfortably. Remember—**don't rush**! You can also skip around in the remaining portion of the test to pick up as many easy points as possible.

Avoiding Errors

When you take the test, you want to make as few errors as possible in the questions you answer. Here are a few tactics to keep in mind.

Control Yourself

Remember that comparison between your mind and a seesaw? Keeping your emotional energy low and your intellectual energy high is the best way to avoid mistakes. If you feel stressed or worried, stop for a few seconds. Acknowledge the feeling ("Hmmm! I'm feeling a little pressure here!"), take a few deep breaths, and send yourself a few positive messages. This relieves your emotional anxiety and boosts your intellectual capacity.

Directions

In many standardized testing situations, a proctor reads the instructions aloud. Make certain you understand what is expected. If you don't, **ask**. Listen carefully for instructions about how to answer the questions and make certain you know how much time you have to complete the task. Write the time on your test if you don't already know how long you have to take the test. If you miss this vital information, **ask for it**. You need it to do well on your test.

Answers

This may seem like a silly warning, but it is important. Place your answers in the right blanks or the corresponding ovals on the answer sheet. Right answers in the wrong place earn no points—depending on the test, you may even lose points for incorrect answers. It's a good idea to check every five to 10 questions to make sure you're in the right spot. That way, you won't need much time to correct your answer sheet if you have made an error.

Choosing the Right Answers by Process of Elimination

Make sure you understand what the question is asking. If you're not sure of what's being asked, you'll never know whether you've chosen the right answer. So determine what the question is asking. If the answer isn't readily apparent, look for clues in the answer choices. Notice the similarities and differences in the answer choices. Sometimes, this helps to put the question in a new perspective, making it easier to answer. If you're still not sure of the answer, use the process of elimination. First, eliminate any answer choices that are obviously wrong. Then, reason your way through the remaining choices. You may be able to use relevant information from other parts of the test. If you can't eliminate any of the answer choices, you might be better off to skip the question and come back to it later. If you can't eliminate any answer choices to improve your odds when you return, make a guess and move on.

If You're Penalized for Wrong Answers

You **must know** whether there's a penalty for wrong answers before you begin the test. If you don't, ask the proctor before the test begins. Whether you make a guess depends on the penalty. Some standardized tests are scored in such a way that every wrong answer reduces your score by one-fourth or one-half of a point. Whatever the penalty, if you can eliminate enough choices to make the odds of answering the question better than the penalty for getting it wrong, make a guess.

Let's imagine you are taking a test in which each answer has four choices and you are penalized one-fourth of a point for each wrong answer. If you have no clue and cannot eliminate any of the answer choices, you're better off leaving the question blank because the odds of answering correctly are one in four. This makes the penalty and the odds equal. However, if you can eliminate one of the choices, the odds are now in your favor. You have a one-in-three chance of answering the question correctly. Fortunately, few tests are scored using such elaborate means, but if your test is one of them, know the penalties and calculate your odds before you take a guess on a question.

If You Finish Early

Use any time you have left at the end of the test or test section to check your work. First, make certain you've put the answers in the right places. As you're doing this, make sure you've answered each question only once. Most standardized tests are scored in such a way that questions with more than one answer are marked wrong. If you've erased an answer, make sure you've done a good job. Check for stray marks on your answer sheet that could distort your score.

After you've checked for these obvious errors, take a second look at the more difficult questions. You've probably heard the folk wisdom about never changing an answer. It's not always good advice. If you have a good reason for thinking a response is wrong, change it.

After the Test

Once you've finished, *congratulate yourself*. You've worked hard to prepare; now it's time to enjoy yourself and relax. Remember that celebration you planned before the test? Go to it!

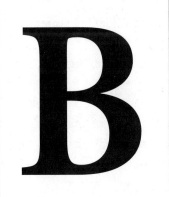

ADDITIONAL RESOURCES

If using this book has whetted your appetite for learning to write better, you may want to continue your study. Many high schools and community colleges offer inexpensive writing courses for adults in their continuing education departments, or you may be able to find a teacher who is willing to tutor you for a modest fee. In addition, you might consult one of the following books:

- *Thirty Days to Better English* by Norman Lewis (Signet)
  Useful for general information; suited to both native and nonnative speakers of English.

- *English Made Simple* by Arthur Waldhorn and Arthur Ziegler (Made Simple Books)
  Designed for nonnative speakers of English; also good for native speakers with little training in grammar.

- *Errors in English and Ways to Correct Them* by Harry Shaw (HarperCollins)
  Addresses specific problems in both writing and grammar; useful for nonnative speakers of English.

- *Grammar* by James R. Hurford (Cambridge University Press)

  Thorough coverage of parts of speech, sentence structure, usage, punctuation, and mechanics; especially good for native speakers of English.

- *Grammar Essentials* by Judith Olson (LearningExpress)

  All the rules of grammar explained in plain English; includes lots of exercises so you can practice what you learn.

- *The Grammar Handbook* by Irwin L. Feigenbaum (Oxford University Press)

  Huge, unfortunately expensive, book; very comprehensive and problem specific.

- *The Handbook of Good English* by Edward D. Johnson (Washington Square Press)

  Well-organized, comprehensive handbook for both grammar and writing.

- *Improve Your Writing for Work* by Elizabeth Chesla (LearningExpress)

  Great instruction on how to write in the business world, as well as tips on good writing in general.

- *Living in English* by Betsy J. Blosser (National Textbook Company)

  Specially designed for nonnative speakers of English.

- *1001 Pitfalls in English Grammar* by Ruth Parle Craig and Vincent F. Hopper (Barron's)

  Problem-solving approach to writing and grammar; very useful for nonnative speakers of English.

- *Practice with Idioms* by Ronald E. Feare (Oxford University Press)

  For nonnative speakers of English.

- *Smart English* by Annette Francis (Signet)

  Thorough general-purpose handbook for both writing and grammar; good for nonnative speakers of English.

- *The New Well-Tempered Sentence: A Punctuation Handbook for the Innocent, the Eager and the Doomed* by Karen Elizabeth Gordon (Houghton Mifflin)

  Interesting general information on punctuation; especially valuable for nonnative and confused native speakers.

- *Writing Smart* by Marcia Lerner (The Princeton Review)

  Good for general writing skills; well organized, so information is easy to find.

In addition to print resources, there are some great websites out there that can provide you with quick references when you need help.

- Grammar Girl: Quick and Dirty Tips
  grammar.quickanddirtytips.com

- University of Chicago Grammar Resources
  writing-program.uchicago.edu/resources/grammar.htm

- University of Illinois at Urbana Champaign Writers Workshop
  www.cws.illinois.edu/workshop/writers/

Glossary

abstract language   words or phrases that refer to intangible ideas or to classes of people and objects rather than the people or things themselves. Abstractions are built on concrete ideas.

active voice   in an active sentence the subject performs the action of the verb. The person or thing that performs the action is named before the verb, or the action word(s).

adjective   word that describes a noun or pronoun in a sentence. Adjectives answer one of three questions about another word in a sentence: *Which one? what kind?* and *how many?*

adverb   word that describes verbs, adjectives, and other adverbs. Adverbs answer one of these questions about another word in the sentence: *Where? when? how?* and *to what extent?*

apostrophe   (') symbol used to show possession; show to whom or what a noun belongs

appositive   a word or group of words that immediately follows a noun or pronoun. The appositive makes the pronoun more defined by explaining or identifying it.

brackets   ([ ]) symbols used to close parenthetical material within parentheses, to enclose words inserted into a quotation, and around the word *sic* to show that an error in quotation was made by the original writer or speaker.

cliché   a tired, overused word or phrase

colloquialism   informal word or phrase such as *a lot, in a bind, pulled it off,* and so on. These words are regularly used in conversations between friends, rather than in official written communication.

colon   (:) symbol used to introduce a list of items, as long as the part before the colon is already a complete sentence

comma   (,) symbol used to separate items in lists of similar words, phrases, or clauses to make the material easier for a reader to understand. Commas are often used before the final conjunction in a sentence.

comma splice   a type of run-on sentence in which a comma is used in place of semicolon to join two independent clauses without a conjunction. Comma splices can be corrected by putting a semicolon in place of the comma or by adding a conjunction after the comma.

complete sentence   a group of words that expresses a complete thought and has a verb and a subject; also called *independent clauses.*

conjunction   a joining word such as *and, but, or, for, nor, so,* or *yet.*

conjunctive adverb   an adverb that joins independent clauses. These are punctuated differently from regular conjunctions.

dangling modifiers   words, phrases, or clauses that begin a sentence and are set off by commas, but mistakenly modify the wrong noun or pronoun

diagonal   (/) also known as a *backslash*; symbol used to join words or numbers. The most frequent use of the diagonal is with the phrase, *and/or*, which shows that the sentence refers to one or both of the words being joined. Diagonals are also used to separate numbers in a fraction, to show line division in poetry, or to indicate *per* or *divided by*.

diction   the use of appropriate words, combining them in the right way to communicate your message accurately

double negative   a negative word added to a statement that is already negative

ellipses   (…) symbol that indicates omitted material or long pauses; used to show that quoted material has been omitted, or to indicate a pause or hesitation.

em-dash   (—) a specialized punctuation mark that can be used to mark a sudden break in thought or to insert a comment; emphasize explanatory material; indicate omitted letters or words; or connect a beginning phrase to the rest of the sentence

future perfect progressive tense   verb form that shows continuing actions that will be completed at a certain time in the future

future perfect tense   verb form that shows actions that will be completed at a certain time in the future

future progressive tense   verb form that shows continuing actions in the future

future tense   verb form that shows action that has yet to happen

hyphen   (-) symbol used to join words in creating compound nouns or adjectives. Hyphens can be used to join two coequal nouns working together as one (e.g., teacher-poet), to join multiword compound nouns (e.g., up-to-date), to join two or more words that function as a single adjective preceding the noun (e.g., a soft-spoken person), and to join prefixes to words (e.g., ex-husband, secretary-elect).

independent clause   a group of words within a sentence that by itself could form a complete sentence

jargon   technical, wordy language used by those associated with a trade or profession

modifiers   words and phrases that describe other words. For example, an *adjective* is modifier because it describes nouns and pronouns. *Adverbs* are modifiers because they describe verbs, adjectives, and other adverbs.

misplaced modifiers   words, phrases, or clauses that describe nouns and pronouns, but are placed too far away (in a sentence) from the words they describe. For example, the words *only, almost,* and *just* should be placed as closely as possible to the words they describe.

nominative case pronoun   word used as subject or as complement following linking verb (*am, is, are, was, were*—any form of *be*)

nonrestrictive clause   group of words that simply adds information, but is not essential to the basic meaning of a sentence (if it is removed, the basic meaning of the sentence is not changed). Nonrestrictive clauses must be set off by commas; also known as a *nonessential clause.*

objective case pronoun   word used as object following an action verb or as object of a preposition

parallel structure   two or more equivalent ideas in a sentence that have the same purpose, presented in the same form

parentheses   ( ) symbols used to enclose explanatory material that interrupts the normal flow of a sentence. They also enclose information when accuracy is essential and enclose letters or numbers in a list, marking a division from the rest of the text.

past perfect progressive tense   verb form that shows continuing action that began in the past

past perfect tense   verb form that shows an action completed in the past or completed before some other past action

past progressive tense   verb form that shows a continuing action in the past

past tense   verb form that shows action that happened in the past

possessive case pronouns   pronouns that show ownership, such as *my, our, your, his, her, their, its*

present perfect progressive tense   verb form that shows action that began in the past and is continuing in the present

present perfect tense   verb form that shows an action that began in the past

present progressive tense   verb form that shows an action happening now, and ends in the suffix *-ing*

present tense   verb form that shows action that happens now or action that happens routinely

pronoun   a word used in place of a noun; includes *I, my, she, he, them, theirs, it*

proper nouns   nouns that name a specific person, place, or thing. Proper nouns must be capitalized. Some examples of proper nouns include days of the week, holidays, historical events, names of people, landmarks, cities and states, names of products, and works of art and literature.

quotation marks   (" ") symbols used to set off a direct quotation or thought within a sentence or paragraph. They are also used to set off unfamiliar terms and nicknames. Do not use quotation marks for paraphrases or indirect quotations.

redundancy   the same idea expressed twice using different words; words with meanings that overlap

reflexive pronoun   a pronoun that includes the word *self* or *selves*: *myself, yourself, himself, herself, ourselves, themselves*

restrictive clause   group of words that, if omitted from a sentence, changes the entire meaning of the sentence, or even makes the sentence untrue. The restrictive clause is not set off with commas; also known as an *essential clause.*

run-on sentence   a sentence in which independent clauses have been run together without punctuation (a period, semicolon, or comma)

semicolon　(;) symbol used to separate independent clauses. This includes independent clauses that are joined without a conjunction, independent clauses that contain commas even if the clauses are joined by a conjunction, and independent clauses connected with a conjunctive adverb.

subject　someone or something that performs the action or serves as the main focus of a sentence

subject-verb agreement　the rule that states that the subject in a clause—the person or thing doing the action— must match the verb in number. For example, if the subject is singular, the verb must be singular; if the subject is plural, the verb must be plural.

subordinate clause　a dependent clause

tone　describes a writer's emotional attitude toward the subject or audience

verb　a word or phrase that explains an action, such as *want, run, take, give*, or a state of being, such as *am, is, are, was, were, be*

Using the codes below, you'll be able to log in and access additional online practice materials!

Your free online practice access codes are:
FVETE4U72G6E73CRJJ0W
FVE32D843UTC7OT02FNS
FVEG3TIQGC11OVBDO46F

Follow these simple steps to redeem your codes:

- Go to **www.learningexpresshub.com/affiliate** and have your access codes handy.

  If you're a new user:
  - Click the **New user? Register here** button and complete the registration form to create your account and access your products.
  - Be sure to enter your unique access code only once. If you have multiple access codes, you can enter them all—just use a comma to separate each code.
  - The next time you visit, simply click the **Returning user? Sign in** button and enter your username and password.
- Do not re-enter previously redeemed access codes. Any products you previously accessed are saved in the **My Account** section on the site. Entering a previously redeemed access code will result in an error message.

  If you're a returning user:
  - Click the **Returning user? Sign in** button, enter your username and password, and click **Sign In**.
  - You will automatically be brought to the **My Account** page to access your products.
- Do not re-enter previously redeemed access codes. Any products you previously accessed are saved in the **My Account** section on the site. Entering a previously redeemed access code will result in an error message.

  If you're a returning user with a new access code:
  - Click the **Returning user? Sign in** button, enter your username, password, and new access code, and click **Sign In**.
  - If you have multiple access codes, you can enter them all—just use a comma to separate each code.
- Do not re-enter previously redeemed access codes. Any products you previously accessed are saved in the **My Account** section on the site. Entering a previously redeemed access code will result in an error message.

If you have any questions, please contact Customer Support at Support@ebsco.com. All inquiries will be responded to within a 24-hour period during our normal business hours: 9:00 A.M.–5:00 P.M. Eastern Time. Thank you!